T0305482

Campus Emergency Preparedness

Meeting ICS and NIMS Compliance

Campus Emergency Preparedness

Meeting ICS and NIMS Compliance

Maureen Connolly

CRC Press
Taylor & Francis Group
Boca Raton London New York

CRC Press is an imprint of the
Taylor & Francis Group, an **informa** business

CRC Press
Taylor & Francis Group
6000 Broken Sound Parkway NW, Suite 300
Boca Raton, FL 33487-2742

First issued in paperback 2021

Version Date: 20150709

ISBN 13: 978-1-03-224269-9 (pbk)
ISBN 13: 978-1-4665-8757-1 (hbk)

CONTENTS

PREFACE

I am a United States Coast Guard Auxiliarist. Because of this affiliation, I was able to work as a Federal Emergency Management Agency (FEMA) disaster assistance employee (DAE) in New Orleans following Hurricane Katrina in September 2005. The devastation to homes, schools, hospitals, and businesses that I witnessed in our country had a life-changing effect on me. The people I met and the stories I heard motivated me to become involved in helping to increase an awareness that through emergency preparedness some aspects of a disaster or emergency could be mitigated. I was appalled and astonished that such devastation could occur in *my* country. After a month of working as a community relations person, assisting survivors in locating resources that were available, I returned home to New York. I joined the local Community Emergency Response Team (CERT), an organization whose focus is to train people who live in the community to provide for their own safety and the safety of their neighbors until assistance is available from professional emergency services. It was then that I began to rethink my dissertation focus.

At the time, I was a college administrator working on my doctorate. Because of my experience with Hurricane Katrina, I began to explore emergency preparedness in colleges and universities. I had been toying with looking into some aspects of the adult education marketing arena, but my time in New Orleans made me think about the vast numbers of students who had been displaced from their home institutions. From the freshmen who had only spent a few days at their new schools, to the sophomores, juniors, and seniors seeking the opportunity to continue their education; life as they knew it was forever changed. This natural event changed the course of many lives at educational institutions—faculty, staff, administrators, as well as students. I wondered what colleges and universities could do to retain their students when their buildings became uninhabitable. I wondered if these institutions had emergency preparedness plans in place and whether there was anything that they could have done to lessen the interruption to the educational process on their campuses. Thus, I began my venture investigating what guidance was available through the United States Department of Education (DOE) and FEMA.

As I reflected on my past administrative positions and the colleges where I had worked, I realized that at least two of these three colleges did not have adequate emergency preparedness plans in place. One of these institutions did not even have fire drills for the administrative buildings, only for the dorms. At one college, the entire emergency preparedness plan was written by one person, who had no prior experience working at a college. I saw fire extinguishers with inspections that were well out of date, students climbing a 40-foot lighting apparatus in the theater with no tethers, and professors who continued to teach during fire drills because they did not know if it was a real fire. I witnessed a blackout once in July on a 100-degree day where the residence life staff had no alternative plans in place for the tower full of students other than to run to Home Depot to buy flashlights. Events such as these happen every day across the country at countless colleges. It is my intention to simply call attention to the guidelines that are available for colleges and universities to follow that could help reduce the risk and help mitigate those situations that are unavoidable.

During my doctoral inquiry period, 32 people on the campus of Virginia Tech were shot to death in April 2007 when one emotionally disturbed student went on a rampage. This horrendous event exposed problems in emergency response at that college campus. Unfortunately, this was not an isolated incident. The next year, in Northern Illinois, an alumnus returned to campus with a guitar case loaded with three handguns and a shotgun. In a geology lecture hall, he stepped from behind a screen on the stage and opened fire, killing five students and then himself. Yet three years following this horrific event, a *New York Times* article, "Colleges Fail to Complete Required Safety Plans" (Pawlowski & Manetti, 2011), reported that even after the State of Illinois put a law into place that required colleges and universities to put emergency preparedness plans in place, very few were in compliance. Sadly, these types of tragedies continue to plague our society. During the first month of preparing this manuscript, holiday shoppers were gunned down in a Seattle mall, and then 2 weeks before Christmas, 20 first graders, 3 of their teachers, their principal, and the school psychologist were murdered at the hand of a psychotic individual armed with an assault rifle as they began their school day in Newtown, Connecticut. Tragically, what is occurring in our schools is a microcosm of what is occurring in society at large.

The purpose of this resource book is to assist colleges and universities in developing and organizing their emergency operation plans in a manner that is easy to read and understand, and incorporate all of the key components recommended by FEMA and the DOE. I have seen far too many campus plans with information that is not pertinent intertwined with critical information, directives for action by students mingled with action items for the preparedness teams, and repetitive unedited information, and some missing critical information. This resource book contains a NIMS/ICS compliant template (see Appendix A) for creating a campus emergency preparedness plan, which is designed to help campus teams develop plans that contain all pertinent information in an orderly, coherent manner so that information can be readily obtained. The information in this resource book has been extracted from FEMA and DOE documents and training programs. Additionally, there are concepts and pieces of plans from countless college and university emergency plans that were melded together to provide the reader with strategies for protecting, preventing, mitigating against, responding to, and recovering from threats and hazards that may materialize at an institution of higher education.

REFERENCE

Pawlowski, S. M., & Manetti, M. (2011, December 23). Colleges fail to complete required safety plans. *New York Times.* http://www.nytimes.com/2011/12/23/education/chicago-area-colleges-fail-to-complete-safety-plans.html?_r=0

1

Is Your School Really Ready for Any Crisis?

Colleges and universities are responsible not only for the education but also for the safety and welfare of their students. That responsibility includes keeping them free from physical and psychological harm from the moment they enter the campus. In recent years, it has become distressingly apparent that these institutions are not well prepared for this challenge. While most institutions across the United States have an emergency management plan, many of these plans are not comprehensive and do not meet federal guidelines.

Ask any president, provost, or director of emergency operations at most colleges and universities across the country and they will tell you that they have an emergency management plan in place. But was the plan written in consultation with the local Office of Emergency Management (OEM), fire and police departments? Are the plans practiced? Most frequently, the only safety training that college/university faculty, staff, and students participate in is fire drills. However, even when fire alarms sound, oftentimes those on campus continue to teach, study, and ignore the sounding alarm. Is this because they perhaps have been involved in what they perceive to be more than their share of false alarms or practice drills? It will be unfortunate for those too busy to drill when a real fire strikes and they will not have evacuated.

Depending on your location, your campus may be affected by natural events, such as earthquakes, fires, and floods. Health hazards such as meningitis, West Nile fever, SARS, a pandemic flu, and other emerging diseases pose a threat for campuses. If your college is located near a nuclear power plant, you must have a plan in place for evacuation and lock-down in the event of a radiation or chemical leak as you would not want to evacuate and send students outside into an approaching poisonous air mass. Colleges near transportation routes such as highways and railways must be prepared in the event of a chemical spill from a transportation vehicle or roadway obstruction due to accidents or derailments. Plans must be in place for a massive food poisoning, water or air supply contamination, student disturbances such as weapons, hostage, and kidnapping incidents on campus. And unfortunately, schools must be prepared for terrorist activities that may affect the school and its surrounding community.

Colleges and universities are responsible not only for the education but also for the safety and welfare of their students. That responsibility includes ensuring that they are free from physical and psychological harm from the moment they enter the campus. In recent years, it has become distressingly apparent that schools are not well prepared for this challenge. Colleges and universities have been the targets of violence, crises, and disasters, many for which had the schools been better prepared the outcomes could have been more favorable. Just during the writing of this book, campuses have fallen victim to deadly shootings, fires, power outages, tornadoes, and floods to name a few such occurrences.

The Government Accountability Office (Ashby, 2007) report states that most colleges and universities have a plan but their plans do not meet federal guidelines. I have seen campus websites state that you should use common sense in an emergency. But unfortunately, unless you have been a recipient of disaster training, it is quite probable that you will not be capable of making competent decisions when involved in an event that evokes high levels of stress. Good decision making comes from people who have been trained in best practices. University teacher preparatory programs, at the undergraduate and graduate levels, focus on teaching methods. They do not address the emergency responsiveness of faculty, but as Pfefferbaum states:

> Over time, expectations for teachers have broadened beyond instruction in academic skills and knowledge to include health and social and emotional growth of students. Unfortunately, few studies address teachers' reactions, perceptions of need, and understanding of issues following large-scale community trauma and how these may influence their ability to meet the needs of their students.
>
> Pfefferbaum (2004, p. 251)

College and university officials have no idea what crisis or disaster will strike next or where. The only thing that they can be certain of is that something will occur and that the community will expect the campus to react swiftly and expertly. Just because your campus has a plan on the books and a crisis team in place does not mean that your campus will be prepared when something unexpected happens in a classroom, not unless each and every faculty member and administrator feels comfortable and confident that they know their role, will your college truly be prepared.

While emergency alert text/phone systems have their value, they should not be relied upon as the sole method for keeping your campus safe. When a shooter opens fire on a classroom full of unarmed, innocent students, the survival of those involved depends on swift and immediate actions of those in the immediate vicinity, and that may be a teacher, an administrator, or another student, and not the Public Safety Officer or a member of the crisis team. There certainly will not be time to look for advice from the text alert system. Without training, the actions will be reactionary, not necessarily best practices unless training has taken place. Most college shooters have a long history of depression. Colleges and universities need to look at developing preventive measures and protocols for identifying and then referring persons of concern, in addition to any emergency planning for a campus. The protocols need to be very specific, describing very clear responsibilities for all faculty and staff. The responsibilities must be clearly understood with prevention, protection, mitigation, response, and recovery strategies. Training and preparation prior to an event will clarify for faculty and staff what the expectations are for their emergency response role.

Institutional communities need to develop and practice all-hazard plans so that they can respond and handle whatever crisis may develop at the campus. When these events take place during the school day, action must be taken to stop the incident from progressing or at least taken at a high level of responsiveness, to keep students out of harm's way. A key finding in the study coauthored by the United States Secret Service and the United States Department of Education (Fein, Vossekuil, Pollack, Borum, Modzeleski, & Reddy, 2002), "Threat Assessment in Schools: A Guide to Managing Threatening Situations and to Creating Safe School Climates", is that most incidents that occurred at schools were interceded by a school official who was on the scene prior to the arrival of law enforcement.

So, which school personnel feel that they are prepared for an emergency? The results of Megumi Kano's research of school officials in

Los Angeles County found that the respondents' preparedness perceptions of their school's current preparedness levels were high when the respondents participated in general and event-specific training activities. Survey participants reported higher levels of perceived preparedness if they had a personal copy of the school emergency plan, if their school conducted various kinds of drills, if their school owned a wide variety of emergency equipment and supplies, if that equipment and the supplies had been inspected during the prior school year, and if their school cooperated with the numerous local agencies and groups on emergency preparedness issues (Kano, Ramirez, Ybarra, Frias, & Bourque, 2007).

The results of a study that this author conducted at a university corresponded with the results of Kano's in that the respondents who felt most confident in their schools emergency responsiveness had participated in training drills and had a personal copy of their school's emergency plan. On the surface, it appeared that 56% of the faculty and staff surveyed felt that the school was prepared for any emergency; however, further questioning revealed that only 44% knew where to find the emergency call box closest to their office or classroom, more than 50% did not have a copy of the pocket emergency plan prepared by the campus security team. Only 56% of the respondents felt it was their responsibility to report persons of concern on campus; and 75% of the adjuncts, 58% of the administrative staff, and 73% of the nonadministrative staff indicated that they did not know how to report a person of concern. The final survey question asked whether the respondent was clear about his or her emergency response role. Seventy-four percent indicated that they were not clear on what was expected of them during an emergency. If almost three-fourths of your faculty and staff are not sure of what is expected of them during a high-stress event, they are putting your school, themselves, and your students at a level of high risk and your school is not prepared for an emergency event.

This resource book will provide the reader with recommendations from the how-to guide *Building a Disaster-Resistant University* (Federal Emergency Management Agency [FEMA], 2003) and the *Action Guide for Emergency Management at Institutions of Higher Education* (Department of Education [DOE], 2009) for emergency preparedness for colleges and universities, as well as contributed exercise scenarios and best practices from college and university emergency managers from across the United States. While most colleges and universities have an emergency preparedness plan on the books, there are many that do not have the resources to develop exercise scenarios. Submissions to this resource book were made with the intent to assist colleges and universities in the development of their emergency preparedness teams. The expectation is that college administrators, faculty, and staff are not only responsible to educate but to also prepare for, react to, and recover from events that could compromise the safety of any person in a classroom, residence hall, office, or any other campus facility, as well as for any event that could jeopardize the continuation of the use of any campus facility.

REFERENCES

Ashby, C. M. (2007). *Emergency management: Most school districts have developed emergency management plans, but would benefit from additional guidance.* Washington, DC: United States Government Accountability Office Emergency.

Federal Emergency Management Agency. (2003). *Building a disaster-resistant university.* Retrieved from http://www.fema.gov/institution/dru.shtm

Fein, R. A., Vossekuil, B., Pollack, W. S., Borum, R., Modzeleski, W., & Reddy, M. (2002). *Threat assessment in schools: A guide to managing threatening situations and to creating safe school climates.* Washington, DC: United States Secret Service and United States Department of Education.

Kano, M., Ramirez, M., Ybarra, W. J., Frias, G., & Bourque, L. B. (2007). Are schools prepared for emergencies? A baseline assessment of emergency preparedness at school sites in three Los Angeles county school districts. *Education and Urban Society, 39,* 399.

Pfefferbaum, R. (2004). Teachers in the aftermath of terrorism: A case study of one New York City School. *Community Health, 27,* 250–259.

U.S. Department of Education. (2009). *Action guide for emergency management at institutions of higher education.* Retrieved from http://www.ed.gov/admins/lead/safety/emergencyplan/remsactionguide.pdf

2

Preparedness Triggers

What triggers a college or university to step up its emergency preparedness? Most colleges and universities have some sort of an emergency preparedness plan. It is safe to say that they are not all created equally. This chapter looks at areas that are sometimes overlooked when managing campus threats and crises.

Granted this is a developing area of practice due to the ever-increasing number of both human-made emergency events and natural disasters affecting colleges. And because of this, higher education administrators must include preparedness planning on their agendas. Why? Because parents and students expect the college to not only educate but also keep their children safe whether they are in a classroom, residence hall, library, office building— or anywhere on campus. The expectation of parents and students is that the highest level of safety and security is in place at the educational institution that their child is attending. Not only should educational institutions be concerned about maintaining a safe environment, but they also need to be concerned about legal action which can be taken against them by a victim or victim's family.

Employees, too, expect their workplace to be a safe environment. If your campus cannot keep everyone safe, you will not be able to sustain your enrollment of students and retention of faculty, staff, and administrators. Adverse legal actions can alter the perception of any school's environment and can affect its ability to recruit faculty, staff, and students. Trump (2000) proposes that the prevention of legal actions and fiscal repercussions should be motivators for engaging in emergency preparedness. The Federal Emergency Management Agency (FEMA, 2003) states, "losses could (be)... substantially reduced or eliminated through comprehensive pre-disaster planning and mitigation actions" (p. iii). So whether the impetus is safety, enrollment, fiscal soundness, being litigation-free, or continuity of business, attention must be stepped up in risk management and emergency preparedness at every campus across the nation.

Trump (2000) states that the "tendency to react rather than act is a national trait" (p. 29) and that "educators...tend to forget about the importance of security and crisis preparation until there is a high-profile incident or series of incidents" (p. XIV). As a result, after each high-profile event or series of incidents occurs, studies are done and papers are produced, each aiming to answer questions such as: Why did this event occur? And, what can we learn from this event to prevent it from occurring again or lessen its effects? This chapter looks at items from this body of knowledge to assist campus administrators examine some preparedness triggers and become more proactive in emergency preparedness.

CHANGES TO PROTOCOL AND PROCEDURE AS A RESULT OF ACTS OF VIOLENCE

The Virginia Tech tragedy of April 2007 left 32 people dead when one emotionally disturbed student went on a rampage and exposed problems in emergency response at that college campus. Following the Virginia Tech tragedy, President George W. Bush directed investigators to find out "how the federal government can help avoid such tragedies in the future" (p. 1). In June 2007, a coauthored "Report to the President—On Issues Raised by the Virginia Tech Tragedy" was released by the Department of Health and Human Services, the Department of Justice, and the Department of Education. The research team investigated whether federal laws were an impediment for an institution to proactively conduct emergency and crisis operations. They spoke with educators, mental health providers, and law enforcement officials. Their key findings were as follows: critical information sharing faces substantial obstacles, accurate and complete information on individuals prohibited from possessing firearms is essential to keep guns out of the wrong hands, and improved awareness and communication are key to prevention and it is critical to get people with mental illness the services they need (Leavitt, Spellings, & Gonzales, 2007). We know what to do, we just have to be better at doing it.

The study also found flaws in the interpretation by college and university personnel of the Family Educational Rights and Privacy Act (FERPA), which was intended to protect the privacy of PK–16 students, and the Health Insurance Portability and Accountability Act (HIPAA), which protects personal health information. As detailed in *Balancing Student Privacy and School Safety: A Guide to the Family Educational Rights and Privacy Act for Colleges and Universities,* the intention of FERPA, a federal law, is to protect the privacy of student education records. FERPA provides parents of children under the age of 18 the opportunity to review and correct their children's education records. Once a student reaches the age of 18, he or she becomes responsible for monitoring their educational records. College and university officials typically only looked at the age of the student and often chose not to inform parents in fear of FERPA violations when a student infraction arose. However, FERPA does permit any college or university to contact parents to inform them of situations regarding the health and safety of their children, even if they are over the age of 18. Regarding HIPAA, as per the U.S. Department of Health and Human Services, the entities that must abide by HIPAA are health plans, health-care providers, and health-care clearinghouses, not schools, employers, or law enforcement agencies.

Not only did the study find that communication between colleges and universities and the home need to be improved, but there was also a need for improved communication between colleges/universities and medical facilities and law enforcement, especially in cases where it was indicated that particular students posed a threat to the community. A recommended federal action is that "the U.S. Department of Education should ensure that its emergency management grantees and state and local communities receive training through the program, and have clear guidance on the sharing of information as it relates to educational records and FERPA" (Leavitt et al., 2007, p. 8).

How does your campus manage information about campus community members involving mental health care and law enforcement? Has your faculty and staff had recent training on FERPA compliance?

Following the Virginia Tech tragedy, Rasmussen and Johnson (2008) conducted a nationwide survey of colleges and universities to assess how this event affected campus safety practices. Rasmussen and Johnson (2008) found that changes were made at colleges and universities across the country following the Virginia Tech incident in a number of areas, including emergency notification systems; training and protocols for identifying and reporting disturbing or threatening student behavior; fiscal and staff resources devoted to campus safety; security enhancement systems and equipment; screening of applicants for admission and employment; and policies and protocols related to student mental health.

Yet even after the studies and reports and the upgrades to procedures and protocols, the murders on campuses continue. Two murders have occurred at Virginia Tech since the April 16, 2007, massacre; in 2009, an international student was decapitated with a kitchen knife by another international student, and in 2011 a Virginia Tech police officer was shot to death by a student from another college in a parking lot of Virginia Tech. In 2011, two students were shot to death in a campus garage at San Jose State University by a fellow student who then killed himself. In 2008, 5 students were shot to death and another 17 wounded at Northern Illinois University; and at Louisiana Technical College, a student shot two classmates to death and then turned the gun on herself. In 2007, two students were shot and wounded at Delaware State University. The killers are not always students or former students. In 2010, at Ohio State University, an employee who received an unsatisfactory personnel performance shot and killed two fellow employees; and at the University of Alabama–Huntsville a professor shot and killed three colleagues and injured another three at a faculty meeting.

Which strategy should a campus employ to prevent these types of murders? While individually each emergency preparedness practice has value, the greatest value comes from a comprehensive integration of multiple strategies with more resources deployed on the front end for prevention and mitigation emergency preparedness. Brett Sokolow, JD, the founder of the National Council for Higher Education Risk Management (NCHERM), is a strong proponent of proactive prevention measures. He is in favor of criminal background checks and secondary screenings for college applicants. However, Sokolow, Lewis, and Schuster (2010) suggest that "most campus violence is perpetrated by individuals whose criminal backgrounds would not indicate a potential for the violence to come." Recommendations include adding a list of questions to the Admissions Screening process. If an applicant answers "Yes" to any of the questions then the college/university should proceed with a criminal background check and secondary screening. Answering these questions falsely would be grounds for dismissal. Sokolow and Lewis (2009) recommend using "trained members of the campus Behavioral Intervention Team (BIT) proficient in assessment of the potential for violence and threat, and have the right skill set to determine who is an eligible applicant and what restrictions or conditions on admission should be imposed." Rather than spending time and energy on the latest knee-jerk reaction to crime on campus, Sokolow's team at NCHERM teaches campus administrators how to instill a campus culture of reporting with the institution of a campus BIT. The NCHERM team advises campuses on how to train all factions of the campus community and the community-at-large to look for red flags among campus community members and arm them with what should be reported, to whom, when, and how. Recommendations include tying training and reporting to compliance policies, procedures, and protocols that reflect the best practices.

What changes has your campus made to its emergency preparedness procedures as a result of the massacres at Virginia Tech in 2007? Does your campus perform student, staff, and faculty background checks? Is there a BIT in place?

CHANGES TO PROTOCOL AND PROCEDURE AS A RESULT OF NATURAL EVENTS

In addition to murders, natural events need to be included in a college/ university emergency preparedness plan. In October 2012, Hurricane Sandy struck the east coast of the United States. Colleges and universities were forced to remain closed after the storm passed due to flooding, structural damage to campus facilities, and loss of electricity on campus and throughout the region. Public transportation, including the New York City subway system, was seriously compromised due to flooding, which significantly affected transportation to and from New York City campuses. DeSantis (2012) reported that the timing of this storm affected the early application process. Early admission deadlines were postponed by many colleges to accommodate students, schools, and counselors affected by Hurricane Sandy. Additionally, campuses of the City University of New York as well as Rutgers University served as shelters for the homeless.

Social media played a significant role in colleges and universities keeping in contact with their students, staff, and faculty before, during, and after the storm. Some colleges and universities used the Internet to connect with students, faculty, and staff. Assignments, course materials, and other resources were accessible for those who had connectivity. Quite a different story than the aftermath of Hurricane Katrina in 2005, which crippled colleges and universities across the Gulf Coast, displacing thousands of

11

students, faculty, staff, and administrators at most institutions for at least the entire fall 2005 semester. Because of the long-term closures in 2005, colleges and universities additionally were dealing with breaches in faculty personnel policies. Robert O'Neill of the Association of Governing Boards recalls in Faculty Personnel Policies—Hurricanes Katrina and Rita: Disaster in New Orleans, (2003) "The devastation that Hurricanes Katrina and Rita inflicted upon the universities of New Orleans in late August, 2005, is undoubtedly the most serious disruption of American higher education in the nation's history." This was not the first or last time that college facilities would be destroyed and academic programs halted for substantial periods. However, the difference with Katrina is that it "destroyed an entire community, not only depriving the affected institutions of usable facilities, but also depleting severely the student populations, leaving faculty and staff without homes, teaching hospitals without critical equipment and patients, and so on through an unprecedented litany of woes." Just one of the many recommendations to come from the American Association of University Professors (AAUP, 2011) report was that "disaster plan(s) should specify the steps that might become prudent or even unavoidable in the event of a prolonged inability of the institution to function."

In addition to your campus plans that address temporary loss of functionality of the campus, does your plan address long-term strategies? Does your campus plan address personnel policies, including contingencies for a long-term campus closure or termination of a program due to lack of students or facilities following a man-made or natural disaster?

CHANGES TO PROTOCOL AND PROCEDURE TO ENHANCE CYBER SECURITY

If your emergency management team has not considered data loss as a threat, it isn't prepared. The purpose of a cyber attack is to disrupt your network. Cyber events can affect multiple areas of your campus not just what you typically think of as a computer event. Cyber events can be very fast moving. Sophisticated adversaries have the capability to change their attack plans multiple times a day.

If your university network is wide open, it is subject to hacking, making confidential student and employee records vulnerable. College and university mainframes host a myriad of data critical to maintaining the business aspects of education, including budgets, planning, financial and operational data, human resources, payroll, requisitions, and purchasing information. The mainframe holds student, staff, and faculty protected personal information, course schedules, grades, and information that falls under the HIPAA requirements. Social security numbers alone are highly sought after on the black market. All of these data are regulated to be securely stored.

You must consider that at some time your system is going to fail at some level. Security breaches originate from internal as well as from external sources. Savvy students have covertly installed programs to record keystrokes to gain access to user accounts to change grades and/or inserted code to corrupt data. Not only do these attacks need to be thwarted but mitigation strategies also need to be developed. Encoding can help to minimize these breaches; however, this should not be the only line of defense as a more sophisticated attack would need more sophisticated mitigation strategies in place.

While many colleges have the resources to provide a robust IT team to manage the ever-increasing responsibilities of the information systems, many do not. Many colleges have no security architecture, providing an open door for data to be compromised. Resources are not allocated to replace antiquated operating systems, and IT personnel are not trained in cyber security measures, nor are they included on the emergency planning team.

The IT team should allocate time to exercise the *What ifs* and devise strategies to overcome possible challenges. The purpose of an exercise is to test your plans, raise questions for discussion, and figure out how to continue your operation if a certain threat, hazard, or critical event occurs at your campus. Colleges and universities most frequently test their evacuation plans and most recently have added *shelter-in-place* and *active shooter* to their repertoire of exercises. Low on the exercise list but very high on the list of possible events is data loss.

If your campus does not have a cyber security coordinator on staff, find outside resources now to help your team think through the potential challenges and position your campus for a successful defense. The role of the cyber security coordinator is to protect your critical infrastructure by securing the network, be the lead in incident response and information sharing, engage the campus in shaping the future by providing training and exercises to ensure that your entire campus network is safeguarded.

As part of the emergency preparedness team, the cyber security coordinator should be positioned in the emergency operations center, not in a remote location! All emergency management team members need to know IT terminology, and all IT team members need to have command of Internet connection sharing (ICS) principles before an event occurs.

As for accessing critical data when the campus is uninhabitable, some institutions are using cloud services. Using the cloud is proving beneficial for not only e-mail storage but also for data security and meeting HIPAA requirements. Data can be accessed from remote locations, an asset when student records and employee payroll systems need to be retrieved.

Breakdowns in cyber security affect confidence in the college or university, which negatively affects student, staff, and faculty retention, as well as security, privacy, and other mandated regulatory requirements.

What safeguards does your campus have in place to mitigate a cyber event? Is there a cyber security coordinator on your emergency preparedness team? Is there training for students, staff, and faculty on best practices for keeping your network safe? Who has access to your computer labs, the network? Is a current student/staff/faculty ID required to gain access? Is it a card swipe system or just flash the card at the attendant? What is your communications system for alerting the campus that a cyber event has occurred?

CHANGES TO PROTOCOL AND PROCEDURE TO INTEGRATE SOCIAL MEDIA

College campuses use a variety of methods to communicate emergency messages to the community. This may include mass emergency alert systems, sirens, public address, web pages, building captains, and residence hall assistants. However, if your emergency preparedness team is not keeping abreast of the latest social media platforms and integrating them into its communications strategies, it is missing an opportunity to reach a wider audience.

The old paradigm for information sharing was that it was received at specific intervals with an occasional special broadcast of breaking news. The morning and evening news, radio broadcasts, and daily newspapers were the mediums. On campuses, breaking news is released from a well-crafted statement by the administration after consultation with the public relations department via website postings and one-way mass broadcast systems. Today's paradigm demands that information be shared as events are occurring and in the arena of emergency management, ample notification and preparedness be built into the communications system. Social media platforms, such as Twitter and Facebook, provide opportunities to deliver news and information as it is occurring using a two-way model. Information that is hours old may not be accurate by the time it is received.

Most colleges have a webpage dedicated to emergency preparedness. It is often filled with facts, phone numbers, and protocols of what to do in the event of an emergency. It is normally static and very often has not been updated recently. If you look at college websites for emergency plans, you will discover that there is no universal format being used across the sites. At some locations, there are full emergency plans on the home page; others have an array of fact sheets with instructions of what to do should a particular event be occurring on campus. How many students actually read them? How many faculty and staff take the time to seek out this information? Unless there is an impending event and specific direction from administration telling the community to familiarize themselves with the information, what is the incentive to read it? As a society we tend to be more reactionary than proactive, especially in the area of emergency management. Why is there not full adaption of social media from colleges and universities? College administrators need to gain an understanding of these new technologies, how they work, and who is using them as this is critical for campus emergency planners. Social media as a component of the campus emergency preparedness plan needs to become a priority.

Following the Virginia Tech tragedy, federal law mandated that all campuses must have mass notification systems in place and that they be tested annually. Mass notification systems are used to announce and provide guidance in an emergency or critical incident and to communicate relevant updates. Mass notification systems push information regarding campus emergencies, natural disasters, and inclement weather closings to the campus community through landline phones, cell phones, text messages, and e-mail. Campuses use one of two methods for capturing contact information of students, staff, and faculty. Depending on the operating system and campus policies, students, staff, and faculty choose the opt-in and opt-out methods. The opt-in method relies on the student, staff, and faculty members to input their contact information into the mass notification system, while the second automatically inputs contact information such as name and campus e-mail and puts the onus of removing information from the system on the individual who chooses not to receive emergency messages. Both systems do require users to update their information as it changes, most frequently this will be cell phone numbers and non-campus e-mail addresses. Campuses are urged to use the mass notification system only to transmit critical information, not general news as this will dilute its effectiveness during an actual emergency.

During an emergency when multitudes of users are all trying to make phone calls at the same time, it can be difficult for mass notification phone messages to be delivered. Since texting uses less bandwidth than phone lines in such situations, it has proven to be the preferred method of communication. Such was the case in lower Manhattan following Hurricane Sandy in October 2012. Students, staff, and faculty from the Metropolitan College of New York (MCNY) were unable to return to campus for 1 week. The New York City subway system, the main transportation route to reach campus, was crippled by floodwaters that had filled the subway stations with over 12 feet of water and there was no electricity in downtown Manhattan, throughout the city, and in many surrounding towns in New York and New Jersey. MCNY had an emergency preparedness plan in place. It called for mass notification messages to be sent out to students. Texting emergency closure messages proved to be the only method that worked, and this was only after Vinton Thompson, president of the college, could locate a hot spot from which to transmit the message!

While mass notification systems have the ability to quickly pass on emergency information to a targeted group of individuals on campus, they are only as good as the people who manage their use. Notification delays have occurred because of a human factor. Perhaps there is confusion as to who has authority to release a mass notification message. Or there is a directive for a message to be crafted and there is confusion as to what should be said. Mass notification systems are important pieces of the campus emergency communications system; however, it must be recognized that they are one-way streets dependent on one person or a small team of administrators crafting and releasing a message for the community. How many campus emergency plans actually test the ability of the mass notification message to be constructed and released within a pre-determined acceptable time? And how many evaluate and take into consideration what is an acceptable notification lag time? Campus mass notification systems do not have the capacity to receive on the ground information from those across the campus with their ear to the ground.

Social media platforms such as Twitter and Facebook can manage the lag time of many campus cumbersome administrative processes for identifying what has occurred, verifying the event, crafting the message, and then releasing the message. It is probable that every person on your campus is carrying a portable mobile device prior to, during, and after an emergency event. It is entirely possible that most of them will be using these devices to capture some aspect of an emergency event with these devices. They may be sending photos, texting, Tweeting, Periscoping, and calling friends and family. By March 2, 2013, there were 1.06 billion active monthly users of Facebook, 680 million mobile users, and 500 million Twitter total users and more than 200 million active Twitter users. These widely used technologies stress the importance for college and university emergency planners to address how to best integrate social media into a campus emergency plan. Students, staff, and faculty triangulating events can capture eyewitness data, which ultimately results in validated data. Social media is about the community talking to each other to keep them up to date with what is occurring.

Social media can be used throughout the emergency management cycle. YouTube videos that demonstrate a safety practice are particularly useful in the preparation phase. Emergency managers can maximize utilization of social media by pushing out information to personal mobile devices via text messaging and Twitter during both the response and recovery phases. You can ask for assistance from your followers in identifying campus community needs. In the recovery phase, you could ask questions of your followers. How are they managing following whatever the event was that took place?

What if an emergency event occurs at your campus and there are folks there who are not connected to your emergency alert mass notification system and you need to get a message out to them? Did you know that they can receive your emergency procedures on their phone via Twitter Fast Follow without them actually being a Twitter account holder? Say for instance, an emergency occurred at a huge event where people who are not connected to the emergency alert system are attending. Maybe it is a graduation that was scheduled for the great lawn and a sudden thunderstorm is causing your ceremony to be delayed. An announcement is made from the podium regarding the rain delay, telling the guests to reconvene in an hour after the storm passes. The guests are asked to find shelter around campus in any open building. An hour passes but the storm has not. Administration makes a last minute decision to hold graduation in the gym. How do you get the message out to the guests who are scattered around the campus that the graduation location and start time have been changed? What if the message at the podium as the rain clouds were approaching included a Twitter Fast Follow direction that told the guests that if they texted "follow SCHOOL NAME" to 40404, they would be kept abreast of when and where the graduation would reconvene? Someone at the school designated as the Public Information Officer (PIO) would then manage messages to the guests regarding what to do, which would greatly decrease the anxiety and apprehension of parents, family, and other guests about the graduation ceremony. Twitter Fast Follow could be built into the emergency plans for sporting events or concerts or any gathering of people who are not connected to the campus emergency alert system. As part of the protocol, guests would know at the beginning of the event that should an emergency occur, they can text "follow SCHOOL NAME" to 40404 to be kept abreast of emergency directions. This information could be relayed to guests either from an announcement at the beginning of the event, a printed message in the event bulletin, or the instructions to text "follow SCHOOL NAME" to 40404 could even be printed on admission tickets.

Twitter, as well as Facebook, when integrated into a campus emergency management plan can add a vital component for open, continuous communication flow, which contributes to ongoing situational awareness. A quick search for usage of Twitter and Facebook in college emergency preparedness will show you that a number of colleges are already using these platforms to communicate with the campus community not only for emergency preparedness messages but also for a wide variety of topics, including marketing of educational programs and sporting events. The University of Texas at Tyler recently posted lightning and thunderstorm warnings. Winter weather driving tips can be found on the Indiana University Public Safety and Institutional Assurance Twitter page. On the Yale Twitter page a user is redirected via a link to the campus emergency preparedness website. The College of William & Mary uses Twitter with a link to Facebook to facilitate emergency management information at its campus. Another advantage of using Twitter or texting is that the information is date and time stamped with geo-locator data unless the individual has that feature turned off. This small sampling demonstrates the various adaptations of Twitter in an overall campus emergency plan.

The benefit to the campus emergency management team is even greater when they can hear what the members of the campus community are saying regarding an event. Why? Those around the campus may be in touch with a greater visibility of situation awareness of whatever is occurring whether it is an active shooter, a flood, or the effects of flu among the campus community. Crowdsourcing, or group contributions of situational awareness in this case, result in a more comprehensive picture of the event.

"Crowdsourcing is a type of participative online activity in which an individual, an institution, a non-profit organization, or company proposes to a group of individuals of varying knowledge, heterogeneity, and number, via a flexible open call, the voluntary undertaking of a task. The undertaking of the task, of variable complexity and modularity, and in which the crowd should participate bringing their work, money, knowledge, and/or experience always entails mutual benefit. The user will receive the satisfaction of a given type of need, be it economic, social recognition, self-esteem, or the development of individual skills, while the crowdsourcer will obtain and utilize to their advantage that what the user has brought to the venture, whose form will depend on the type of activity undertaken" (Estellés-Arolas, González-Ladrón-de-Guevara, 2012). If those participants feeding information to the campus emergency management team come from across the campus in positions such as residence life directors, building captains, and faculty, staff, and students selected to be part of the crowdsourcing team, the information is rich data from trusted sources.

College students use social media to communicate their activities more than any other population segment. Social media posts are increasingly generated from smart phones and other smart devices that attach geographic coordinates identifying the user's location. It is no surprise to campus emergency professionals that many campus adversaries have had a social media presence prior to causing harm to themselves and/or others. As part of proactive campus emergency preparedness planning, institutions may choose to monitor the campus for chatter that could lead to illegal activities, or perhaps prevent a suicide. As campus administrators, you want to hear the messages so your team can react more appropriately. It also provides an opportunity to correct misinformation that may be circulating around campus.

Location-based social media listening and monitoring sites such as Monitter.com, Tweetgrid.com, and Twitterfall.com allow you to observe Twitter activity on anyone's accounts. You can narrow your search to a specific location, like a campus and monitor for a set of keywords, thus allowing your preparedness team to get a pulse of campus activity. Taking it to the next level is Geofeedia.com that currently aggregates posts from five sources: Twitter, You Tube, and three photo-sharing sites—Instagram, Picasa, and Flickr. All five locations can be monitored on one screen. Future plans include a monitoring and analytics platform that will allow comprehensive data analysis. Currently, the user identifies the geographic area to be monitored, and the data is available to monitor instantly as it is gathered and archived. Data analysis can be performed by any number of filters, including keywords and author. These location-based social media listening and monitoring sites only collect publicly available information.

Used as part of a campus preparedness plan, this technology can be instrumental in assisting the emergency management team in recognizing emerging campus issues. This could prove beneficial in providing opportunities for intervention and, thereby, preventing a liability before it has an opportunity to develop. Think of the added security benefit this could provide at a large sporting or special event on campus.

Information is moving at an incredible speed across social networks as more and more people share their experiences during a disaster or critical event. Campuses must recognize the importance of social media as it relates to college and university emergency planning and build social media management tools into their emergency management plans. The emergency planning team needs to choose which social media strategy best meets the needs of the campus. Whether it be a one-way engagement with mass notification, a two-way engagement with social media sites such as Twitter and Facebook, or monitoring, campus emergency and disaster management teams can no longer ignore social media or neglect to include it in emergency planning.

What social media strategies are integrated in your campus emergency management plans?

In spite of the federal government's best efforts, there are still problems with the state of preparedness of post-secondary educational organizations (Department of Education [DOE], 2007, 2009; FEMA, 2003; Graham, Shirm, Liggin, Aitken, & Dick, 2009; Mitroff, Diamond, & Alpaslan, 2006; Rasmussen & Johnson, 2008). As colleges and universities strive to improve emergency preparedness, they need to keep abreast of new mitigation strategies to be integrated into their underdeveloped and outdated plans.

What trigger will initiate a review of your campus emergency response plan and create an all-hazards strategy for all five phases of emergency preparedness?

REFERENCES

American Association of University Professors (AAUP). (2011). *Ensuring academic freedom in politically controversial academic personnel.* http://www.aaup.org/report/ensuring-academic-freedom-politically-controversial-academic-personnel-decisions

DeSantis, N. (2012). How colleges are responding to Hurricane Sandy. *The Chronicle of Higher Education.* Retrieved from http://chronicle.com/blogs/ticker/how-colleges-are-responding-to-hurricane-sandy/51262

Estellés-Arolas, E., & González-Ladrón-de-Guevara, F. (2012). Towards an integrated crowdsourcing definition. *Journal of Information Science. 38*(2), 189–200.

FEMA. (2003). *Building a disaster-resistant university.* Retrieved from http://www.fema.gov/institution/dru.shtm

Graham, J., Shirm, S., Liggin, R., Aitken, M. E., & Dick, R. (2006). Mass-casualty events at schools: A national preparedness survey. *Pediatrics, 117,* e8–e15.

HIPPA. (2011) *Balancing student privacy and school safety: A guide to the family educational rights and privacy act for colleges and universities.* Retrieved from www2.ed.gov/policy/gen/guid/fpco/brochures/postsec.pdf

Leavitt, M. O., Spellings, M., & Gonzales, A. R. (2007). *Report to the President on issues raised by the Virginia Tech tragedy.* Washington, DC: United States Government.

Mitroff, I. I., Diamond, M. A., & Alpaslan, C. M. (2006, January/February). How prepared are America's colleges and universities for major crises? *Change, 38*(1), 60–67.

Number of active users at Facebook over the years—Yahoo. (May 1, 2013). Retrieved from news.yahoo.com/number-active-users-facebook-over-2304

O'Neill, R. M. (2013). *Faculty personnel policies—Hurricanes Katrina and Rita: Disaster in New Orleans.*

Rasmussen, C., & Johnson, G. (2008). *The ripple effect of Virginia Tech: Assessing the nationwide impact on campus safety and security policy and practice.* Minneapolis, MN: Midwestern Higher Education Compact.

Sokolow, B. A., & Lewis, W. S. (2009). *2nd Generation behavioral intervention.* Malvern, PA: National Council for Higher Education Risk Management (NCHERM). Retrieved from https://www.ncherm.org/resources/publications/#WhitePapers

Sokolow, B. A., Lewis, W. S., & Schuster, S. K. (2010). *Murder at UVA: Preventing the preventable.* Malvern, PA: National Council for Higher Education Risk Management (NCHERM). https://www.ncherm.org/resources/publications/#WhitePapers

Trump, K. S. (2000). *Classroom killers? Hallway hostages? How schools can prevent and manage school crises.* Thousand Oaks, CA: Corwin Press.

Twitter Fast Follow. SMS follow. https://support.twitter.com/articles/20170004-fast-following-on-sms#

U.S. Department of Education. (2009). *Action guide for emergency management at institutions of higher education.* Washington, DC: U.S. Department of Education. Retrieved from http://www.ed.gov/admins/lead/safety/emergencyplan/remsactionguide.pdf

U.S. Department of Education. (2012). *Family educational rights and privacy act (FERPA).* Washington, DC: U.S. Department of Education. Retrieved from http://www2.ed.gov/policy/gen/reg/ferpa/index.html

3

A Case for Including Retention Strategies in the Campus Emergency Management Plan

This qualitative study tells the stories of four students who prior to Hurricane Katrina were attending colleges and universities along the Gulf Coast. The colleges and universities had emergency plans in place; however, the plans were underdeveloped in comparison to the magnitude of Hurricane Katrina. The institutions were forced to close, and these students had decisions to make regarding the continuation of their education. Included in this resource book as a close-up view of the effects of not including a retention strategy as part of the campus emergency management plan.

Based on this study, it is clear that there were several factors that overwhelmingly affected whether a student continued his or her education at the college or university he or she was attending prior to Hurricane Katrina. These factors included the individual student's future orientation; their connectedness or lack of connectedness to their schools and the people in them; the learning environment, which included the ability of the institution to maintain communication with the students, offer online courses, provide flexibility in courses, both at the campus when school reopened and in accepting courses that students took elsewhere during fall 2005 when the students' home campus was closed; and the structural limitation of finances and housing.

A goal of this study was to heighten the awareness for university and college administrators of the importance of having a comprehensive campus emergency plan in place, which includes retention strategies in the event that the closure of their brick-and-mortar institution is imperative. Based on the findings of this study, recommendations for higher education administrators include being prepared to offer their courses online and to develop transitional housing arrangements should their campus be affected by a dormitory closure. However, this small study also found that when students feel that they are cared about, when they feel that they matter, they are more inclined to stay retained at an institution, disaster or not, providing that housing and finances remain unchanged.

INTRODUCTION

In August and September 2005, Hurricanes Katrina and Rita struck the U.S. Gulf Coast leaving long-lasting economic devastation. This natural event in conjunction with a lack of emergency preparedness on the part of the local government crippled the citizens from New Orleans, Louisiana to Biloxi, Mississippi, closed businesses and schools and left an entire region uninhabitable. Families evacuated to communities near and far, neighborhoods and communities were lost. The hurricanes and floodwaters that followed reached unprecedented heights, destroying thousands of buildings including homes, businesses, churches, and schools. In its wake, students from 10 colleges and universities in the New Orleans area found themselves cutoff from a typical college experience (Appleseed, 2006).

This qualitative study attempts to tell the stories of four students who prior to Hurricane Katrina were attending colleges and universities along the Gulf Coast. Their schools were forced to close, and they had decisions to make regarding the continuation of their education. The literature review takes a look at some student retention efforts that colleges employed (Johnson, Nolan, & Siegrist, 2006; Sumner, 2007; Tarr, Birdwhistell, & Schmehl, 2007) and also makes recommendations for creating a more comprehensive emergency and crisis plan (Mitroff, Diamond, & Alpaslan, 2006) that includes retention strategies.

LITERATURE REVIEW

In order to put the magnitude of the Hurricane Katrina event in perspective and understand how it affected the New Orleans education system, it is necessary to understand the environment. Appleseed conducted 350 interviews to capture a snapshot of the housing, health care, education, employment, and legal services status of the more than 1 million Katrina evacuees. Their findings provide a foundation for understanding of the challenges an educational system, college, or university faces with a catastrophic event that shut down not only a city but an entire region of the United States (Appleseed, 2006). Thousands of college students were unable to return to school for fall 2005. Nontraditional college students experiencing the loss of their homes, their livelihoods, lack of child care, and schools for their children would have their own education put on hold indefinitely. In areas such as St. Bernard Parish, where every one of the 27,000 homes was uninhabitable, students lost everything—their homes, clothes, and all possessions. The Southern Education Foundation report (2007) indicated that 2 years after the storms, 26,000 students in Louisiana still had not returned to college. Extraordinary circumstances contributed to this high attrition rate.

Dr. Theresa Perry, president of the United Teachers of New Orleans, reported (2006) that even before Katrina struck, plans were underway for what ultimately was the takeover by the state of 102 underperforming K–12 schools. What became the "Post Katrina ACT 35" authorized the state to take over these schools. Graduates from these high schools were among the enrollees of the colleges and universities in New Orleans. Extensive multilayered retention strategies for high-risk students (college freshmen with low entrance grades, lack of college prep in high school, low SES) are necessary to retain them in ordinary times.

The first year is critical to laying the foundation for a successful college experience (Habley & McCanahan, 2004; Tinto, 2004). Prior to Hurricane Katrina, the K–12 education system in New Orleans, a feeder for post-secondary schools was collapsing (Perry, 2006). Briggs (2008) interviewed Ron Maggiore, associate vice chancellor for enrollment management and dean of admissions at the University of New Orleans (UNO). Maggiore stated that 25% of the students that did not return to UNO after Hurricane Katrina were freshman and sophomores. As students become more committed and involved with their college/university, it is easier for them to be retained as students. Kuh (2005) stated that invested ties that solidify their commitment, which include their time vested in their academic programs, friends, faculty, and institutional support assist a student in staying in a particular school. If students are satisfied with the education they are receiving and the services available to them, they will stay.

Online courses can contribute to retention. Tarr et al. (2007) and Jarrell, Dennis, Jackson, and Kenney (2008) found that some schools made an attempt to continue to serve their students through the online environment, but this was difficult for schools that had not yet made preparations to convert their courses to the online platform. It was also quite challenging for students who had lost their homes and possessions. Lessons learned include the following: provide Internet access at a predetermined evacuation site and provide more training for faculty in the use of BlackBoard, move online course management to a hosted site, develop a Listserve for faculty and student contact, and provide an outline shell for uploading faculty course curriculum.

Johnson et al. (2006) reported that "focused leadership, open lines of communication, flexibility in college operations, and the involvement of a steadfast faculty and staff all united at the right moment to reopen the college" (p. 46) at Delgado Community College contributed to its retention success and ability to reopen in spring 2006. Even with 20 of its 25 buildings destroyed and a 40% loss of tuition revenue, the college was able to reopen with 60% of the spring 2005 enrollment.

Delgado Community College advises the following: identify an emergency headquarters; include prevention, protection, and mitigation strategies; create communications procedures; cultivate relationships with government officials and private foundations; provide an emergency hotline for students who are taking classes at other schools across the country so that they can speak with the registrar or faculty to confirm that the courses they are taking would transfer back to Delgado; provide online courses; and conduct classes in unconventional available space such as movie theatres and hospitals.

Delgado administrators stated that if faced with this situation again, they would additionally

- Issue laptops with wireless capabilities as the leadership team was evacuating
- Provide alternate e-mail addresses
- Supply cell phones with paging capabilities and area codes outside the region
- Select in advance a headquarters, including provisions for lodging for the emergency management team
- Secure information technology at a distant site, outside the range of a possible disaster

- Provide faculty with CDs to store course outlines, syllabi, class rosters that include the addresses, cell phone numbers, and alternate e-mail addresses of students
- Have a well-established communications protocol—preferably using the web
- Provide access for emergency and government workers to all buildings on campus
- Provide group and individual counseling immediately for students, staff, and faculty

A single causal event such as a hurricane is not enough to destroy the determination for a program to succeed (Sumner, 2007; Tarr et al., 2007). For Sumner and other faculty at the Louisiana State University Health Sciences Center (LSUHSC) School of Nursing in New Orleans, even a lack of a building could not deter them from using creativity and a willingness to do things differently to retain 96% of the nursing students in fall 2005. With no facility to call their own nor established clinical sites, they were able to reestablish a headquarters at the Baton Rouge campus, began a telephone call-in center and were able to get their website up and running—all critical communication facets in reaching and retaining students. The housing need was met when LSUHSC purchased a refurbished ferry and set it on the Mississippi River. Undergraduate lectures were given in a movie theater in the mornings before it opened for theater goers. Space was made available for graduate students at Southern Louisiana University on Friday nights and Saturdays. This school was able to retain its students with the dedication of the faculty, staff, and the students all in sync to accomplish their goals with a "whatever it takes" attitude.

Tarr et al. (2007) report that using creativity and having a willingness to do things differently contributed to the success of Loyola University in retaining 90% of its chemistry majors. Advising was conducted online and was key to their success. Success in using good academic advising to increase retention is supported by the study conducted by Habley and McCanahan (2004). Tinto (2004) proposes that successful retention strategies include providing academic advising interventions, learning support such as a reading, math, writing, and foreign language lab; learning communities; and programs for minorities as necessary components. Tinto (1987) theorizes that when students adapt socially on campus, they are more likely to persist with their studies. Braxton (2003) states "when students feel that someone in the institution cares about them, takes an interest in them, and pays attention to their experience, they feel they matter." Faculty members, Irons, Carlson, Duncan, and Wallace (2007), of Lamar University, conducted a mixed methods survey capturing the students' perspective on the impact of Hurricane Rita that supports Braxton (2003). The survey of 179 respondents containing quantitative and qualitative questions was distributed to Lamar University classes, 9 months following the evacuation. Findings included that the respondents would have liked to have more communication with faculty during the evacuation and suggested that faculty have students' e-mail and cell phone information available in order to contact the students. Also noted was that students felt the faculty were not considerate of the student's emotional state following this traumatic event. Kiernan (2005) and Lipka (2005) concur that communication is the most important component of a crisis plan.

Success happens more frequently with planning. Only 41% of the colleges that responded to a survey conducted by Habley and McCanahan (2004) employed a person whose primary function was to monitor retention. Retention activities cannot be conducted satisfactorily by one person with a designated title of retention officer, but rather, it should be by a team that meets on a regular basis moderated by the retention officer. Tinto (1987) states that "successful retention programs encompass virtually everything an institution does to improve the quality of student life and learning" and "retention should not be an institutional goal but rather a by-product of improved educational programs and services for students."

Student retention is vital to the fiscal health of a college/university. Jarrell et al. (2008) state that "in the wake of Hurricane Katrina, it behooves us as educators to be proactive with our crisis management plans" (p. 14). Mitroff et al. (2006) conducted a survey of 350 colleges and universities and found that participant colleges and universities did "not follow the best-practice model of crisis management" (p. 64). Most were prepared for fires, lawsuits, and crimes, but few had broad-based crisis management plans or broad-based teams. When asked to rank the "current degree of support" (p. 65) given to crisis/management prevention along with 10 other activities or programs at their institutions, crisis/management prevention was at the bottom of the list. Mitroff et al. (2006) state that crisis management "must be viewed as a key element in the strategic governance of colleges and universities" (p. 66), and those that include an interdepartmental crisis management team that meets regularly to train for a broad range of situations will be better positioned to attend to whatever event strikes their institution.

Strategies employed by colleges to retain their students under ordinary circumstances may or may not be effective in extraordinary circumstances such as a Hurricane Katrina. No one has asked students who have been affected by the closure of their college/university following Hurricane Katrina what their institution could have done to help retain them as students. Research exists on retention and on the compilation of what constitutes an effective campus emergency management team. A study is needed to generate an understanding of effective retention strategies following extraordinary events and the effect of having a broad-based campus emergency team that meets regularly to train for a broad range of situations has on retention.

What follows is an excerpt of an unpublished qualitative study, factors that influence students' decisions to return or not to return their home college or university following its closure due to Hurricane Katrina. It looks at the student perception of the factors that influenced their decisions to return, or not return, to the colleges and universities they were attending when Hurricane Katrina struck in the fall of 2005. The schools were forced to close, and students had decisions to make regarding the continuation of their education. The goal here is to listen to what students have to say regarding their immediate post-Katrina experience regarding their education, to look at the retention techniques their schools may or may not have used to retain them, to look at other factors that influenced the students' decisions, and to provide a foundation for further study of the effect that a focus on retention in a campus emergency plan can have on retaining students after an extraordinary event.

CONCEPTUAL FRAMEWORK

A college/university has to close temporarily due to a catastrophic event. Institutions whose leadership is supportive of crisis and emergency planning will be better prepared to return their campuses to its pre-event status, including preventing student attrition. There will be events that are beyond the reach of the campus administration that will affect the students' ability to return to campus following an event. However, when an institution does all it can do to improve the quality of student life and learning (Tinto, 2004), including having solid retention strategies in place, as well as making provisions for health and safety, most students will not flee. Mitroff et al. (2006) claim that a broad-based crisis management team that meets regularly and trains for a broad range of situations will be best

29

prepared to deal with the wide range of events that may affect the health, safety, and learning at a campus.

METHOD

Students who were attending colleges/universities that were affected by Hurricane Katrina were not only from the immediate area or even from across the United States, but also from countries around the globe. Kvale and Brinkman's (2009) analogy of an interviewer/researcher is a miner, digging and chipping away until the answers that they know are there, are uncovered; however, before the mining could begin a net was cast wide. How does one locate students who were displaced from their colleges? If you want to locate college students you need to go where they go. Initial contact was made with the subjects through a Facebook interest group called *Students Affected by Hurricane Katrina*.

The Narratives

The students wrote free-flowing narratives in response to the main prompt: *Tell me your story describing your student experience involving Hurricane Katrina*. Additional prompts included the following:

- What was communication with your school like for you regarding the continuation of your education during fall 2005 following Hurricane Katrina?
- What were you thinking about as you packed your things to evacuate prior to the hurricane striking?
- What was it like when you realized the magnitude of this event?
- It is important for me as a researcher to understand something about the institutional support from your school so that I can make some comment for institutions to assist their students in the future.

Respondents

There were four student participants, three females and one male. The three females were undergraduate students; the two from University of New Orleans (UNO) were unmarried and lived on campus in the dormitories. One of the two was a freshman; the other's academic status is unknown. The third female student was from William Carey College (WCC) in Gulfport, Mississippi. She was beginning her junior year, was married and lived in her own home 10 minutes away from campus with her husband. The one male student was an unmarried foreign exchange graduate MBA student from Turkey, attending classes at UNO.

The four individual case studies were obtained via e-mail in the form of unstructured narratives where the participants responded to a single research question: *What factors influenced your decision to return (or not return) to your home institution following Hurricane Katrina?*

Debbie

Debbie, a native of Louisiana, was living at home with her parents and siblings in Lafayette prior to arriving at University of New Orleans (UNO) on August 19, 2005, 10 days before Hurricane Katrina struck on August 29. Debbie had her sights set on the Ivy League schools, but finances did not permit such applications. The State of Louisiana has a program called TOPS that awards scholarships to students attending any public school in Louisiana based on the students' high school grades. As a TOPS scholarship recipient, Debbie received full tuition money for food, textbooks, and cash every semester. Debbie was thrilled to be attending UNO. On August 26th, the Friday before the storm struck, she made a trip home to Lafayette, 2 hours west of New Orleans, for what she thought was a weekend trip. On Tuesday, August 30, when it was obvious that UNO and New Orleans would not be operational for the fall of 2005, Debbie registered at University of Louisiana, Lafayette (ULL). Debbie took one online class during the fall semester through UNO as well as attended a full load of classes at ULL. In spring 2006, she returned to UNO as a full-time student.

> Debbie: I was displaced from the University of New Orleans, and I transferred to the University of Louisiana at Lafayette for one semester before returning back to UNO.

For Debbie, the impact of Hurricane Katrina was distressing. Instead of being at the school that she loved, she attended ULL for 2005 fall semester until UNO opened again in the spring of 2006. Things that worked in her favor were that she could use her TOPS scholarship at ULL and then at UNO for the spring semester; and her grandfather lived within commuting distance, which allowed her to attend classes on the UNO campus, as housing was very scarce in New Orleans in the spring of 2006.

Cathy

Cathy, an art major, was starting her junior year at William Carey University (WCC), a small Baptist college in Gulfport, Mississippi. She lived locally, in her own home, with her husband. After the hurricane, she did initially attend classes offered through her home school; however, due to the annihilation of the campus, the classes were offered at Gulfport High School. Cathy's husband's place of employment was also obliterated. Rather than travel 3 hours each way to and from work, he opted to seek employment out of state. He took a position in Wyoming in December 2005, and Cathy ultimately transferred to the State University of Wyoming. Many of her classes, however, did not transfer into her new degree audit. At the time of this data collection, Cathy had a 2½-year-old child, was unable to find affordable child care, which resulted in her having to drop to part-time status, and hence she lost all financial aid. At WCC, she received a full scholarship of $20,000 per year. Cathy anticipated that it would take another 3 or 4 years to complete her BFA.

> Cathy: I was going to school full time at William Carey University on the coast, also right off Highway 90 in Gulfport. I was going to graduate with my BFA in 1 year. I am thinking it'll take approximately another 3–4 years, which means it will have taken around 8–9 years to get my BFA instead of graduating (in) December 2006 like what was originally planned before the storm hit.

Hurricane Katrina had a profound effect on Cathy's life. Not only was it necessary to leave her family and friends in Mississippi so that her husband could find employment, but the impact on her education was enormous. Since she no longer had a full scholarship, she could only attend college attended part time because she could not afford child care, and many of her courses did not transfer to the State University of Wyoming.

Gail

There is limited information regarding the third participant, Gail. She only responded to the initial inquiry on Facebook seeking student participants. Her limited information has been retained in the study as it does add to the body of knowledge. Gail was a UNO student when Hurricane Katrina struck. She was living in an apartment and lost everything she owned.

> Gail: I finished college in a quite interesting way (first tried to stay and finish in New Orleans, but that wasn't possible so I did a National Student Exchange Program) and am now living in Los Angeles, California.

Henry

Henry was the only graduate student in the study; he was an international exchange student from the University of Innsbruck, Austria, with the intention of studying at the University of New Orleans for 1 year. At the time Katrina struck, he had been living on campus for 2 weeks. He and a new friend evacuated to the home of the friend's parents in New Iberia, Louisiana. Henry stayed there for 2 weeks before transferring to Georgia State University (GSU) for the 2005 fall semester. He attempted to return to UNO for the 2006 spring semester but was unable to find affordable housing. He was finally able to secure another student exchange program at the University of Bogazici in Istanbul, Turkey, and then went on to study international economics in Austria.

> Henry: About me, I have been studying international economics in Austria. During Hurricane Katrina, I was an MBA student at the University of New Orleans with a Joint Study Program between the University of Innsbruck and University of New Orleans for 1 year.

Because of Hurricane Katrina, Henry was unable to study in America for 1 year as he had intended. However, he was able to attend MBA classes at Georgia State University (GSU), and because of funding provided by GSU to those affected by the hurricane, Henry paid no tuition for the 2005 fall semester. He was able to complete a study abroad program in Istanbul. Communications with the student president of the MBA program at UNO supported the correspondence from Henry.

Emerging Themes

A decision was made to analyze and code the cumulative data from each individual and then cross analyze to compare the differences and the similarities between the cases. The narratives were initially coded for attachment with their home school, communication during and after the hurricane with their home school, detachment from home school, detachment from school enrolled in while home school was closed, e-learning as it pertained to their home school, financial aspects of tuition pre- and post-Katrina, personal financial situation, housing pre- and post-Katrina, personal motivation, faculty influence, and flexibility of the institutions.

As the codes were formulated into categories, four themes (theories) emerged. The themes are (1) future orientation, (2) connectedness to people and place, (3) learning environment, and (4) structural influences. "The development of categories, properties, and tentative hypotheses through the constant comparative method is a process whereby the data gradually evolve into a core of emerging theory" (Merriam, 1998, p. 191).

Future Orientation

Future orientation is defined by the participants as what they intended to accomplish with or without the storm and/or the assistance of their home school. This includes their personal motivation and what they intended to do with their completed degree. The term *home school* refers to the college or university that the participants were attending when Hurricane Katrina struck on August 29, 2005. All four of the participants had a determination to complete college. None of them dropped out. Debbie attended ULL for 2005 fall semester and returned to UNO to complete her bachelor's degree; Cathy was still in an undergraduate BFA program at the end of this study; Gail completed her degree through the National Student Exchange Program; and Henry completed his MBA through the University of Innsbruck. Both Debbie and Cathy mentioned a desire to attend graduate school. Debbie intends to complete a doctorate degree as her aspiration is to become a clinical psychologist.

> Debbie: The main thing that kept me interested in UNO had little to do with how they handled the situation. Rather, what kept me interested was simply my interest. The amazing thing is that I planned to graduate in 3 years, and even with all the confusion and disaster that occurred, I still graduated in 3 years. My own personal motivation is mostly to blame.

> Henry: I went to Atlanta and proceeded with my education at the Georgia State University in Atlanta. I could not complete my 1-year education in the United States. What I want to add is that after I returned to Austria, I arranged another Student Exchange Program at the University of Bogazici in Istanbul in Turkey.

Connectedness to People and Place

Connectedness is defined by the participants as attachment with their home school. In this section, focus is on the disconnect some of these participants had with either their home school and/or the school that they located to following the closure of their home school. It is by analyzing the connection and disconnection that brings clarity to what helped a student to return to their home school.

Two of the four participants, Debbie and Cathy, had formed attachments to their home schools prior to the storm. Debbie was only at UNO for a week before Katrina. She wrote of her attachment to the school, but she also wrote of her love of the city of New Orleans. Her writing states her love of how UNO struggled and tried its best in the midst of this crisis, and with a lack of resources. She mentions several times that she loves UNO.

> Debbie: I liked New Orleans a lot for starters, and I think that's why I went there in the first place, but once I got there I was instantly attached. The teachers are amazing; each of them loves their job, and it shows.

Cathy was starting her junior year and lived locally in her own home with her husband. She too had no thoughts of transferring to another school. Her attachment to William Cary College (WCC), her classmates, her teachers was evidenced by her joining them just days after the storm to clean up the art lab. Cathy received a phone call from a fellow student asking if she could assist with cleaning up the art classrooms and labs.

> Cathy: The professors were also there at the cleanup of the art complex, and we were able to discuss some things then, such as if art classes would resume or not. As evening approached, there were more tears as people realized friends and teachers were without homes. We made time to meet and discuss what to do about the rest of the trimester, as well as contact information for fellow students that were still missing.

When she arrived at the campus, she worked with other students and faculty members in clearing debris as well as removing mold-covered drywall from the walls of the sculpture room. Cathy was very attached to her campus community and talked a lot about her sorrow for the destruction of the campus and the homes of her classmates. She expressed compassion for her teacher whose art tools were destroyed. She worried that he would never be able to get past this tragedy and return to his art.

> Cathy: Professor Jeff lived in a tent for several weeks. Doc lost all his tools, his beautiful mesquite stumps, and various stones of alabaster and marble, as his studio was completely underwater, and the flooding of the bayou reached up to 3 feet in the second floor of his house. He hasn't done any art since.

Both Debbie and Cathy spent time talking about the faculty and their commitment to the students and to the learning environment. Debbie stated that the UNO faculty members were interested in teaching and in providing the best education for their students. Both Debbie and Cathy had been contacted by their schools regarding the state of the school and what steps were being put into place to assist them in the continuation of their education.

Debbie: I wish I could remember more about how they communicated with us during the fall, and what they did in the spring that welcomed back so many more students, but I don't think I could remember if I tried. ...All I know is that I checked my e-mail every day, and they were actually pretty good at keeping everyone updated.

Cathy: Margot from Student Services contacted me and told me that most classes would be resuming at the Gulfport High School.

Henry mentions that UNO had no idea where he was until he contacted them. It was only after that connection was made by Henry that he received additional information regarding the happenings of UNO.

Henry: UNO did not know where I was before I contacted the Austrian Center based on the UNO campus. ...After I contacted them, I was asked to return to UNO after finishing my 2005 fall semester for the 2006 spring semester.

Debbie recalls that all communication was handled via e-mail and was current, keeping the community apprised of its progress regarding reopening. I am not sure why the experiences of Debbie and Henry at UNO were so different. Henry was a foreign exchange graduate student, and Debbie was a domestic undergraduate student, but one would think that the application process that includes collecting personal contact information would have included phone numbers and e-mail addresses whether a domestic or international student. Since Debbie did not recall the date that UNO contacted her nor did Henry recall the date that he contacted UNO, it could be possible that Henry contacted UNO prior to the time when Debbie was contacted by UNO. Keep in mind that the university was not fully staffed due to the situation and needed time to organize its resources before contacting students and making public statements as to the "next-steps."

Detachment is defined as a lack of attachment to school and those within the campus community. All mention of ULL from Debbie was with words of detachment. She was not open to being at ULL. Her perception was that the teachers there did not care and that the classes were not helpful. She thought that they just wanted to capture her as a student without listening to what it was that she wanted.

Debbie: Before the hurricane I had no intention of ever going to ULL, and while I was there I had no intention of staying there. The teachers were apathetic to their jobs, which was the polar opposite of what I had seen in only 5 days at UNO... I loved UNO; I hated ULL; it was pretty simple.

36

There was never a thought that Debbie would stay at ULL for more than the 2005 fall semester. She talks about how unhelpful ULL was in assisting her in selecting courses that would work for her in her transfer back to UNO.

> Debbie: ULL was so unhelpful...they told me I had to take a ...math class (because it was required for all of THEIR programs), which did not help me at all with anything at UNO, and I later discovered that the math class that I needed was available; they simply failed to tell me about it. They put me in the next English class but wouldn't allow me to take the honors version (what I needed because I was in the honors program at UNO) because I had not tested into *their* honors program.

The transfer to the University of Wyoming has not been easy for Cathy. They were not flexible with transferring in courses that she had taken at WCC, and she states that by the time she completes her BFA it will have taken her 8–9 years to complete the degree.

> Cathy: I must say that transferring from a private Baptist college to a state university has been the biggest pain. I am still having problems getting classes and credits accepted.

Both Debbie and Cathy use words that reflect that they felt that the schools they transferred to did not care about them as individuals or take into account what they had been through. Because of this, they had a difficult time "connecting" with ULL and University of Wisconsin, respectively.

Gail and Henry did not talk about any attachment to UNO, their home school for the 2005 fall semester. Henry talked about the fellow student with whom he evacuated with to the family home. He also mentioned the MBA president who was helpful, but there was no attachment noted in his writing. His writings indicated that he had a goal of completing a student exchange program, not that he had to be a student at UNO. He found another student exchange program at the University of Bogazici in Istanbul, Turkey, and then went on to international economics in Austria.

> Henry: What I want to add is that after I returned to Austria, I arranged another Student Exchange Program at the University of Bogazici in Istanbul in Turkey, where you can attend the classes in English. Turkey is my country of origin.

For Henry, while UNO was his home school for the 2005 fall semester, his true home school was the University of Innsbruk, Austria. This may have factored into his inability to connect to UNO. Gail's short correspondence lacked any sense of attachment to UNO, or to anyone at the school.

Learning Environment

Learning environment is defined by the administrative and faculty activities that took place at the campus immediately before, during, and following the hurricane. It includes communication, facility availability, e-learning, course availability, faculty influence, and flexibility of the institutions.

Cathy received a phone call from an administrative office to let her know that classes would resume the third week of September 2005, at Gulfport High School. The damage at WCC was extensive with many buildings completely destroyed and others deemed an unsafe environment in which to hold classes. Cathy mentions that she and the other students were tearing down mold-covered walls.

> Cathy: About a foot of water had gotten into the back studios, more in the front sculpture building and foundry. I helped remove the lower drywall from the walls of the sculpture room, as they were completely covered with mold.

There was no mention by Cathy of any courses being offered online at WCC; however, they were able to reopen at Gulfport High School just 3 weeks following the storm. When classes resumed at Gulfport High School, Cathy found that none of her art classes were to be offered.

> Cathy: …Art classes were canceled for the term. I wound up taking my health and my world civilization class. My ceramics and sculpture classes did not continue. I still think back on it and know that if the storm hadn't hit, I would be working on my MFA right now instead of slowly attempting to finish by BFA.

Cathy thought that WCC not offering art classes for the 2005 fall semester would set her back at least one semester once WCC was back to full order for the following fall. Communication for Debbie was through the online environment. She states that she checked her e-mail daily for updates. Debbie, who prior to Katrina, was a communications major, found that she would need to change her major as the communications department had collapsed. She then switched her major to psychology.

> Debbie: Because of the hurricane, many teachers had to be laid off, and many programs were shut down, communications being one of them, leaving me with no major and forcing me to make a quick decision about

the direction I wanted to go in my life.... It just took a hurricane to show me that psychology is exactly what I wanted to study.

Debbie registered for an online course through UNO during the 2005 fall semester in addition to attending classroom-based courses at ULL. In the 2005 fall semester, after Katrina, she was registered to take French III through the UNO online environment. The class was canceled and she was put into French IV, even though French III was a prerequisite for French. She states that UNO was the first to reopen with online classes and then the first to open its doors in the spring of 2005. Debbie was not sure how many online courses were offered prior to Katrina at UNO, but she feels that there were more offered for the 2005 fall semester and the 2006 spring semester in an effort to retain students, especially since housing was not available in the New Orleans area.

> Debbie: The Internet side of UNO remained open and available through-out the hurricane semester.... I know plenty of people who remained as full-time UNO students through online classes that semester, and some continued to do this during the spring semester if they could not yet return.... I do not know how many were offered prior to my enrollment, but after the hurricane they were forced to continue offering many of their classes online in order to save money and desperately hold onto as many displaced students as they could.

Debbie expressed that UNO offered her flexibility, which she felt made it easy to return; first with the online classes and then with a flexible schedule.

> Debbie: They made it easy to come back and jump right back into the routine, and they left room for change, and restructure.

When she returned to UNO, they worked with her regarding transferring in the classes that she had taken at ULL and did not penalize her for courses that she had taken at ULL but rather found flexible ways to transfer those classes back into her UNO degree audit.

Neither Gail nor Henry made mention of any courses offered via the online environment, and both attended UNO as did Debbie.

For both Debbie and Cathy, when they initially returned to their home schools, UNO and WCC, respectively, they both found that their schools were forced to cut out certain courses, either due to a lack of students, lack of faculty, or lack of a facility. For Cathy, that ultimately did not factor into her completion goal since she had to relocate to Wyoming due to her husband's job relocation because of Hurricane Katrina.

Structural Influences

Structural influences are defined by the limitations that were unable to be altered by the college/university due to overwhelming circumstances that were beyond the scope of capabilities of the individual institutions such as the lack of housing in the broader New Orleans area and the financial impact of the hurricane on the personal finances and economics of the area. It also includes any references made to tuition and scholarships. Finances are described by the participants as any financial aspects of tuition pre and post-Katrina and any reference to how the hurricane impacted their lives financially.

Cathy did not complete her 2005 fall semester at WCC at the Gulfport High School location. While her home withheld the storm with minor damage, the facility that housed her husband's place of business was completely destroyed. His employer had another facility 3 hours away. Rather than face that commute, he sought employment elsewhere, and ultimately took a position in Wyoming. Cathy and her husband left Gulfport, Mississippi, on November 30, 2005 for Wyoming. While at WCC, she was receiving a full-time student annual scholarship of $20,000. At the University of Wyoming she returned as a part-time student and received no financial aid. She had a 2½-year-old child and could not afford child care, so she could not attend full time, so she received no aid. Cathy stated that the University of Wyoming had done little to help her. She received no Katrina-related scholarship or grant. It was her understanding that other colleges/universities offered such scholarships/grants for other students who were victims of Hurricane Katrina.

> Cathy: I was offered no Katrina-related scholarship or grant like other schools (from what I heard) were doing for displaced students. This means I'm paying for a state university out of pocket when I had a $20,000 scholarship to William Carey University.

Debbie was the recipient of a TOPS scholarship and was planning on using it for the 2005 fall semester at UNO. TOPS is a scholarship program that covers tuition, housing, books, and personal expenses for scholastically gifted high school students who are attending a public university in New Orleans. Her tuition was paid for at UNO and ULL, with the exception of the 2005 fall semester when she took the online UNO class as well as classes at ULL. The source of her frustration regarding the online course not being covered was that she was given incorrect information. When she registered for classes at ULL after Katrina struck, her TOPS scholarship was then used for tuition at ULL. Debbie, however, was also taking

40

an online course through UNO. She was told by everyone she asked that TOPS would cover this unique situation. She was told, yes, that TOPS was making exceptions to their ruling that a student could only take classes at one institution per semester. Three years later, Debbie received a bill from UNO for the online course for which TOPS had declined tuition payment.

> Debbie: When Hurricane Katrina hit, I transferred to ULL and signed up for 15 hours and also took the one online class with UNO. Before I did this, I asked several people whether or not TOPS would cover this unique situation. I was told by everyone that I asked, probably for lack of a better answer, yes. They told me TOPS was making exceptions for everyone that was affected by the hurricane, and that my semester would be covered. Apparently, however, TOPS thinks that it's okay to change their minds about what they want to pay for 3 years after the fact. I was just billed for $923 for the one online class that I took with UNO. The reason is TOPS took back that money because they "cannot" pay for more than one university per student per semester. Thank you TOPS.

Henry did not pay tuition for the fall; he received a full tuition waiver from GSU for 2005 fall semester.

> Henry: I got a tuition waiver; I did not have to pay any tuition fee for the 2005 fall semester.

Housing is defined by pre- and post-Katrina housing and how it affected the education of the participants. Following Hurricane Katrina, the City of New Orleans was uninhabitable for a number of months. In some places it has yet to return to its pre-Katrina state, and for some areas it never will. The city was a ghost town except for disaster workers, and some business and home owners returning to assess the damage to their properties. In many sections of the city, mold and mildew had destroyed whatever the floodwaters and winds did not. Remediation included extensive demolition and rebuilding.

For each of the students who had attended UNO, the lack of housing was an issue. Due to the water damage and mold, not only were the academic buildings unavailable but also the dormitories as well as off-campus housing in the immediate area was not possible. The housing situation affected not only the student population but also the residential as well as business communities of New Orleans. FEMA was providing housing trailers in the vicinity, and Debbie talked about the anticipation of FEMA trailers to replace student housing. That never became a reality. When UNO resumed some of its classroom learning in the spring of 2006, housing remained an issue.

41

Debbie: There was nowhere to live, and every option that FEMA provided was a dead end. They said they would find a hotel for me to stay in, and they didn't. They said that they would put FEMA trailers on campus for us to stay in, but they didn't. Fortunately, I had a relative who lived not too far away, so I was able to commute, but I'm sure there were more students who would have returned to UNO if they would have had a place to live. My grandfather lived about 40–50 minutes away from campus, give or take traffic.

Debbie's grandfather lived within commuting distance of UNO. Had he not, it is uncertain of how she would have continued her education at UNO for 2006 spring semester.

Henry stated that housing was the only reason that he did not return to UNO. After his fall semester at GSU, he was contacted by UNO that school was open and he could return to classes. He contacted the Austrian Center at UNO and was told that the dorm where he was previously situated was condemned and there was no other housing alternative. He therefore made the decision, based on this information to return to his home school, the University of Innsbruck in Austria. He then applied for another student exchange program at the University of Bogazici in Istanbul, Turkey.

Gail too stated that the only reason that she did not continue at UNO was due to housing. She ultimately relocated to California through the National Student Exchange Program and completed her undergraduate education.

Cathy was the only student participant for whom housing was not an issue. Her home in D'Iberville, Mississippi, sustained damage but was in a repairable state. Cathy was unable to continue at WCC, as mentioned previously, due to the destruction of the building that housed her husband's employer's place of business, which resulted in their moving to Wyoming and the continuance of her studies at the University of Wyoming.

DISCUSSION

Based on this study, it is clear that there were several factors that overwhelmingly affected whether a student continued their education at their home institution. Those factors included the individual student's future orientation; their connectedness or lack of connectedness to their schools and the people in them; the learning environment, which included the ability of the institution to keep up communication with the students, offer online courses, provide flexibility in courses, both at the campus when school reopened and in accepting courses that students took elsewhere during the 2005 fall semester when the home school was closed; and the structural limitations of finances and housing.

The students in this study came with the recognition that they needed to complete a college degree. Their personal motivation was intact. Trying to make sense of why some stayed at their home school rather than transfer to any other school in the country is the challenge of this analysis. When students feel that they matter, that their school is interested in connecting with them, they will be more inclined to stay. Two of the four, Henry, and Gail, easily made transitions to schools other than their home schools following Katrina. Their writing painted a picture of detachment. For Henry, he spoke about the lack of communication. Henry was detached from UNO and because of this was able to quickly adjust to Georgia State University where he spent the 2005 fall semester and then for spring 2006 moved on to the University of Bogazici. Gail's short correspondence lacked any sense of attachment to UNO, but rather spoke of her detachment to UNO. She found a college program in Los Angeles, California, through the National Student Exchange program and moved on.

Perhaps we can conclude that rather than deal with the issues surrounding reopening a college/university following a catastrophic event such as Hurricane Katrina, for those who are not feeling connected, it is easier to transfer to a new school, especially if you felt that the school was lax in reaching out to the students following the traumatic event. As for students whose writing spoke of a love for the people and place, Debbie and Cathy, we could conclude it would be very difficult to pick up and go elsewhere. This was evidenced by Debbie's stories about ULL. There was nothing that anyone at ULL could have done that would have made her happy. Consistent with Schuh and Laanan's findings (2006), "by leaving their college in New Orleans, the students are leaving what has become familiar and they are moving to a college not of their choosing. They will need to feel someone at the new college cares about them and is welcoming them to their new surroundings" (p. 93). Cathy had friends and professors who she held close to her heart at William Carey College. The transfer to the University of Wyoming was not easy for Cathy. She mentioned how the school had not extended themselves to understand her personal situation. They had not been at all accommodating. Cathy was already detached from the University of Wyoming. These findings are consistent with Braxton (2003) "when students feel that someone in the institution cares about them, takes an interest in them, and pays attention to their experience, they feel they matter" (p. 324).

When looking for a meta-analysis for structural limitations one could issue that for those who could overcome the housing issue, retention at their home school would be an easy task, provided that the financial situation of the individual was being taken care of, even when presented with a loss of educational departments, faculty, and facilities. Schools such as UNO who were able to offer online courses fared better than those who were unable to keep students retained through online courses. Jones, Das, and Huggins (2008) qualify this finding with their statement, "Many institutions decided to offer online course instruction in an effort to keep currently enrolled students. There is no doubt the use of technology had an impact on student retention" (p. 173).

Debbie, who prior to Katrina was a communications major, found that she needed to change her major as the communications department had collapsed. That did not present a huge problem for Debbie; she switched her major to psychology, switching to a school that offered communications was not even a thought that Debbie considered. For Cathy, even when her major art courses were not being offered due to the destruction of the art lab in the fall of 2005, she had no intention of transferring to another school. Cathy spoke of the camaraderie she felt with her fellow students and faculty members as they attempted to clean their school. Yet because of her husband's employment situation, Cathy did ultimately need to transfer schools.

None of these students experienced a financial situation that prevented them from continuing with their education. For Debbie, she continued to receive her TOPS scholarship. For Cathy, the transfer from WCC to the University of Wyoming had a negative impact on her, but she was still able to attend school. It had proved to be stressful and costly due to the fact that she had a child, could not afford child care, and did not receive any scholarship money. Henry fared best with regard to tuition. As a foreign student, he did not qualify for any student loans, yet he did receive a full tuition waiver from GSU for the 2005 fall semester.

While each of these factors affected student retention, it appears that housing had the greatest affect on the students attending UNO. Henry clearly states that if he was able to find housing, he would have stayed at UNO; Gail also makes a similar claim. Even Debbie would not have been able to return for the spring 2006 semester if it had not been for her grandfather living within commuting distance from UNO. The students in the study were not unique to being affected by the lack of housing. Jones et al. (2008) state that "housing shortages will continue to be a monumental barrier" (p. 173).

As a side note—Cathy mentioned that she and other students and faculty were removing mold-covered drywall from the walls of the sculpture room. Mold exposure has been known to cause serious health consequences including respiratory and neurological problems. While that speaks volumes for the sense of community and attachment, it also screams loudly at the physical dangers that these people placed themselves. All colleges/universities need to have a remediation plan in place and to vocalize the proper procedures for faculty, staff, and students following an event that involves flooding and mold. This will prevent well-meaning students, faculty, and staff from putting themselves in physical danger. By not addressing this issue, a college/university opens up an opportunity for future action by the community members.

CONCLUSION

The primary goal of this study, to explore the experiences of a small group of students who due to the closure of their colleges and universities following Hurricane Katrina had their life plans altered, was met. The secondary goal of this study was to heighten the awareness for university and college administrators to the importance of having a comprehensive campus emergency plan in place that includes retention strategies in the event that the closure of their brick-and-mortar institutions is imperative. It is my hope that this research will be used as a resource for college/university administrators who may be faced with such a future extraordinary event.

This study of four students is too small to make any generalizations except regarding housing, since it affected each of the four students. While colleges/universities had emergency plans in place, it was clear that the plans were underdeveloped in comparison to the magnitude of Hurricane Katrina. When institutions are forced to close due to extreme conditions, students may be unable to continue their education at these institutions for some period of time. Based on the findings of this study, recommendations for higher education administrators is to be prepared to offer courses online and to develop transitional housing arrangements should the campus be affected by a dormitory closure. A more comprehensive study could include interviews with administrators from UNO to get their impression of how the housing situation was handled and what they could have done, if anything, given the widespread housing shortage in the entire city of New Orleans following the hurricane.

Because student retention is vital to the fiscal health of a college/university, it is imperative that emergency plans include retention strategies. In addition to reporting the financial and enrollment impacts, administration of affected institutions need to develop action plans for student retention. Institutions need to start taking seriously the federal government's warnings regarding understanding the risks associated with hazards that can affect the campuses and develop action plans not just emergency management plans written for the sake of having a written document. Institutions need to be talking with their counterparts at other schools and becoming familiar with the resources available to them through such organizations as FEMA, and National Center for Higher Education Risk Management (NCHERM). FEMA's *Action Guide for Emergency Management at Institutions of Higher Education* (2009) is a good starting point.

Regarding student finances and transfer evaluation, schools need to look at each student case individually and not make blanket rulings that treat everyone with the same pen stroke. There are unique situations that occur during catastrophic disasters where the students would be better served if colleges could use flexibility when making decisions. But perhaps the most important lesson learned is one that transcends all settings. It is that people need to feel that they matter. The stories of these students reflected that they felt good about themselves and their schools when they were connected to people there, when they felt that they mattered. My recommendation is to offer professional development training programs for staff and faculty that include sensitivity training so that all community members recognize that their behavior, the way they speak to and act toward students, affects the way students feel about the institution. When students feel that they are cared about, when they feel that they matter, they are more inclined to stay at an institution, disaster or not, providing that housing and finances remain unchanged.

REFERENCES

Appleseed. (2006). *A continuing storm: The ongoing needs of Hurricane Katrina evacuees—A review of needs, best practices, and recommendations.* Washington, DC: Appleseeds.

Briggs, L. (2008). Technology helps New Orleans University rebuild environment. *Campus Technology.* Retrieved February 5, 2009, from http://campustechnology.com/Articles/2008/06/Technology-Helps-New-Orleans-University-Rebuild-Enrollment.aspx

FEMA. (2009). *Action guide for emergency management at institutions of higher education.* Washington, DC: FEMA.

Habley, W. R., & McCanahan, R. (2004). *What works in student retention?* Iowa City, IA: ACT Inc.

Irons, E. J., Carlson, N. L., Duncan, B., & Wallace, F. (2007). The academic impact of Hurricane Rita: Voices of students. *National Social Science Perspectives Journal, 35*(1), 92–99.

Jarrell, C., Dennis, R., Jackson, M., & Kenney, C. (2008). Academic and student affairs issues post hurricane Katrina. *Community College Journal of Research and Practice, 32*(3), 235–250.

Johnson, A., Nolan, G., & Siegrist, C. (2006, September/October). Lessons learned from a Bout with Hurricane Katrina: The Delgado Community College story. *Change, 38,* 42–46.

Jones, J., Das, N., & Huggins, D. (2008). Enrollment management issue analysis: Operating in a post Katrina education environment. *Community College Journal of Research and Practice, 32*(3), 167–183.

Kiernan, V. (2005). Ready for the next Katrina. *The Chronicle of Higher Education, 52*(8), A31.

Kuh, G. D. (2005, October 14). *Student success in college: Creating conditions that matter.* San Francisco, CA: Jossey-Bass.

Kvale, S., & Brinkman, S. (2009). *Interviews: Learning the craft of qualitative research interviewing.* Thousand Oaks, CA: Sage Publications.

Lipka, S. (2005, October 14). After Katrina, colleges nationwide take a fresh look at disaster plans. *Chronicle of Higher Education, 52*(8), A28.

Merriam, S. (1998). *Qualitative research and case study applications in education.* San Francisco, CA: Jossey-Bass.

Mitroff, I. I., Diamond, M. A., & Alpaslan, C. M. (2006, January/February). How prepared are America's colleges and universities for major crisis? *Change, 38*(1), 60–67.

Perry, T. (2006). The plight of the education systems—Post hurricane Katrina: An interview with Dr. Brenda Mitchell and Dr. Linda Stelly. *The High School Journal, 90*(2), 16–22.

Schuh, J. H., & Laanan, F. S. (2006). Forced transitions: The impact of natural disasters and other events on college students. *New Directions for Student Services, 2006,* 93–102.

Southern Education Foundation. (2007). *Education after Katrina.* Atlanta, GA: Southern Education Foundation.

Sumner, J. (2007). Post Katrina: The story of the LSUHSC school of nursing. *Nursing Education Perspectives, 28,* 180–182.

Tarr, M. B., Birdwhistell, K. R., Birdwhistell, T. T., & Schmehl, R. (2007). Hurricane Katrina: Impacts at four university chemistry departments in New Orleans. *Journal of Chemical Health and Safety, 14,* 15–24.

Tinto, V. (1987). *Leaving college: Rethinking the causes and cures of student attrition.* Chicago, IL: University Press.

Tinto, V. (2004). *Student retention and graduation: Facing the truth, living with the consequences.* Washington, DC: The Pell Institute.

4

Federal Emergency Management Agency and Department of Education Guidelines

Colleges and universities have been the sites of previous and very likely will be future targets for both natural and man-made hazardous events. As we continue to develop as a nation, we continue to put in place laws as a result of actions that have taken place among our citizens.

On March 30, 2011, President Barack Obama issued *Presidential Policy Directive 8* (PPD-8): *National Preparedness,* which directed the establishment of the National Preparedness System (NPS) to support the National Preparedness Goal (NPG), which is that we become "a secure and resilient nation with the capabilities required across the whole community to prevent, protect against, mitigate, respond to, and recover from the threats and hazards that pose the greatest risk." College and university campuses as a unique composition of the whole community fall under this directive. While an individual campus may not have functions that align with all of the 31 core capabilities, there are certainly many that fall under the campus jurisdiction that need to be adopted. Worth noting is that this directive provides a mechanism for funding for emergency planning.

Listed here are the 31 core capabilities as identified by the NPG, mission area, as well as a description as listed at: http://www.fema.gov/core-capabilities.

PLANNING

Mission areas: All.

Description: Conduct a systematic process engaging the whole community as appropriate in the development of executable strategic, operational, and/or community-based approaches to meet defined objectives.

PUBLIC INFORMATION AND WARNING

Mission areas: All.

Description: Deliver coordinated, prompt, reliable, and actionable information to the whole community through the use of clear, consistent, accessible, and culturally and linguistically appropriate methods to effectively relay information regarding any threat or hazard, as well as the actions being taken and the assistance being made available, as appropriate.

OPERATIONAL COORDINATION

Mission areas: All.

Description: Establish and maintain a unified and coordinated operational structure and process that appropriately integrates all critical stakeholders and supports the execution of core capabilities.

FORENSICS AND ATTRIBUTION

Mission area: Prevention.

Description: Conduct forensic analysis and attribute terrorist acts (including the means and methods of terrorism) to their source, to include forensic analysis as well as attribution for an attack and for the preparation for an attack in an effort to prevent initial or follow-on acts and/or swiftly develop counter-options.

INTELLIGENCE AND INFORMATION SHARING

Mission areas: Prevention, Protection.

Description: Provide timely, accurate, and actionable information resulting from the planning, direction, collection, exploitation, processing, analysis, production, dissemination, evaluation, and feedback of available information concerning threats to the United States, its people, property, or interests; the development, proliferation, or use of WMDs; or any other matter bearing on U.S. national or homeland security by federal, state, local, and other stakeholders. Information sharing is the ability to exchange intelligence, information, data, or knowledge among federal, state, local, or private sector entities, as appropriate.

INTERDICTION AND DISRUPTION

Mission areas: Prevention, Protection.

Description: Delay, divert, intercept, halt, apprehend, or secure threats and/or hazards.

SCREENING, SEARCH, AND DETECTION

Mission areas: Prevention, Protection.

Description: Identify, discover, or locate threats and/or hazards through active and passive surveillance and search procedures. This may include the use of systematic examinations and assessments, sensor technologies, or physical investigation and intelligence.

ACCESS CONTROL AND IDENTITY VERIFICATION

Mission area: Protection.

Description: Apply a broad range of physical, technological, and cyber measures to control admittance to critical locations and systems, limiting access to authorized individuals to carry out legitimate activities.

CYBER SECURITY

Mission area: Protection.

Description: Protect against damage to, the unauthorized use of, and/ or the exploitation of (and, if needed, the restoration of) electronic communications systems and services (and the information contained therein).

PHYSICAL PROTECTIVE MEASURES

Mission area: Protection.
Description: Reduce or mitigate risks, including actions targeted at threats, vulnerabilities, and/or consequences, by controlling movement and protecting borders, critical infrastructure, and the homeland.

RISK MANAGEMENT FOR PROTECTION PROGRAMS AND ACTIVITIES

Mission area: Protection.
Description: Identify, assess, and prioritize risks to inform Protection activities and investments.

SUPPLY CHAIN INTEGRITY AND SECURITY

Mission area: Protection.
Description: Strengthen the security and resilience of the supply chain.

COMMUNITY RESILIENCE

Mission area: Mitigation.
Description: Lead the integrated effort to recognize, understand, communicate, plan, and address risks so that the community can develop a set of actions to accomplish Mitigation and improve resilience.

LONG-TERM VULNERABILITY REDUCTION

Mission area: Mitigation.
Description: Build and sustain resilient systems, communities, and critical infrastructure and key resources lifelines so as to reduce

their vulnerability to natural, technological, and human-caused incidents by lessening the likelihood, severity, and duration of the adverse consequences related to these incidents.

RISK AND DISASTER RESILIENCE ASSESSMENT

Mission area: Mitigation.

Description: Assess risk and disaster resilience so that decision makers, responders, and community members can take informed action to reduce their entity's risk and increase their resilience.

THREATS AND HAZARD IDENTIFICATION

Mission area: Mitigation.

Description: Identify the threats and hazards that occur in the geographic area; determine the frequency and magnitude; and incorporate this into analysis and planning processes so as to clearly understand the needs of a community or entity.

CRITICAL TRANSPORTATION

Mission area: Response.

Description: Provide transportation (including infrastructure access and accessible transportation services) for response priority objectives, including the evacuation of people and animals, and the delivery of vital response personnel, equipment, and services into the affected areas.

ENVIRONMENTAL RESPONSE/ HEALTH AND SAFETY

Mission area: Response.

Description: Ensure the availability of guidance and resources to address all hazards, including hazardous materials, acts of terrorism, and natural disasters in support of the responder operations and the affected communities.

FATALITY MANAGEMENT SERVICES

Mission area: Response.

Description: Provide fatality management services, including body recovery and victim identification, working with state and local authorities to provide temporary mortuary solutions, sharing information with mass care services for the purpose of reunifying family members and caregivers with missing persons/remains, and providing counseling to the bereaved.

INFRASTRUCTURE SYSTEMS

Mission area: Response, Recovery.

Description: Stabilize critical infrastructure functions, minimize health and safety threats, and efficiently restore and revitalize systems and services to support a viable, resilient community.

MASS CARE SERVICES

Mission area: Response.

Description: Provide life-sustaining services to the affected population with a focus on hydration, feeding, and sheltering to those who have the most need, as well as support for reunifying families.

MASS SEARCH AND RESCUE OPERATIONS

Mission area: Response.

Description: Deliver traditional and atypical search and rescue capabilities, including personnel, services, animals, and assets to survivors in need, with the goal of saving the greatest number of endangered lives in the shortest time possible.

ON-SCENE SECURITY AND PROTECTION

Mission area: Response.

Description: Ensure a safe and secure environment through law enforcement and related security and protection operations for people and communities located within affected areas and also for all traditional and atypical response personnel engaged in lifesaving and life-sustaining operations.

OPERATIONAL COMMUNICATIONS

Mission area: Response.

Description: Ensure the capacity for timely communications in support of security, situational awareness, and operations by any and all means available, among and between affected communities in the impact area and all response forces.

PUBLIC AND PRIVATE SERVICES AND RESOURCES

Mission area: Response.

Description: Provide essential public and private services and resources to the affected population and surrounding communities, to include emergency power to critical facilities, fuel support for emergency responders, and access to community staples (e.g., grocery stores, pharmacies, and banks), and fire and other first response services.

PUBLIC HEALTH AND MEDICAL SERVICES

Mission area: Response.

Description: Provide lifesaving medical treatment via emergency medical services and related operations and avoid additional disease and injury by providing targeted public health and medical support and products to all people in need within the affected area.

SITUATIONAL ASSESSMENT

Mission area: Response.

Description: Provide all decision makers with decision-relevant information regarding the nature and extent of the hazard, any cascading effects, and the status of the response.

ECONOMIC RECOVERY

Mission area: Recovery.

Description: Return economic and business activities (including food and agriculture) to a healthy state and develop new business and employment opportunities that result in a sustainable and economically viable community.

HEALTH AND SOCIAL SERVICES

Mission area: Recovery.

Description: Restore and improve health and social services networks to promote the resilience, independence, health (including behavioral health), and well-being of the whole community.

HOUSING

Mission area: Recovery.

Description: Implement housing solutions that effectively support the needs of the whole community and contribute to its sustainability and resilience.

NATURAL AND CULTURAL RESOURCES

Mission area: Recovery.

Description: Protect natural and cultural resources and historic properties through appropriate planning, mitigation, response, and recovery actions to preserve, conserve, rehabilitate, and restore them consistent with postdisaster community priorities and best practices and in compliance with appropriate environmental and historical preservation laws and executive orders.

In addition to the core capabilities directive there are laws, codes, regulations, and guidelines aimed at providing a safe college and university environment; U.S. Public Law 110-315, Higher Education Opportunity Act (HEOA), and the Code of Federal Regulations (34 CFR). Consistent with this directive, the U.S. Department of Education, Emergency Management for Higher Education, has developed regulations that require colleges and universities to have in place an emergency management plan that integrates all departments and facilities across the campus and include all-hazards capabilities for all four emergency management phases: preparedness, response, recovery, mitigation. A critical component that must now be included in the campus emergency preparedness plan is a mechanism to address the mental health needs of students, staff, and faculty and have in place a written plan of action for identifying and managing those identified as persons of concern. The intention is to prevent acts of violence on campus by unstable individuals whose intent is to harm others and or themselves. For a full understanding of the capabilities of the U.S. Department of Education and its dedication to providing a safe educational environment, one can look to the Center for School Preparedness housed in the Office of Safe and Healthy Students (OSHS).

Competitive grants are available for college and universities under the Project School Emergency Response to Violence (SERV) for campuses recovering from a violent or traumatic event where the learning environment has been compromised. There are two types of grants available: the Immediate Services Grant, limited to $50,000 for a period of 6 months, is limited to use in meeting immediate needs for restoring the campus learning environment and the Extended Services Grant, limited to $250,000 for a period of up to 18 months, used to meet longer term needs surrounding recovery efforts in restoring the campus learning environment for students, staff, and faculty. There needs to have been a significant impact to the campus and a very clear *research-based plan and effective practices related to recovery from traumatic events*, included in the proposal for restoring the campus to its pre-event status in order for this award to be granted.

Grant money has been available in the past through the Emergency Management for Higher Education grant fund for the purpose of developing or updating all-hazards emergency management plans for colleges and universities. In order to be awarded money under this grant, all four phases (Prevention-Mitigation, Preparedness, Response, and Recovery) of the emergency management cycle must be addressed. The plans must integrate development, planning, and training across the campus, as well as inclusion of community partners. The emergency preparedness plan must be inclusive across the campus (to include students, staff, and faculty, with or without special needs whether they be physical or cognitive) with procedures detailed for communication, medical access, and mental health programs. The plan must address both short-term (such as Methicillin-resistant Staphylococcus aureus (MRSA) or food-borne illnesses) and long-term infectious disease outbreaks (such as pandemic influenza and Ebola); violence prevention programs that focus on identifying and monitoring students, staff, and faculty who are in danger of doing harm to themselves and/or the community; and a plan for the continuation of business operations, which include the business of educating students, as well as all other key functions across the campus during and following an emergency event. For the complete guidelines on the Project SERV Immediate Services and Extended Services Grant Program, visit: www.http://www2.ed.gov/about/offices/list/oese/oshs/aboutus.html.

The Readiness Emergency Management program has grants available for reviewing and revising emergency management plans, training school staff, conducting building and facilities audits, implementing the National Incident Management System (NIMS), developing an infectious disease plan, developing or revising food defense plans, conducting drills and tabletop simulation exercises, and preparing and distributing copies of emergency management plans.

In addition to enacting regulations, the federal government has written numerous documents to assist colleges and universities in prevention, mitigation, response, and recovery strategies for emergency and crisis events. In addition to the Leavitt, Spellings and Gonzales (2007) "Report to the President—On Issues Raised by the Virginia Tech Tragedy," the federal government funded research for *Building a Disaster-Resistant University* (FEMA, 2003) and *Practical Information on Crisis Planning: A Guide for Schools and Communities* (DOE, 2007). All these documents are well worth reading. The *Practical Information on Crisis Planning: A Guide for Schools and Communities* (DOE, 2007) focuses on what all schools need to be doing in order to prevent injuries, protect the lives of students and staff, as well as minimize damage to the facilities. This study produced key principles for effective crisis planning that includes ideas for leadership development and creating an effective crisis plan that incorporates the integration of community partners such as law enforcement, fire safety officials, and emergency medical services. The DOE (2007) research team conducted focus groups across the country with educators and emergency response personnel. What surfaced was the importance of using a common vocabulary during a crisis event and the benefits of training with all facets of the community: students, staff, faculty, and community partners, so that when and if an event occurs members can appropriately respond and recovery will be attended to with practiced efficiency (DOE, 2007). The National Response Framework (FEMA, 2008), the *Action Guide for Emergency Management at Institutions of Higher Education* (DOE, 2009), and *Building a Disaster-Resistant University* (FEMA, 2003) are the three overarching documents that set the cornerstone for this resource book. Let us explore these three documents and how they set the stage for all college and university emergency preparedness plans.

FEMA AND DOE WORKING TOGETHER

The National Response Framework (NRF) developed by the U.S. Department of Homeland Security, Federal Emergency Management Agency in 2008, is an all-hazards guide that defines the roles and responsibilities for all levels of government, nongovernmental organizations, and the private sector. FEMA (2008) states that education and training for safety must first begin with individuals, families, communities, local organizations, workplaces, and schools. *Building a Disaster-Resistant University* (FEMA, 2003) and the *Action Guide for Emergency Management at Institutions of Higher Education* (DOE, 2009) are guidelines for emergency management at institutions of higher education to help them to be better prepared to meet the needs of students, staff, and faculty at college and university campuses in the event that a natural or man-made hazardous event occurs. They provide frameworks for colleges and universities to follow regarding keeping campuses safe from both man-made and natural hazards. The guidelines include minimizing the risk to students, staff, and faculty, safeguarding the continuity of business operations with the development of an all-hazards plan, having a well-practiced team following an ICS structure, and integrating campus emergency preparedness activities with the community external to the campus.

FEMA (2003) states that "Higher education institutions…are realizing that improving their campus' resistance to disaster will not only protect their own lives and those of their students, it will also safeguard their campus' instruction, research, and public service" (p. 1). Aligning campus emergency preparedness plans with the government documents not only will assist in keeping college and university campuses safe, but it will also provide support for the continuity of business operations should such a critical event befall the community.

The DOE (2009) and FEMA (2003) were specifically aimed at emergency preparedness in institutions of higher education. Neither document makes reference to the NRF (devised before DOE, 2009 and after FEMA, 2003) whose objective is to protect the American people and our critical infrastructure and key resources. "The (NRF) strategy sets forth that to protect the lives and livelihoods of the American people, we must undertake measures to deter the threat of terrorism, mitigate the Nation's vulnerability to acts of terror and the full range of manmade and natural catastrophes, and minimize the consequences of an attack or disaster should it occur" (FEMA, 2008, p. 13). As this is a national strategy, it is then logical that all other strategies are subordinate and should align with its structure and objectives. Accordingly, the FEMA (2003) and the DOE (2009) documents should then be aligned to the NRF as institutions of higher education fall into the categories stated in the NRF.

The article "A Study of Emergency Preparedness of U.S. Colleges and Universities" (Connolly, 2010) used alignment with the NRF as a proxy to measure emergency preparedness in institutions of higher education. This study is important because it dissects the emergency preparedness guidelines that both FEMA and DOE have put in place for institutions of higher education and suggests that as entities that fall within the government, private-sector, and/or nongovernmental organizations, such guidelines should adhere to the NRF. The following is a synopsis of the study.

Government agencies are in place to provide assistance, but it is the responsibility of individuals and organizations to develop personal and organizational contingency plans that fit and align with the State and federal guidelines. The five principles of the NRF are critical to preparation, response, and recovery from man-made and natural hazards whether the incident takes place at an educational institution or the community at large. For the institution of higher education, this alignment of its emergency preparedness plans to the NRF increases the probability that no stone is left unturned in the preparation of its plans to keep students, faculty, and staff safe in the event of a man-made or natural emergency.

The five principles are:

1. Engaged partnership
2. Tiered response
3. Scalable, flexible, and adaptable operational capabilities
4. Unity of effort through unified command
5. Readiness to act

NRF Principle 1: Engaged Partnerships

Engaged partnership refers to the overarching need for all members of the community—internal and external to the campus—to participate in emergency preparedness measures. In order to be able to quickly assimilate into an active response scene, the community responders need to know the composition and makeup of not only the physical structure but also the human components. This is best accomplished by developing and nurturing relationships prior to an incident. A campus community is located within a larger community: a town, a county, a state. Therefore, the crisis or disasters that plague the campus are of concern to the community at large. NRF Principle 1 suggests that "preparedness activities should be coordinated among all involved agencies within the jurisdiction, as well as across jurisdictions" (FEMA, 2008, p. 9).

The Department of Education (DOE, 2009) specifically recommends that training be conducted with community partners such as fire, police, and other emergency responders. It also recommends that these same parties have input when designing the policies, procedures, and protocols. As experts in their respective areas, they can offer expertise in the specifics of law enforcement, medical assistance, and other public health parameters. The DOE recognizes that it is advantageous to have developed mutual aid agreements with these community partners and others prior to an event taking place. In order to quickly offer assistance it is imperative that community partners have access to a detailed or GIS map of the campus. The DOE recognizes that during a critical event is not the time to be searching for a detailed campus map.

FEMA (2003) also recognizes that "the local government and the university or college should have a close working relationship" to reduce risk (p. 12). It also makes mention of the advantages of a detailed or GIS campus map. Regarding mutual aid agreements, FEMA states that "the university should be familiar with local nonprofit organizations and their services and should enter into mutually supportive agreements where appropriate" (p. 15).

NRF Principle 2: Tiered Response

The second principle of the NRF states that "incidents should be handled at the lowest jurisdictional level capable of handling the work" (p. 27). Tiered response refers to a campus's need to recognize that management of an event may be handled by the first on scene; whether that is a student, staff, or faculty member. It also embraces the concept that input in developing the campus emergency preparedness plan is necessary from all levels of campus staff and administration. It recognizes that the eyes and ears at the lowest level may have valuable information that can quickly defuse an incident and bring the campus to its pre-incident state. In order to have the capability to do so, emergency preparedness planning must include everyone on the campus in emergency preparation, response, and recovery activities.

Statements found in DOE (2009) that link to NRF Principle 2 include, "Responsibility for developing, testing, and implementing an emergency management plan should be shared and communicated across all departments and functions" (p. 4). The DOE also states that "routine, multi-hazard training should be conducted with faculty, staff, and other support personnel, focusing on the protocols and procedures in the emergency management plan" (p. 5).

The Department of Education (2007) states

> Knowing how to respond quickly and efficiently in a crisis is critical to ensuring the safety of our schools. The midst of a crisis is not the time to start figuring out who ought to do what. At that moment, everyone – from top to bottom – should know the drill and know each other. (p. 1-1)

When looking to develop skills for the lowest level of response, FEMA (2003) recommends, that it "start with a thorough inventory of all potential stakeholders across the three traditional divisions of academia—administration, faculty, and students" (p. 5). To be considered truly comprehensive, all stakeholders must be involved.

NRF Principle 3: Scalable, Flexible, and Adaptable Operational Capabilities

NRF Principle 3 states "as incidents change in size, scope, and complexity, the resource must adapt to meet requirements" (p. 10). Scalable, flexible, and adaptable takes into account that there are countless incidents that can befall a campus, and it may be impossible to have an exact plan for every incident. Therefore, a good all-hazards plan is the foundation and the campus community should be trained to expand or modify its plan, to respond to the circumstances. The types of incidents that can befall a campus are innumerable and impossible to predict. It is unlikely that a campus will have a written response to every possible type of emergency that it may encounter. The necessary asset is the ability to be flexible to expand and/or scale back operations as the scene dictates (Hough & Spillan, 2005; Pearson & Mitroff, 1993; Trump, 2000; Zdziarski, Dunkel, & Rollo, 2007).

Questions for administrators to ask when looking to measure a college/university's alignment with Principle 3 include asking if, in creating the emergency preparedness plan, an analysis was conducted to identify potential hazards, threats, and vulnerabilities; if the emergency preparedness plans define procedures for students, faculty, staff, visitors, and persons with special needs, shelter-in-place, lock-down, evacuation, educational continuity, and business continuity; whether there is a mechanism in place for referring students, staff, and faculty of concern. If so, what is that mechanism? These questions contribute to making a college/university emergency preparedness plan adaptable to any number of incidents involving any number of people who may be found on campus.

Having multiple modes of communication is a critical component in a campus's ability to relay information and adapt its operational capabilities. Colleges include a number of the following modes of communication in their emergency preparedness plans: e-mail, cell and landline phone broadcasts, text message broadcasts, social media, website postings, warning alarms, signs posted around campus, and PA systems. Many have created communications templates so that at a time of heightened activity, the foundation of the message is ready for pertinent incident-specific information to be added for communicating with the media, students, faculty, staff, external community, and families.

There is evidence that the DOE supports an emergency response plan that has scalable, flexible, and adaptable operational capabilities. DOE (2009) states, "The Institution of Higher Education (IHE) emergency management plan must be based on a comprehensive design, while also providing for staff, students, faculty, and visitors with special needs" (p. 4). DOE recommends adding flexibility to the plan as it would be impossible to script every event that could occur.

FEMA (2003) states that "the first step in conducting a hazard identification and risk assessment is to identify the natural and man-made hazards that present risk to your college or university" (p. 21). FEMA (2003) recommends that campus and community mental health professionals are included "for evaluating persons who are at-risk of causing harm to themselves or others" (p. 10). Other recommendations are to "establish an emergency notification system using multiple modes of communication to alert persons on campus that an emergency is approaching or occurred" (p. 10). As internal and external communication is imperative, FEMA

63

recommends "...develop(ing) a campus emergency communications plan that may include drafting template messages for communicating with the media, students, faculty, staff, community, and families prior to, during, and after an emergency" (p. 10). This will assist in relaying important information that could aid in the recovery from an incident. "By recognizing the hazards your institution faces and estimating potential losses from these events, your long-range planning efforts will improve and your institution will be more likely to make strategic choices that incorporate the principles of disaster mitigation" (p. 28). Taking all of these factors into account contributes to a campus's ability to include scalable, flexible, and adaptable operational capabilities to its emergency response plan.

NRF Principle 4: Unity of Effort through Unified Command

Unity of effort takes into account that all members of the community need to know what the plan is, who is in charge, what the response expectations are, and how information will be communicated throughout the event. Each and every campus member needs to know what is expected of them and the roles and responsibilities of each member of the community. There is agreement by researchers that by providing a job description for crisis responders that summarizes their tasks, duties, and responsibilities will provide a clearer understanding of the expectations of the college/ university (Clement, 2002; Trump, 2000; Zdziarski et al., 2007).

During an emergency, it is sometimes unclear as to who is in charge. When an incident occurs, there may be leadership from multiple departments involved with resolving the event. However, they must all work together and not undermine each other. In order to prevent leadership chaos, the incident command system (ICS) has been integrated into campus emergency preparedness plans. To be considered ICS consistent, the campus is managed under five functional areas: command, operations, planning, logistics, and finance and administration. The leadership comprises the command staff that includes the Incident Commander, the Public Information Officer (PIO), Safety Officer (SO), and Liaison Officer (LNO). The general staff consists of personnel who represent the five functional areas. Both DOE and FEMA documents mention items that assist the general staff in areas of the ICS functions. This includes such items as the need for constant communication between all internal and external stakeholders, and making sure that all radio systems (campus police, security personnel, local law enforcement, local first responders) are interoperable.

DOE (2009) states that "establish(ing) an incident command system (ICS) is consistent with the National Incident Management System (NIMS) for organizing personnel and services to respond in the event of an emergency" (p. 9). The first person on the scene is called the incident commander since they have the most information about what occurred. This could be a professor, an administrator, or anyone who was there first and has taken control of managing the situation. As others who have a higher level of skills arrive on the scene, the incident command position is handed off. FEMA (2003) states that "it is imperative that you establish and cultivate relationships with campus leadership and acquire permanent authority to manage disaster resistance efforts."

NRF Principle 5: Readiness to Act

Readiness to act refers to a college or university's ability to respond appropriately to any event that befalls the campus community, as quickly as possible. In order to do so, there needs to be a plan in place, which includes emergency preparedness training for those on the emergency preparedness team as well as for those not on the team. Once an incident is in progress, an emergency response is executed. Those that have a practiced plan are in a better position to respond effectively. Most colleges and universities have emergency preparedness plans in place; however, many of them do not meet the recommended government guidelines (DOE, 2009; FEMA, 2003). Additionally, most plans are not updated regularly and few train their employees on the content and procedures of their emergency preparedness plans and as a result are not ready to act. Recommendations found in the guidelines include keeping the campus community practiced by training all personnel with an all-hazards focus at least once a year.

FEMA (2003) recognizes that it is the responsibility of the campus to maintain a safe environment for its students, staff, faculty, and visitors as well as to protect its facility. "Higher education institutions...are realizing that improving their campus' resistance to disaster will not only protect their own lives and those of their students, it will also safeguard their campus' instruction, research, and public service" (FEMA, 2003, p. 1). FEMA and DOE both agree that the plan needs to be reviewed at least annually and that it is imperative to test and practice the plan in training sessions, drills, and exercises. Additionally, having a well-integrated campus CERT team in place can only add to the readiness to act capably.

Table 4.1 lists each of the five NRF principles, the expectations for colleges/universities looking to align their emergency preparedness plans

Table 4.1 Principles for Establishing the EM Plan

NRF Principles	Expectations	Questions for Administrators
Principle #1: Engaged Partnership	• Community participation	How well established are relationships with (town, city, county, state) community partners, government officials, and first responders (police, fire, and office of emergency management)?
	• Campus-community wide emergency preparedness training: • Communication • Scenarios	How often does your college/university train for emergencies with the (town, city, county, state) community partners, government officials, and first responders (police, fire, and office of emergency management)?
	• Mutual aid agreements	Does your college/university have mutual aid agreements in place with outside providers to provide resources (such as food, transportation, medical services, and volunteers) in the event of an emergency?
	• Availability of maps	Does your plan include a map of campus facilities? Is the map GIS based?
Principle #2: Tiered Response	• Development of emergency preparedness plan	Who was involved in developing your campus emergency preparedness plan?
	• Participation in emergency preparedness training	Who is included in the emergency preparedness training at your college/university?
Principle #3: Scalable, Flexible, Adaptable, Operational Capabilities	• Hazard analysis conducted	In creating the emergency preparedness plan at your college/university was an analysis conducted to identify potential hazards, threats, and vulnerabilities?

(Continued)

Table 4.1 (*Continued*)   Principles for Establishing the EM Plan

NRF Principles	Expectations	Questions for Administrators
	• Emergency preparedness plans in place for students, faculty, staff, visitors	Does your college/university emergency preparedness plan define procedures for students, faculty, staff, visitors, and persons with special need? Does it include shelter-in-place, lock-down, evacuation, educational continuity, and business continuity?
		Are there mechanisms in place for referring students, staff, and faculty of concern?
	• Referral systems in place for persons of concern	What mechanism does your college/university use to refer individuals of concern?
	• Multiple communications systems in place	What modes of communication are included in your college/university emergency preparedness plan: e-mail, cell and landline phone broadcasts, text message broadcasts, website postings, warning alarms, signs posted around campus, PA system.
		Are templates in place for communicating with the media, students, faculty, staff, external community, families?
Principle #4: Unity of Effort	• Leadership clarification	Would it be clear who is in charge and how leadership responsibility will be handled as an emergency evolves at your campus?
	• ICS and NIMS compliance	Is your college/university emergency preparedness plan organized using the ICS and NIMS structure?

(Continued)

Table 4.1 (*Continued*)   Principles for Establishing the EM Plan

NRF Principles	Expectations	Questions for Administrators
	• Radio interoperability	Are radio systems of college/university police or security personnel interoperable with local first responders (police, fire, and office of emergency management)?
Principle #5: Readiness to Act	• Presence of emergency preparedness plan	Does your campus have an emergency preparedness plan?
	• Annual review of the emergency preparedness plan	How often is your campus emergency preparedness plan reviewed and updated?
	• Presence of an emergency preparedness team	Does your campus have an emergency preparedness team?
	• Frequency of emergency preparedness training	How often is emergency preparedness training provided for: review of the plan, evacuation drill, shelter-in-place drill, table-top exercises, training with local responders?
	• Existence of CERT team	Does your campus have a CERT team in place?

with the NRF, as well as specific questions to be asked of administrators and the emergency preparedness team.

Now that we have examined how the NRF (FEMA, 2008), *Building a Disaster-Resistant University* (FEMA, 2003), and the *Action Guide for Emergency Management at Institutions of Higher Education* (DOE, 2009) coalesce, let us look at two questions addressed in Connolly (2010). To what extent do the emergency preparedness plans of colleges and universities align with the NRF, FEMA (2008)? And, does the institution type play a role in alignment with the National Response Framework (NRF)?

To determine alignment with the NRF, a 20-question survey was developed based on FEMA (2003) and the DOE (2009) guidelines written specifically for such institutions. There were 254 respondent colleges/universities; of these, data from 138 were usable. The institutions were categorized as they are listed by the New York State Education Department

Table 4.2 Emergency Preparedness Index (EPI) Means by College/University Classification

Classification	N	Mean	SD
Independent	51	25.73	6.664
State	73	27.96	6.661
City	7	32.29	4.821
Proprietary	7	21.86	9.990
Total	138	27.04	6.985

(NYSED) in the New York State Directory of Colleges and Universities found at www.highered.nysed.gov. There was usable data from 138 respondents; 51 (37%) from institutions categorized as independent colleges/universities, 73 (53%) from state colleges/universities, and 7 (5%) from city colleges/universities, and 7 (5%) from proprietary colleges/universities. An Emergency Preparedness Index (EPI) was constructed where an EPI of 40 is the highest score a college/university could receive and is equivalent to the college/university receiving a score of 2 (*aligned*) for each of the 20 survey questions or guidelines. The mean EPI for the 138 respondents was 27. If 40 is a perfect EPI score equivalent to 100% alignment, then a mean of 27 is equivalent to 67% alignment with the government recommendations for emergency preparedness (Table 4.2).

Principle 1: Engaged Response

72% had developed relationships with community partners
60% train with community partners
63% have mutual aid agreements in place
15% had a detailed or GIS map

Results of the study found that there were only 7% of institutions that achieved *alignment* with Principle 1: *Engaged Response*. A campus community is located within a larger community: towns, a county, a state, and, therefore, the crisis or disasters that plague the campus are of concern to the community at large. The first principle of the NRF suggests that "preparedness activities should be coordinated among all involved agencies within the jurisdiction, as well as across jurisdictions" (FEMA, 2008, p. 9). Consistent with this doctrine, Helsloot and Jong (2006) found that "the risks falling under the domain of higher education as a microcosm of society are the risks that face society at large" (p. 3). Donald (2002) too agrees that "minimizing risk and creating safer communities must be integrated into the local political, cultural and planning-development framework" (p. 17). Unfortunately, a very small percentage of the respondents have taken the time to develop these relationships and make mutual aid agreements in advance. This is consistent with the findings of previous studies where emergency preparedness is typically found at the bottom of the list of an educational institution's agenda (Mitroff, 2008; Zdziarski et al., 2007).

Principle 2: Tiered Response

Emergency plans were not created with input from across the institution.

Emergency preparedness training was not being conducted across all departments.

Principle 2 *Tiered Response* had the lowest alignment with only 2% of colleges and universities meeting the guidelines. Zdziarski et al. (2007) state to "understand and be well prepared for their roles in responding to crisis" (p. 184), the entire community needs to be aware of the plan and its intricacies. The DOE states that "routine, multi-hazard training should be conducted with faculty, staff, and other support personnel, focusing on the protocols and procedures in the emergency management plan" (p. 5). Most colleges and universities that responded to this survey that conducted emergency preparedness training, most frequently did not include everyone on the campus in its training. More often it was only the emergency preparedness team which most often only conducted a review of the emergency preparedness plan.

Principle 3: Scalable, Flexible, and Adaptable Operational Capabilities

86% conducted a hazard analysis before constructing the emergency preparedness plan

76% had referral systems in place for individuals of concern

68% had individual procedures in place for a variety of potential incidents

57% had a mechanism in place to refer individuals of concern

30% had communications templates in place

When examining alignment with Principle 3, *Scalable, Flexible, and Adaptable Operational Capabilities*, it was discovered that respondents indicated their emergency response plans did not consider the multi-hazards that could occur at the campus, and emergency preparedness training was lacking for all constituents on the campus. Unfortunately this, too, was consistent with the literature. Borodzicz (2004) conducted a review of studies that used simulations for crisis management training exercises. His study found that "a crisis typically develops fast, confronting decision makers with large quantities of conflicting or erroneous information" (Borodzicz, 2004, p. 417). He argues that "qualitative skills, such as flexibility, negotiation, and the ability to effectively communicate, may be key to facilitating crisis management" (Borodzicz, 2004, p. 419). Borodzicz found "that in every single case of a successfully managed crisis event, the positive outcome could be directly linked to creative or flexible rule breaking by key decision makers in the response" (p. 418). The findings indicate that campuses need to develop plans and initiate training that could assist those who encounter an emergency event with the tools to manage it successfully. It is unlikely that a campus will have a written response to every possible type of emergency that it may encounter. The necessary asset is the ability to be flexible to expand and/or scale back operations as the scene dictates (Hough & Spillan, 2005; Pearson & Mitroff, 1993; Trump, 2000; Zdziarski et al., 2007). Additionally, only 17% had 5 or more of the 8 various modes of communication in place that would give them the alignment designation.

Principle 4: Unity of Effort through Unified Command
Principle 5: Readiness to Act

The closest alignment was with Principle 4: *Unity of Effort through Unified Command* and Principle 5: *Readiness to Act*. What contributed to the high alignment?

99% have an emergency preparedness plan
90% reviewed their emergency preparedness plan at least once a
    year
90% have clear leadership
91% had an emergency preparedness team
77% are NIMS compliant
63% have radio interoperability
28% conduct training exercises
29% have a CERT team in place

Why aren't the EPI scores and alignment with the DOE and FEMA guidelines higher? Colleges and universities, like many other organizations, have placed emergency and crisis planning near the bottom of their priorities. College and universities, like most other organizations in America, tend to be reactionary rather than proactive when it comes to emergency preparedness (Mitroff, Diamond, & Alpaslan, 2006). Or you may prefer an alternative mindset; as Bolman and Deal (2003) state, when people are faced with an issue (regardless of its topic) that, "the problem is not a lack of intellectual wattage but a lack of understanding of what they (in this case college administrators) are up against and what remedies might work" (p. 4) (Table 4.3).

No matter what focus you take, action must move forward in more assertive emergency management practices at colleges and universities. Colleges and universities that were aligned with the NRF principles were more inclined to have participated in training activities, such as an evacuation drill, a shelter-in-place drill, a table top exercise, and a full-scale drill, and to have trained with local responders. They also were more inclined than other respondents to have a campus CERT in place. This is consistent with a study done by Pearson and Mitroff (1993) outside of academia. They investigated why some organizations are better prepared to act during emergency events. They found that the companies that were better prepared have crisis plans and teams in place that regularly conduct practice drills in "conditions which simulate the informational and emotional overload that they will face during the heat of a real crisis" (p. 54).

Does institution type play a role in alignment with the NRF?

Colleges/universities that were defined as city yielded the highest mean EPI of 32 or 80% alignment, followed by state with an EPI of

Table 4.3 Emergency Preparedness Index (EPI) by Principle and Institution Type

	Mean EPIs by Principle					Mean EPI by Category
	Principle 1	Principle 2	Principle 3	Principle 4	Principle 5	
Independent	4.82	1.66	7.92	7.76	3.54	26
State	5.65	1.80	8.20	8.60	3.72	28
City	6.28	1.85	10.42	8.85	4.85	32
Proprietary	4.28	1.14	7.42	6.28	2.71	22
Total	5.25	1.61	8.49	7.87	3.70	27

28 or 70% alignment, independent with an EPI of 26 or 65% alignment. While the mean EPT was highest for city colleges/universities, there were more state colleges/universities than any other institution type that were aligned with every principle on government recommendations. Proprietary colleges/universities had the lowest mean EPI of 22 or 53% alignment.

SUMMARY AND DISCUSSION

Colleges and universities have been the sites of previous and very likely will be future targets for both natural and man-made hazardous events. FEMA (2003) and DOE (2009) have written guidelines for emergency management at institutions of higher education to help them to be better prepared to meet the needs of students, staff, and faculty at college and university campuses in the event that a natural or man-made hazardous event occurs. FEMA (2003) states, "Higher education institutions...are realizing that improving their campus' resistance to disaster will not only protect their own lives and those of their students, it will also safeguard their campus' instruction, research, and public service" (p. 1). Aligning campus emergency preparedness plans with the government documents not only will assist in keeping college and university campuses safe, but it will also provide support for the continuity of business operations should such a critical event befall the community.

REFERENCES

Bolman, L. G., & Deal, T. E. (2003). *Reframing organizations: Artistry, choice, and leadership.* San Francisco, CA: Jossey-Bass.

Borodzicz, E. (2004). The missing ingredient is the value of flexibility. *Simulation & Gaming, 35,* 414–426.

Clement, L. M. (2002). *Confronting undesirable traditions: A case study.* In C. K. Wilkinson (Eds.), *Addressing contemporary campus safety issues* (pp. 47–55). San Francisco, CA: Jossey-Bass.

Code of Federal Regulations. *34CFR.* Retrieved from http://www.gpo.gov/fdsys/browse/collectionCfr.action?collectionCode=CFR

Connolly, M. (2011). *A study of emergency preparedness of U.S. colleges and universities.* Retrieved from http://eric.ed.gov/?id=ED539413

Donald, G. (2002). *The Shanghai principles for creating safer cities and societies through sustainable urban development.* FEMA Emergency Management Institute. Retrieved from https://training.fema.gov/EMIWeb/downloads/Theshanghai- principles.doc

Emergency Management for Higher Education Grant Program. Funding. Retrieved from http://www2.ed.gov/programs/emergencyhighed/legislation.html

FEMA. (2003). *Building a disaster-resistant university.* Retrieved from http://www.fema.gov/institution/dru.shtm

FEMA. (2008). *National response framework.* Washington, DC: U.S. Department of Homeland Security. Retrieved from http://www.fema.gov/nrf

Helsloot, I., & Jong, W. (2006). Risk management in higher education and research in the Netherlands. *Journal of Contingencies and Crisis Management,* 125–141.

Hough, M. G., & Spillan, J. E. (2005). Crisis planning: Increasing effectiveness, decreasing discomfort. *Journal of Business & Economics Research, 3*(4), 19–24.

Leavitt, M. O., Spellings, M., & Gonzales, A. R. (2007). Report to the President on issues raised by the Virginia Tech Tragedy. Washington, DC: United States Government.

Mitroff, I. I. (2008, August 15). *Two challenges: Crisis management and spirituality.* Retrieved from Bernstein Crisis Management, Inc. http://www.bernsteincrisismanagement.com/newsletter/crisis-manager-080915.html

Mitroff, I. I., Diamond, M. A., & Alpaslan, C. M. (January/February 2006). How prepared are America's colleges and universities for major crises? *Change, 38*(1), 60–67.

Pearson, C. M., & Mitroff, I. I. (1993). From crisis prone to crisis prepared: A framework for crisis management. *Academy of Management Executive, 7*(1), 48–59.

Presidential Policy Directive/PPD-8: National Preparedness. (2011). Retrieved from http://www.dhs.gov/presidential-policy-directive-8-national-preparedness

Project SERV (Immediate Services and Extended Grant Program). Retrieved from www2.ed.gov/about/offices/list/oesc/oshs/aboutus.html

Project SERV (School Emergency Response to Violence). Retrieved from www2.ed.gov/programs/dvppserv/index.html

Trump, K. S. (2000). *Classroom killers? Hallway hostages? How schools can prevent and manage school crises.* Thousand Oaks, CA: Corwin Press.

U.S. Department of Education. *Office of safe and healthy schools.* Retrieved from www2.ed.gov/about/offices/list/oese/oshs/index.html

U.S. Department of Education. (2007). *Practical information on crisis planning: A guide for schools and communities.* Retrieved from http://www.ed.gov/admins/lead/safety/emergencyplan/crisisplanning.pdf

U.S. Department of Education. (2009). *Action guide for emergency management at institutions of higher education.* Retrieved June 29, 2009, from http://www.ed.gov/admins/lead/safety/emergencyplan/remsactionguide.pdf

U.S. Public Law 110-315. *Higher education opportunity act.* Retrieved from http://www.gpo.gov/fdsys/pkg/PLAW-110publ315/content-detail.html

Zdziarski, E. L., Dunkel, N. W., & Rollo, J. M. (2007). *Campus crisis management: A comprehensive guide to planning, prevention, response, and recovery.* San Francisco, CA: Jossey-Bass.

5

Organizing an Incident Command System/National Incident Management System Compliant Team

Both the Department of Homeland Security and the Department of Education state that colleges and universities that use a whole community, multihazards approach to emergency planning, and adopt the National Incident Management System (NIMS) and Incident Command System (ICS) are better prepared to respond in partnership with local, state, tribal, and federal agencies. As this organizational system is not the typical campus configuration, this chapter will attempt to clarify how a college can organize itself to be ICS and NIMS compliant.

The understanding of how a college or university can comply with federal initiatives for emergency planning begins with an understanding of the directives. The National Incident Management System (NIMS) was developed by the U.S. Department of Homeland Security (DHS), under Homeland Security Presidential Directive 5 (HSPD-5) issued by President George W. Bush on February 28, 2003. It is designed to structure the framework used nationwide for both governmental and nongovernmental agencies to respond to natural disasters and/or terrorist attacks at the local, state, and federal levels of government. HSPD-5 also requires all federal agencies to make adoption of NIMS by state, tribal, and local organizations a condition for federal funding. Presidential Policy Directive (PPD-8), issued on March 30, 2011, by President Barack Obama, provides guidance that further strengthens the nation's ability to respond to threats and hazards. It identifies five core mission areas necessary to improve preparedness capabilities: Prevention, Protection, Mitigation, Response, and Recovery. The five mission phases defined:

Prevention, for the purposes of this PPMRR guidebook, means the action that colleges/universities take to avoid or deter an emergency event from occurring.

Protection focuses on ongoing actions that protect the campus community: students, teachers, staff, visitors, networks, and property from a threat or hazard.

Mitigation means reducing the likelihood that threats and hazards will happen.

Response means the actions taken to stabilize the campus once a critical event has occurred or is about to happen in an unpreventable way.

Recovery means the actions taken to return the campus to its pre-event status.

These mission areas align with the three time frames associated with an incident: before, during, and after. The majority of Prevention, Protection, and Mitigation activities generally occur before an incident, although these three mission areas do have ongoing activities that can occur throughout an incident. Response activities occur during an incident, and Recovery activities can begin during an incident and continue to occur after an incident.

All federal funding received by a college or university requires that the institution adopt NIMS. The Department of Homeland Security defines NIMS as:

- A comprehensive, nationwide, systematic approach to Incident Management
- A set of preparedness concepts and principles for all hazards
- Essential principles for a common operating picture and interoperability of communications and information management
- Standardized resource management procedures
- Scalable, so it may be used for all incidents
- A dynamic system that promotes ongoing management and maintenance

NIMS focuses on five key areas, or components:

1. Preparedness
   a. Planning
   b. Procedures and Protocols
   c. Training and Exercises
   d. Personnel Qualifications and Certification
   e. Equipment Certification

2. Communications and Information Management
   Promotes flexible communications and information systems.

   Built on the concepts of
   a. Common Operating Picture
   b. Interoperability
   c. Reliability, Scalability, and Portability
   d. Resiliency and Redundancy

3. Resource Management
   NIMS describes standardized resource management practices such as typing, inventorying, organizing, and tracking that allows for effective sharing and integration of critical resources across jurisdictions as well as activating, dispatching, and deactivating those systems prior to, during, and after an incident. Managing people, their skills, and equipment needed to manage a critical event fall under NIMS resource management practices.

4. Command and Management
   NIMS enables effective and efficient incident management and coordination by providing a flexible, standardized incident management structure. This structure integrates three key organizational constructs:
   a. Incident Command System
   b. Multi-Agency Coordination System
   c. Public Information

5. Ongoing Management and Maintenance
   The FEMA National Integration Center (NIC) provides strategic direction, oversight, and coordination of NIMS. NIMS curriculum recommends that emergency operations plans (EOPs) identify Goals, Objectives, and Action Items for each identified threat and/or hazard.

If campuses are to incorporate NIMS and the presidential directives, including the five mission areas into the campus plans,
rather than call them emergency preparedness or crisis management plans, a more inclusive term should be used to identify plans
that include Preparedness, Prevention, Mitigation, Response, and
Recovery strategies. Until a better term is identified, this resource
book will call these PPMRR strategies when referring to campus
emergency and crisis planning.

NIMS requires the implementation of the incident command system (ICS).
The Department of Homeland Security defines the ICS as a standardized,
on-scene, all-hazards incident management approach that

- Allows for the integration of facilities, equipment, personnel, procedures and communications operating within a common organizational structure
- Enables a coordinated response among various jurisdictions and
functional agencies, both public and private
- Establishes common processes for planning and managing
resources

The goal of the ICS system is to ensure the safety of responders and others, achievement of tactical objectives and the efficient use of resources.
Its characteristics include common terminology; correct terminology for
organizations, positions, resources, facilities; clear plain language; chain
of command; and a three-to-seven person span of control.

Many colleges and universities are not familiar with ICS terminology, its characteristics, or how to organize their personnel following the
ICS structure. The first concept to understand is that incident command
only pertains to the Response and Recovery phases. The campus organizational chart may in fact look very different during non-critical event
times; the Prevention, Protection, and Mitigation phases.

This chapter provides an organization and assignment of duties section to assign clarity to the roles and responsibilities of campus personnel
before, during, and after a critical event. The responsibilities found under
the Prevention, Protection, and Mitigation phases are typically conducted
during nonemergency, steady-state chain of command. The responsibilities found under Response and Recovery phases are conducted during and after a critical event occurs on campus and hence follow the

ICS structure. Even though the Prevention, Protection, and Mitigation responsibilities are not controlled by the ICS organizational chart, in the pages that follow these actions will be listed to help define the roles and responsibilities in the four sections, under the following headings: Operations, Planning, Logistics, and Finance and Administration.

The "Organization and Assignment of Duties" section that follows is meant to provide a suggested functional description of responsibilities for campus personnel for all five core mission areas necessary to improve preparedness capabilities. Use the following sections as a template for your campus strategies for Prevention, Protection, Mitigation, Response, and Recovery. And, use the suggested responsibilities listed to help identify the assignment of duties for a campus-specific organizational chart both during steady-state times as well as in response to a critical event. As the titles of PPMRR positions vary from campus to campus, so do their responsibilities. Where necessary replace the title of the person who has been delegated for this responsibility at your campus.

The "Organization and Assignment of Duties" is the most important component necessary for a campus to successfully overcome a critical event. Once it is completed, include it at the beginning of the PPMRR following the contact lists for each position. Backup, hard copy, and a USB record of contact information should be accessible in the event that the campus network experiences problems during an incident. Distribute the PPMRR Organization and Assignment of Duties to the entire PPMRR team and provide training. Do not assume that they know what their emergency response role is, unless you have provided training!

ORGANIZATION AND ASSIGNMENT OF DUTIES

Executive Policy Group

During steady-state times, the Executive Policy Group: the president, provost, chancellor, board of directors or any leadership position designated by the campus to be included, heads the organizational chart. They are responsible for the overall well-being of the campus community. Together they are accountable for any threat or hazard that affects the campus community. This group provides guidance on priorities and objectives of threats and hazards. Individually their critical event responsibilities might be:

> *President*: Responsible for the safe day-to-day operation of the campus.
> *Provost*: Responsible for ensuring continuity of operations for all academic activity during an emergency event and assumes the President's responsibilities when not available.
> *Director of Emergency Management*: Responsible for the overall direction and control of the implementation of the PPMRR operations.

When implementing the Executive Policy Group, be sure to designate a line of succession for leading the team. Example: President, Provost, Director of Emergency Management.

There is no place in a regular ICS organizational structure for an Executive Policy Group, however, this is the structure in place at most colleges and universities. In a true ICS organizational structure, the Unified Coordination Group (UCG) formulates common objectives, allocates resources, and decides on financial reimbursement for the participating agencies. Overall, they are in charge of the incident. The UCG is normally comprised of decision makers from the respective agencies participating in the critical event. In the college/university environment, the UCG and the Executive Policy Group work together effectively without affecting individual agency and campus authorities.

For incidents that do not involve outside agencies, the Executive Policy Group works directly with the command staff to bring resolution to the critical event.

DIRECTOR OF EMERGENCY MANAGEMENT

If the campus has a Director of Emergency Management, it makes sense to have this person chair the Executive Policy Group for emergency operations. Responsibilities should include overall management for the coordination between entities internal and external to the campus regarding initiatives to implement PPMRR strategies for all mission phases: Prevention, Protection, Mitigation, Response, and Recovery.

Prevention, Protection, and Mitigation Responsibilities

In order to have comprehensive strategies that involve all campus entities, it is imperative that the Director of Emergency Management works across the campus to ensure that all campus departments are included in the planning stages of the PPMRR. Together a strategy must be devised to ensure that all new faculty and staff receive a copy of the campus policies and procedures, including the PPMRR strategies at the new employee orientation. The PPMRR strategies must be available to the campus community electronically as well as in hard copy. Not only does the community need to know what the strategies are before a critical event occurs but they must also have an opportunity to attend and participate in training activities to help prepare for such events. It is the responsibility of the Director of Emergency Management to conduct and/or facilitate these trainings as well as maintain a database of employee compliance with training.

Training for appropriate department heads will ensure that an adequate number of individuals are trained to the Incident Commander (IC) level. For instance, it is probable that the facilities director will be designated IC should an event such as a collapsed roof or failure of the HVAC system should occur at the campus. Or the athletic director could be the IC should a bus accident occur while a campus athletic team is traveling. Without training, it is very possible that steps and protocols may be overlooked or skipped due to inexperience with managing critical events.

As PPMRR strategies are updated, the Director of Emergency Management will ensure that the campus community receives communications and updates with the assistance of the campus communications department. These strategies must be tested at least annually through planned drills and exercises. It is imperative that the campus include community agencies in the development and testing of these strategies.

Response Responsibilities

When a critical event occurs at the campus, the Director of Emergency Management or a designee with the full authority of the emergency manager must be accessible throughout an emergency. If not already taking place, activate the *Response* component of the PPMRR Plan. Order the evacuation, shelter-in-place, lock-down, and "All Clear" directives as warranted. Depending on the level of the incident, when appropriate, establish the incident command post, open the EOC, coordinate on-site response. Be sure to provide a copy of the campus PPMRR strategies including the campus map, as needed, to any internal and external units and/or agencies responding to the critical event.

Schedule and convene the Initial Action Planning meeting as soon as possible. Ensure that all Command Staff (CS) and Section Chiefs, and other key agency representatives are in attendance. Based on current status reports and in coordination with the UCG, CS, and Section Chiefs, establish initial and subsequent strategic objectives for the Incident Action Plan (IAP). The Director of Emergency Management in conjunction with the UCG and Section Chiefs will monitor staff activities to ensure that strategic objectives are being met and policy decisions are documented.

The Director of Emergency Management works together with the Public Information Officer (PIO) to provide regular communication and updates to the campus community of incident actions.

Recovery Responsibilities

The Director of Emergency Management with authority from the Executive Policy Group and the CS will declare termination of the emergency response and proceed with recovery operations. This will include the deactivation of the Emergency Operations Center (EOC) and demobilization of the PPMRR team. Open action items not concluded when the EOC is deactivated will be managed after demobilization and the Director of Emergency Management will follow-up until these items are closed.

In the event that a critical incident affects class attendance, the Director of Emergency Management may be the person designated at the campus to notify the appropriate faculty and the registrar. Additionally, the Director of Emergency Management may be the designee to notify the family of any victimized or deceased campus community member. The Executive Policy and/or the Director of Emergency Management will determine and assign a campus representative to the family as a contact should the family have any questions or intend to come to campus to pick up the injured or deceased's belongings.

Together with the Safety Officer (SO), the Director of Emergency Management will coordinate the mental health support needed for the campus community. Additionally, the Director of Emergency Management works collaboratively with the Director of Communications in the preparation of media/campus communications and provides input to the After Action Report.

During the Response and Recovery phases of a critical event on campus, the Executive Policy Group is aided in its decision making by a Unified Coordination Group (UCG) and delegates authority to the IC. The UCG may be comprised of a representative of the Executive Policy Group, the Director of Emergency Management, and depending on the severity of the event, outside agencies such as local police, fire, EMS, utility company representatives, town, county, state, and even federal representatives. One of those individuals, again depending on the situation, is the IC; even if that individual is not a campus employee. The IC will be a representative in the UCG, based on the incident itself and who is most qualified to lead. The IC along with other members of the UCG manages the incident from start to finish, authorizes the opening of the emergency operations center (EOC), determines the activation level, and determines the length of the initial and subsequent operational periods and staff briefings. Based on input from the UCG, the Executive Policy Group commits resources, obligates funds, and when appropriate, makes and changes policy.

FUNCTIONS OF THE COMMAND STAFF

Reporting directly to the UCG is the Command Staff, consisting of a Public Information Officer (PIO), Safety Officer (SO), and a Liaison Officer (LO). While the Command Staff are tasked with independent functions, all are working toward the accomplishment of the incident objectives. As the Command Staff positions are ICS positions, they are only activated during the Response and Recovery phases.

Public Information Officer

The Public Information Officer (PIO) will serve as the official spokesperson for the campus; the "one voice" of the campus to the public and the media. It is the PIO who prepares the information to be released to the media/campus community after consultation with the Executive Policy Group and the Command Staff. The PIO could be the Vice President of Communications, Vice President of Public Relations, or any other person that is designated by the UCG to be the person speaking with the media. The PIO representative's title is campus specific. He/she delivers information about life safety procedures, public health advisories, relief and assistance programs, and other vital information. The PIO has the responsibility for disseminating information that has been approved by the Executive Policy Group and the Command Staff, through all communications channels during emergencies, major disasters or matters that have potential to impact the reputation of the college/university. While the PIO may be one individual, there will most likely be a support team of personnel from the communications department aiding in the facilitation of the responsibilities. The PIO and UCG ensure that adequate staff is available to provide support for the PIO in all his/her duties. During the protection and prevention stages, designate the campus PIO as well as a media center where media conferences can be conducted.

Response Responsibilities

During or immediately after a critical event, depending on the situation, the campus community and the public need timely and accurate information on the status of the emergency. Critical events will draw the attention of the media. The campus must be prepared to provide information. When possible, media representatives, as well as all government agencies, should be provided with the contact information of the PIO prior to a critical event.

Depending on the severity of an emergency that befalls the campus, it may be imperative for the President to be the bearer of the message from the campus. In other instances, the PIO serves as the backup to the President as the campus spokesperson. However, even if the President is the bearer of the message, it is the PIO who coordinates all crisis communication with the media including media interviews, prepared statements, talking points, fact sheets, and press releases, all under the direction of the Executive Policy Group and Command Staff. Any media information released should contain standardized items such as name of the school, point of contact—name, phone, and e-mail. They should be numbered

84

consecutively as they are issued, include a date and time, and be approved by the Executive Policy Group and the UCG before release. Provide copies of all media releases to the UCG and ensure that file copies are maintained of all information released.

A high priority is to ensure that the faculty, staff, and students know that only the PIO is authorized to provide information or any commentary to the news media regarding any phase of the event. The PIO should provide faculty, staff, and students with messaging for the media such as, "To ensure that you have the most up-to-date and accurate information all media inquiries and interviews are being handled by the Vice President of Communications, Ann Smith. Her contact information is 555-555-1234 e-mail Ann.Smith@campus.edu." Include in the message to the campus community that should they encounter or be approached by a member of the media, in addition to delivering the PIO contact information to the media spokesperson that they should also get the media person's contact information and promptly deliver that to the campus PIO.

Information regarding the event that has occurred at the campus is not a one-way communication. It is also the responsibility of the PIO to monitor what is being said about the campus by the media and the campus community via all modes of communication: television, radio, print, and social media outlets. Including a rumor control function is essential to correcting false or erroneous information. Establishing a "Disaster Hotline" with an up-to-date recorded message can help to facilitate factual information that is readily available.

Recovery Responsibilities

The work of the PIO will not be concluded at the end of the emergency event. He/she will prepare final news releases and advise media representatives of point-of-contact for follow-up stories. The PIO will be an instrumental contributor to the After Action Report. Upon its completion, the PIO will distribute the After Action Report to the campus community as well as to its external partners.

Safety Officer

The Safety Officer (SO) monitors incident operations and provides advice on all matters related to operational safety, including the health and safety of emergency responder personnel and building and facility safety. The SO has emergency authority to stop or prevent unsafe acts during incident operations.

Response Responsibilities

The SO and his/her team's primary responsibility is to ensure a safe campus environment during a campus incident. During a critical event at the campus, the SO is tasked with keeping the UCG apprised of unsafe conditions and when necessary takes action. The SO prepares and presents safety briefings for the UCG as well as for the campus at large. The SO provides technical advice to the IC about the incident or response activities as they relate to the safety of the students, staff, faculty, and visitors. The SO assesses and communicates hazardous and unsafe situations and ensures an incident safety plan is developed. He/she prepares and includes safety messages in the IAP.

Issuing identification badges for outside agency representatives and checking IDs of all who report to the EOC are also responsibilities of the SO. Additionally, the SO is responsible for monitoring the well-being of the responders in the EOC. This could be as simple as ensuring that there is food and beverages available for the staff to monitoring the emergency operations staff for stress or psychological issues. It is in their realm of duties to then obtain appropriate support from available resources such as onsite counseling, early relief, and so forth.

Recovery Responsibilities

As the critical event comes to a conclusion, the SO will contribute to the After Action Report. Depending on the situation that has just concluded, this may include strategies for creating awareness and education on how to promote safety. If there were injuries or deaths as a result of the incident, the SO will work with the Financial/Administrative Section in preparing personnel injury claims or records necessary for proper case evaluation and closure. And if the event involved hazardous materials that require notification to local, state, and federal authorities, the SO will manage those entities.

Liaison Officer

The Liaison Officer (LO) is the person designated as the point of contact for assisting and coordinating with agencies that are responding to the campus critical event such as governmental agencies, volunteer organizations, and the Red Cross, to name a few. Designate a person with good communication and organizational skills as the LO. Prior to a critical event, a database of these agencies and their contact persons should be available from the Communications/Public Relations Director.

Response Responsibilities

Once an event occurs and it becomes necessary to call in outside agencies, the role of the LO is to correspond and collaborate with the outside agencies on behalf of the campus. Prior to the arrival of the agency representatives, the LO should establish and maintain a central location for incoming agency representatives to be greeted and signed in and then escorted to a designated workspace within the EOC. It is imperative to coordinate identification badging with the SO and maintain a roster with contact information for agency representatives located at the campus EOC. The LO provides the agency representatives with access to policies, directives, guidelines, IAPs, and situation reports (SITREPs) to help facilitate assistance.

For events where there are many outside groups responding to a campus critical event, it will be necessary to establish and maintain an Interagency Coordination Group comprised of representatives of the agencies. The IC or a representative of the UCG must conduct regular briefings for the Interagency Coordination Group and be sure to provide access to the current Action Plan and SITREPs.

Recovery Responsibilities

When the agency representatives are no longer required on campus to assist with the critical event, it is the responsibility of the LO to release them and to invite the agency contacts to contribute to the campus After Action Report and update, as necessary, the agency database.

FUNCTION OF THE FOUR SECTIONS

In addition to the Command Staff, the Section Chiefs of each functional section: Operations, Planning, Logistics, and Finance and Administration, also report to the UCG. The Section Chiefs advise the UCG and execute their responsibilities with the cooperation of the various Branch Directors that report to each Section Chief, all supporting the incident objectives. Based on the situation, the Section Chiefs activate branches/units within their section and designate Branch Directors and Unit Leaders.

The concept is that each section is tasked with specific responsibilities to meet the incident objectives. Typically a briefing is held where the UCG, Command Staff, and Section Chiefs share information and make decisions and set goals to meet the incident objectives. These goals are recorded by the Planning Section Chief to be incorporated into the Action

Plan. At the conclusion of the briefing, each Section Chief reports back to their Branch and Unit Leads the new action plan for the Section for the next operational period. The same format is followed for each subsequent briefing. The length of the operational period may vary from hours to days to weeks, depending on the event.

Not every threat or critical event at the campus will require the mobilization of all sections. Mobilization is dependent on the incident itself and the incident planning objectives. The incident command structure is flexible; expanding and contracting as needed. However, if a section is not mobilized, the IC will typically manage those functions.

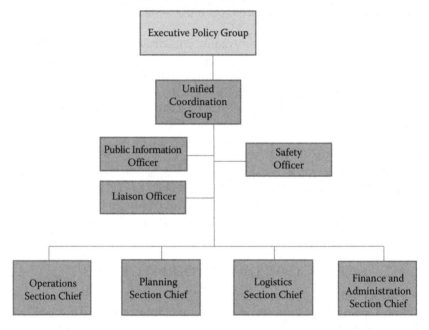

Operations Section

Operations is an incident command function. The Operations Section Chief takes direction from the Executive Policy Group and the UCG in implementing the campus Action Plans. The Operations Section Chief position will vary depending on the actual incident. If it is a safety or criminal event, a likely choice for Operations Section Chief is the Public Safety Director; if the threat is a pandemic health event, a likely choice for Operations Section Chief is the Health Services Director. Think of this position as a role for someone who leads in the development and implementation of strategies to meet the incident objectives.

In the Operations Section, you will find people who hold roles and responsibilities for taking actions; carrying out specific actions to meet incident objectives. Typical branches of the Operations Section that might be utilized in the campus environment include Public Safety, Communications/Public Relations, Academic Affairs, Student Affairs, Health Services, Food Services, Housing, Food Services, and Enrollment Services. Not all branches are activated for every critical event. The IC and the actual critical event will determine which branches need to be activated.

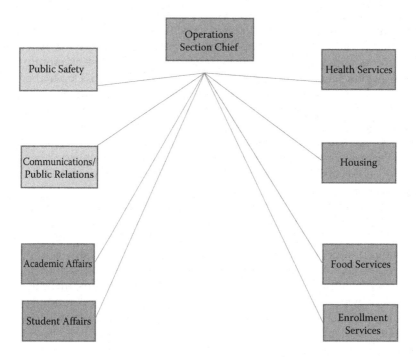

Public Safety Branch
The role of the Public Safety Branch Director is to manage the personal safety of students, staff, faculty, and visitors to the campus. He/she may also be the initiator of campus-wide timely notices. Additionally, Public Safety Officers manage the flow of traffic on campus, a critical component to a successful response and recovery.

Protection, Prevention, and Mitigation Strategies

During the Protection, Prevention, and Mitigation phases, the Public Safety Branch assesses hazardous and unsafe conditions and develops measures for promoting safety. This includes providing the campus community with tools to help them mitigate a critical event. These tools should include campus-wide safety programs and presentations.

The Public Safety Director is responsible for ensuring that Public Safety Personnel are equipped with the tools needed to perform their duties. It is imperative to develop strategies and training for Public Safety personnel based on content of the PPMRR. Public Safety Officers may be the first people alerted to a critical event that is occurring on campus. There must be protocols and procedures in place to monitor campus threats, alert the campus of critical threats, activate the campus PPMRR team, call for backup resources such as local police, fire, and other emergency personnel. Public Safety Officers must be monitoring the Campus Emergency Alert System, as well as the U.S. Department of Commerce, National Oceanic and Atmospheric Administration (NOAA) Weather Alert Systems, local news and weather stations around the clock, every day of the year. Together with the other PPMRR team members, a communications system and campus notification process must be developed to relay threats as determined by these monitoring agencies. Other Public Safety training may include First Responder and CPR/AED certifications.

When developing Protection, Prevention, and Mitigation strategies, much of the focus should be on developing a plan to manage traffic flow. Typically, this function falls upon the Public Safety Branch. Without a strong traffic management plan in place, chaos will ensue and response vehicles and personnel will not be able to reach the scene in a timely manner. In addition to developing traffic maps, include storage, retrieval, and placement of barricades, signage, and sandbags for traffic control and road closures. The plan should include information on how to block areas for ambulances, police and fire vehicles, emergency equipment, and heli-spots.

Response Strategies

The Public Safety Director takes direction from the Operations Section Chief who is taking direction from the Executive Policy Group and the UCG in implementing the campus Action Plans. The Public Safety Director serves as the Branch Director. All department heads that report to the Public Safety Director serve as Unit Leaders. Every Unit Leader has an obligation to provide Protection, Prevention, Mitigation, Response, and Recovery strategies for those who report to them.

As an emergency event unfolds, it is very likely to be reported to the Public Safety Office, the Public Safety Director, or a duty officer. Depending on the situation, this individual determines the incident level as defined in the PPMRR, and immediately contacts as appropriate the Public Safety Director, the Emergency Management Director, police, fire, and ambulance. The Public Safety officers exercise authority to immediately stop unsafe acts or conditions when appropriate and respond to all emergency and critical incidents on campus. It is their responsibility to assess and communicate hazardous and unsafe situations to the Public Safety Director, and the Emergency Management Director as detailed in the campus incident reporting chain.

The Branch Director in consultation with the Section Chief will identify objectives to be accomplished during each Operational Period. This may include activating strategies to manage traffic and road access by the campus community, as well as response personnel, media, parents, and other community members. Maintaining order throughout the incident is a high priority of the Public Safety Branch.

Recovery Strategies

During the recovery phase, the Public Safety Branch will continue to maintain order on campus. The Public Safety Branch Director will notify the appropriate local, state, and federal authorities of all hazardous materials emergencies that require such notification if they were not notified during the Response phase. Where appropriate, collaborate with the Communications Branch Director and the PPMRR team on creating safety awareness and education programs. The Public Safety Branch Director contributes to the After Action Report all actions pertaining to the function of the Public Safety Branch throughout the critical event.

Communications/Public Relations Branch

The Communications/Public Relations Branch Director is responsible for gathering, sharing, and managing incident-related information for constituents internal and external to the campus. Depending on the campus notification system and policies, the Communications/Public Relations Branch may play an integral role in the creation and dissemination of a Timely Notice.

TIMELY NOTICE

A Timely Notice is identified as a notification delivered to the campus community of an ongoing or continuing threat. These threats can include crimes such as arson, criminal homicide (or any suspicious death), robbery, or any emergency situation that may cause a threat to the health and safety of the campus community. These threats may include an active shooter, a hostage situation, a riot, weather events such as an impending tornado or hurricane, a fire or explosion, a biological threat, a gas leak, hazardous materials spill, and so on. A good campus Timely Notice policy aligns with statements in the Campus Annual Security Report. It indicates the types of events for which a Timely Notice will be issued; an acceptable time frame for issuance; who has the authority to issue it; and the method the Timely Notice will be disseminated. The Clery Act does not qualify what is considered a "Timely Manner" so therefore when setting strategies for Timely Manner indicators at the campus, consider using a time frame that a reasonably prudent person would deem appropriate. Methods for dissemination can include an Emergency Alert System that includes e-mails, text messages, phone calls, campus Internet postings, social media postings, radio broadcasts, bullhorn messages, and paper postings.

Prevention, Protection, and Mitigation Strategies

During the Prevention, Protection, and Mitigation phases, the Communications/Public Relations Branch assesses its communication mechanisms for both internal and external constituents. This includes creating communication templates and developing strategies for inputting incident-specific information into the messages as well as the approval chain as per the PPMRR for releasing such messages to the campus community as well as to the community outside of the campus as appropriate. Prior to a critical event, the Communications/Public Relations Branch must develop and maintain a database of local and regional media contacts along with telephone and e-mail contact information and prepare a media kit on a CD or in USB format: campus fact sheet, campus map, and list of key contacts. In the Prevention, Protection, and Mitigation phase, the PPMRR should identify a location that can be utilized as a media center, equipped with Internet connections, telephone lines, and which is located away from the EOC.

Before a critical event occurs is the time to create a database of agencies that could support the campus during a critical event. Agencies such as the local police department, fire department, hospital, local emergency management, utility companies along with a contact person and their phone number, e-mail, and physical address should be included in this database. The town, county, and state representatives as well as the Red Cross, Salvation Army, and other voluntary agencies should also be added to the database. This database should be ready and available in print, online, and on USB for use by the LO at the start of a campus critical event.

The Communications/Public Relations Branch Director is responsible for ensuring that Communications/Public Relations personnel are equipped with the tools needed to perform their duties. It is imperative to develop strategies and enroll staff in training courses. FEMA offers training courses: Basic Public Information Officers (G290); Advanced Public Information Officers (E388); Public Information Awareness (IS-29). Information regarding content and availability of these courses can be obtained at: http://www.training.fema.gov.

Response Strategies

During the Response and Recovery phase, the Communications/Public Relations Branch takes direction from the Operations Section Chief who is taking direction from the Executive Policy Group and the UCG in implementing the campus Action Plans. The Communications/Public Relations Director serves as the Branch Director. All departments that report to the Communications/Public Relations Branch serve as Unit Leaders. Every Unit Leader has an obligation to provide Protection, Prevention, Mitigation, Response, and Recovery strategies for those who report to them.

The Branch Director in consultation with the Section Chief will identify objectives to be accomplished during each Operational Period. During a critical incident, the Communications/Public Relations branch may play a significant role in disseminating Timely Notices to the campus community. Activate the media center and disseminate approved information through the appropriate communication channels such as text messages, e-mails, phone blasts, social media, and the campus website.

Recovery Strategies

Continue to work with the campus community and external parties in delivering information pertaining to the recovery from the critical event. Update templates and databases as necessary. The Communications/Public Relations Branch Director contributes to the After Action Report all actions pertaining to the function of the Communications/Public Relations Branch throughout the critical event and works cooperatively with the Situation Analysis Branch in the distribution of the After Action Report to the campus community as well as to its external partners.

Academic Affairs Branch

The Provost or VP of Academic Affairs may be the conduit at the campus responsible for making sure that teaching schedules and other faculty needs that have been disrupted due to the critical event are being addressed and managed. All campus department heads and academic chairs serve as Unit Leaders, all reporting to the Provost. Every Unit Leader has an obligation to provide Protection, Prevention, Mitigation, Response, and Recovery strategies for those who report to them.

Prevention, Protection, and Mitigation Strategies

All academic and administrative departments share in the responsibility for preparing for critical events. In addition to the campus PPMRR strategies, each department develops PPMRR strategies that fit into the overall campus PPMRR strategy. Faculty and staff possess knowledge and understanding of layout and operation of their specific department, classroom/laboratory or work area, evacuation routes and sheltering areas, and are therefore well-equipped to contribute to the department PPMRR strategies. Each department should assign an emergency coordinator to assist in developing and implementing department-specific PPMRR strategies. The emergency coordinator's responsibilities include ensuring that adequate emergency procedures, training, drills, exercises, personal protective equipment (PPE), and safety equipment are in place to work safely as well as to respond safely and effectively to foreseeable emergencies.

Department PPMRR strategies:

- Protect the safety of students, faculty, and staff and provide for continuity of operations
- Know how to provide, receive, and distribute communications from the Executive Policy Group

- Know how to report an individual of concern
- Have emergency reporting and notification procedures in place for offices and classrooms
- Develop and practice evacuation and shelter-in-place assembly areas
- Designate floor and building wardens to assist with evacuation and/or shelter-in-place and lock-down procedures
- Prepare a database of self-identified individuals who have indicated that in the event of an emergency that they will need help evacuating
- Ensure that department heads and Section Chiefs have contact lists, and understand the roles and responsibilities of its members
- Ensure that department members are familiar with the campus PPMRR strategies, the department strategies, and their individual role and responsibility
- Ensure that departments have basic emergency supplies and equipment to be as self-sufficient as possible after an emergency
- Secure storage locations to safeguard resources for first aid and emergency supplies
- Encourage employees to keep a personal emergency kit in their work area that contains a personal flashlight, backup eyeglasses and medications, sturdy shoes, a sweater, a wrapped snack and water packet, and personal emergency contact numbers
- Identify and refer safety or security deficiencies to the appropriate department for remediation
- Define predefined recall procedures for essential personnel
- Develop and document PPMRR training

SAMPLE SUPPLY AND EQUIPMENT LIST FOR EVERY DEPARTMENT

While the situation will dictate what supplies are needed, each department should be equipped with the following items:

- First aid supplies, with instructions
- Flashlights/batteries, approved power strips, and extension cords
- Portable AM/FM radios/batteries
- Laboratory spill kits

- Portable emergency water
- Megaphones
- Two-way radios
- Employee rosters

Response Strategies

During the Response and Recovery phase, the Academic Affairs Branch Director takes direction from the Operations Section Chief who is taking direction from the Executive Policy Group and the UCG in implementing the campus Action Plans. The Provost or whoever is in charge of Academic Affairs and the Faculty at the campus serves as the Branch Director. The Branch Director in consultation with the Section Chief will identify objectives to be accomplished during each Operational Period. Based on the situation, the Provost will ensure that all department heads and academic chairpersons are prepared to respond as needed to in supporting the overall operation and ensuring that all appropriate safety and security directions are followed. The Provost responsibilities may include relaying to faculty information for them to relay to staff and students within their area of communications and directions from the Command Staff. The Academic Affairs Branch Director may also serve as the conduit to other Branch Directors on behalf of the faculty where housing, food services, transportation, and counseling services needs arise.

Recovery Strategies

Throughout the Recovery phase, the Academic Affairs Branch Director continues to work cooperatively across the campus with other Branch Directors to assist faculty with struggles due to the critical event that occurred on campus. The Academic Affairs Branch Director contributes to the After Action Report all actions pertaining to the function of the Academic Affairs Branch throughout the critical event.

Student Affairs Branch

The Vice President of Student Affairs may be the conduit at the campus responsible for making sure that student housing, food services, transportation, class schedules, and counseling needs due to the critical event are being managed. All departments that report to the Vice President of Student Affairs serve as Unit Leaders. Every Unit Leader has an obligation to provide Protection, Prevention, Mitigation, Response, and Recovery strategies for those who report to them.

Prevention, Protection, and Mitigation Strategies

During the Prevention, Protection, and Mitigation phases, the Vice President of Student Affairs and other department heads work cooperatively to develop strategies that can be activated should a critical event disrupt the steady-state operation of these services at the campus. These strategies may include working with Housing, to account for students and their need for temporary or alternative student housing; with Food Services, to ensure that all students with and without a meal plan have access to food and water; with Transportation to move students and their personal belongings to their temporary or alternative housing. The Vice President of Student Affairs also works with the Registrar and Counseling outlets preemptively to develop strategies that can be put into action as needed.

Response Strategies

During the Response and Recovery phase, the Student Affairs Branch takes direction from the Operations Section Chief who is taking direction from the Executive Policy Group and the UCG in implementing the campus Action Plans. The Vice President of Student Affairs or whoever is in charge of Student Affairs at the campus serves as the Branch Director. The Branch Director in consultation with the Section Chief will identify objectives to be accomplished during each Operational Period. During the Response phase, the Student Affairs Branch Director will work with the Branch Directors of Housing, Food Services, Transportation, and any others as necessitated by the critical incident to activate strategies to assist students with life and scholastic struggles due to the critical event that occurred on campus.

Recovery Strategies

Throughout the Recovery phase, the Student Affairs Branch Director continues to work cooperatively across the campus with other Branch Directors to assist students with life and scholastic struggles due to the critical event that occurred on campus. The Student Affairs Branch Director contributes to the After Action Report all actions pertaining to the function of the Student Affairs Branch throughout the critical event.

Health Services Branch

Health Services as it pertains to critical events is an entity that pertains to all campuses, even those campuses that do not provide any medical services to students, staff, or faculty. Areas of concern include personnel safety and health issues. Guidance for Occupational Health and Safety is provided from Health and Hospital Services (HHS), the Department of Labor (DOL), the Department of Homeland Security (DHS), and the Department of State Health Services (DSHS).

Prevention, Protection, and Mitigation Strategies

Identify the Health Services Branch Director, and all areas that report to the Health Services Branch and departments across the campus that work cooperatively to ensure that the Occupational Health and Safety of the campus community is being monitored. Identify strategies to keep the Branch as well as the campus community up to date.

Identify qualified safety and health personnel to ensure infection control measures are identified and implemented, including (if applicable) the appropriate selection and use of personal protective equipment, based on Health and Hospital Services and Department of Labor guidance. Perform and regularly update risk assessments based on occupational exposures and assess whether the risk can be controlled through engineering, administrative and work practice measures, and if not, procure appropriate types and quantities of infection control-related supplies (e.g., personal protective equipment [PPE], hand sanitizers, surface wipes, cleansers, and tissues).

Develop strategies for receiving information from the Department of Homeland Security (DHS) and the Department of State Health Services (DSHS) for events such as a pandemic or hazardous materials affecting air quality. Work with the Communications Department in devising strategies to push out such information to the campus community.

Create training programs to increase campus awareness of methods for thwarting the spread of germs such as stay home if you or a household member is sick, cough etiquette, hand hygiene, use of a face mask for respiratory protection, and social distancing strategies. Work with the Communications Department to create messaging. Create strategies to have health-care providers administer flu vaccinations, antiviral and supportive medications, or perform other health service related duties during a pandemic. Consider creating links from the campus website to www.flu.gov for pandemic flu–related guidance and information (e.g., signs and symptoms of influenza, modes of transmission, developing individual and family plans, when to return to work and school).

Review and/or create strategies and identify resources available to ensure that the campus community (students, staff, and faculty) are equipped to prepare and respond to the psychological and social needs of employees prior to, during, and after a critical event.

Response Strategies

During the Response and Recovery phase, the Health Services Branch takes direction from the Operations Section Chief who is taking direction from the Executive Policy Group and the UCG in implementing the campus Action Plans. The Health Services Director serves as the Branch Director and will activate the appropriate units as the situation demands. The Branch Director in consultation with the Section Chief will identify objectives to be accomplished during each Operational Period.

Recovery Strategies

Throughout the Recovery phase, the Health Services Branch Director continues to provide services to the campus community as indicated by the incident and the directives of the Executive Policy Group, UCG, and IC. The Health Services Branch Director contributes to the After Action Report all actions pertaining to the function of the Health Services Branch throughout the critical event.

Food Services Branch

The Food Services Director is responsible for managing all kitchen facilities and food distribution locations across the campus during nonemergency times as well as during times of emergency and recovery. All departments that report to the Food Services Director serve as Unit Leaders. Every Unit Leader has an obligation to provide Protection, Prevention, Mitigation, Response, and Recovery strategies for those who report to them.

Prevention, Protection, and Mitigation Strategies

If during nonemergency times, the Food Services Branch provides meals (breakfast, lunch, and dinner) to students with meal plans and/or if students without meal plans, faculty and staff may purchase breakfast, lunch, and dinner, the campus PPMRR should include strategies to be used in the event that a critical event befalls the campus. In this section, list the amount of food and water that is available in nonemergency times as well as the amount of food and water and the estimated time that it will be depleted if unable to be restocked. Determine strategies for ordering and delivering food during times of campus critical events. Consider contracting with a national or regional food service rather than a local provider for food, water, and ice. In the event that the critical event is a hurricane or tornado, it is possible that a local provider may not be operational.

If the campus meal plan is accessed via swiping the individual's ID and there is a loss of electricity, it may be impossible to determine who has purchased a meal plan. Additionally, the cash register may not be functional without electricity. Create a strategy for overcoming these challenges.

Identify alternative locations to serve food in the event that the cafeteria is damaged. Create food service strategies in the event that the kitchen sustains damage. Consider mutual aid agreements with neighboring schools, and the services of the American Red Cross, Salvation Army, and other local voluntary agencies. If during nonemergency times food service is not available at the campus, consider strategies to feed EOC personnel.

Response Strategies

During the Response and Recovery phase, the Food Services Branch takes direction from the Operations Section Chief who is taking direction from the Executive Policy Group and the UCG in implementing the campus Action Plans. The Food Service Director serves as the Branch Director. The Branch Director in consultation with the Section Chief will identify objectives to be accomplished during each Operational Period. Activate the strategies for providing food to faculty, staff, students, as well as the EOC staff that may be comprised of community responders such as police, fire, utility personnel, and so on. If needed, implement a food delivery plan to the EOC with the Transportation Branch. Activate, if necessary, the backup plan as determined in the Prevention, Protection, and Mitigation phases of overcoming the challenges associated with paying for meals.

Recovery Strategies

During the Recovery phase, the Food Service Director will replenish food and water supplies. The Food Services Branch Director contributes to the After Action Report all actions pertaining to the function of the Food Services Branch throughout the critical event.

Housing Branch

The Housing Director is responsible for the management of residential locations both on and off campus during nonemergency times as well as during times of Response and Recovery. All departments that report to the Housing Director serve as Unit Leaders. Every Unit Leader has an obligation to provide Protection, Prevention, Mitigation, Response, and Recovery strategies for those who report to them.

Prevention, Protection, and Mitigation Strategies

The Housing Director is responsible for ensuring that an accountability system is in place for tracking residents and visitors staying in campus housing and securing temporary and/or long-term housing, if/when campus housing becomes uninhabitable due to a campus threat, hazard, or emergency event. During the Prevention, Protection, and Mitigation phase, identify residential student and staff accountability strategies, as well as possible locations to be used for short- and long-term residences should campus housing become compromised. Before a critical event occurs is the time to create a strategy for housing EOC staff. This may include campus personnel as well as noncampus personnel who are manning the EOC.

Develop relationships and create agreements with local hotels, other campuses, housing developments, and other community resources. Create and maintain a database of these facilities and the agreements as well as the 24/7 contact information for a decision maker from these facilities. Update these agreements and contact lists as needed but at least annually. Student accountability databases, agreements, and databases must be available in hard copy as well as electronically and/or on an external drive.

Response Strategies

During the Response and Recovery phase, the Housing Branch Director takes direction from the Operations Section Chief who is taking direction from the Executive Policy Group and the UCG in implementing the campus Action Plans. The Housing Director serves as the Branch Director. The Branch Director in consultation with the Section Chief will identify objectives to be accomplished during each Operational Period. Work cooperatively with the Student Affairs Branch Director to account for students and their need for temporary or alternative student housing. As necessary activate accountability plans, alternate housing plans, including agreements with local hotels, other campuses, housing developments, and other community resources. Work cooperatively with the Transportation Branch to relocate students and their personal belongings. The Housing Branch Director coordinates with the Food Services Branch Director under the direction of the Operations Section Chief and with the Human Resources Branch Director under the direction of the Finance and Administration Operations Section Chief to provide food and lodging for EOC staff.

Recovery Strategies

The Housing Branch Director works with the Executive Policy Group and the Operations Section Chief in determining the long-term strategy for campus housing. The Housing Branch Director contributes to the After Action Report all actions pertaining to the function of the Public Safety Branch throughout the critical event.

Enrollment Services Branch

In the campus environment, the departments or units that comprise Enrollment Services are typically Admissions, Academic Advising, and Financial Aid.

Prevention, Protection, and Mitigation

Prevention, Protection, and Mitigation are not IC functions; however, developing strategies before a critical event occurs can aid in the Response and Recovery phases. In addition to Admissions, Academic Advising and Financial Aid consider adding the Office of the Registrar, Transcripts and Career Services if these departments are not already managed under your Student Affairs Branch. What do these departments have to do with emergency planning you may ask? Plenty if the critical event occurs in the middle of Admissions, Academic Advising, and Financial Aid decision time frames! Or, if you are an alumnus seeking an official copy of your transcript for submission of a graduate application or for verification of your education for a potential employer. The last thing you want to hear is that the office is closed due to—name any critical event. And as I suggested in Chapter 3, "A Case for Including Retention Strategies in the Campus Emergency Plan," someone somewhere on campus needs to be reaching out to current students who may be displaced due to the current critical event as these students may be considering transferring to another school due to whatever the critical event is at your campus.

In the Prevention, Protection, and Mitigation phases, develop strategies based on what-if scenarios. What if the campus is not operational due to a regional power loss or extensive flooding of the local transportation system preventing students, staff, and faculty from traveling to campus during critical Admissions and Financial Aid deadlines? Hurricane Sandy affected many campus deadlines when it struck in October of 2012. What if the campus was not operational for an entire semester? Hurricane Katrina closed down many campuses for extended periods of time in 2005. What if a student needed an official transcript and the campus was not operational? Is it possible for the staff in the Transcript Unit to print, seal, and mail transcripts remotely? What if the nonoperational status of the campus resulted in students' seeking to transfer to another institution? Is it possible to convert classes to an online format or develop articulation agreements with neighboring schools on a temporary basis? The situations and possibilities are endless.

The Vice President of Enrollment Services is responsible for the management of Enrollment Services during nonemergency times as well as during times of Response and Recovery. All departments that report to the Enrollment Services VP serve as Unit Leaders. Every Unit Leader has an obligation to provide Protection, Prevention, Mitigation, Response, and Recovery strategies.

Response

During the Response and Recovery phase, the Enrollment Services VP takes direction from the Operations Section Chief who is taking direction from the Executive Policy Group and the UCG in implementing the campus Action Plans. The Enrollment Services VP serves as the Branch Director. The Branch Director in consultation with the Section Chief will identify objectives to be accomplished during each Operational Period.

Recovery

The Enrollment Services Branch Director will continue to work on long-term strategies however leadership may be transferred to the Recovery Branch in the Planning Section. The Enrollment Services Branch Director contributes to the After Action Report all actions pertaining to the function of the Enrollment Services throughout the critical event.

Planning Section

The Planning Section is an incident command function activated during the Response and Recovery phases. Do not confuse it with the planning that every department is involved with during the Prevention,

Protection, and Mitigation phases. The Planning Section takes direction from the Executive Policy Group and the UCG in implementing the campus Action Plans. Those in the Planning Section collect, evaluate, and disseminate information within the EOC. During an incident, the Planning Section collects information from the Executive Policy Group, UCG, Operations, Logistics, and Finance and Administration Sections to enter into the IAP, which at a minimum includes an accurate and current description of the incident and the resources available, probable course of events, and strategies to achieve incident objectives set for the operational period. The Planning Section holds the responsibility of maintaining status boards and maps, performing data analysis and preparing reports. At the end of each operational period, the IC, Command Staff, and appropriate Section Chiefs review the incident objectives to see if they have been met or need to be redefined. This information is recorded in the situation report (SITREP) for that operational period, and provides the necessary information to develop objectives for the next operational period and IAP.

Branches that fall under the Planning Section Chief are the Situation Analysis Branch, the Damage Assessment Branch, and the Recovery Branch. Depending on the scope of the campus critical event, these responsibilities may be managed by separate individuals or all fall under the responsibilities of one person. Select the position at your campus that can best manage these roles and responsibilities.

Situation Analysis Branch

During the Response and Recovery phase, the Situation Analysis Branch takes direction from the Planning Section Chief who is taking direction from the Executive Policy Group and the UCG in implementing the campus Action Plans. The Branch Director must be a person who has access to information from the Executive Policy Group, UCG, and all Branch Directors. The Situation Analysis Branch Director is responsible for collecting, evaluating, and analyzing all critical incident information and providing updated status reports to Executive Policy Group and Command Staff. Typically, a briefing is held where the UCG, Command Staff and Section Chiefs share information and make decisions and set goals to meet the incident objectives. These goals are recorded by the Planning Section Chief to be incorporated into the Action Plan.

Prevention, Protection, and Mitigation Strategies

Prevention, Protection, and Mitigation are not IC functions. However, during the Prevention, Protection, and Mitigation phases, the PPMRR team will identify which campus personnel will be delegated to work in the Situation Analysis Branch. Mechanisms for collecting, evaluating, and analyzing critical incident information from the sections and their Branches will be determined as will the process and the individual(s) tasked with writing briefings, the IAPs and SITREPs. This individual will work cooperatively with the Communications/Public Relations Branch Director who will manage the dissemination of the reports, briefings, IAPs, and SITREPs under the direction of the Operations Section Chief, the Executive Policy Group, and the UCG. As the Situation Analysis Branch is also responsible for tracking personnel deployed to the EOC, working cooperatively with Human Resources is imperative as is developing a system for tracking personnel.

Response Strategies

The Branch Director in consultation with the Section Chief will identify objectives to be accomplished during each Operational Period. The Situation Analysis Branch Director will activate the strategies developed during the Prevention, Protection, and Mitigation phases: receive, evaluate, and analyze all critical incident information and provide updated status reports to the Executive Policy Group and Command Staff in the form of oral reports, briefings, IAPs and SITREPs. The Branch Director will work cooperatively with the Communications/Public Relations Branch Director who will manage the dissemination of briefings, IAPs and SITREPs, as well as issue news releases, and disseminate information through appropriate communications channels. It is the responsibility of the Situation Analysis Branch to keeps records and documentation of all EOC activities including the tracking system for personnel deployed to the EOC.

Recovery Strategies

During the Recovery phase, the Situation Analysis Branch continues to collect, evaluate, and analyze critical incident information from the Sections and their Branches. All actions pertaining to the function of all Sections and Branches from throughout the critical event are collected by, and are included in, the After Action Report and written by the Situation Analysis Branch.

Damage Assessment Branch

The Branch Director must be a person who has the ability to assess damage at the campus. Damage may be physical damage of structures and facilities, injuries and fatalities, as well as damage to the reputation of the institution. It may also include damage to the reputation of an individual, such as a faculty member, which could affect the reputation of the institution. The position of the Damage Assessment Branch Director will depend on the critical event.

Prevention, Protection, and Mitigation Strategies

Prevention, Protection, and Mitigation are not IC functions. However, during the Prevention, Protection, and Mitigation phases, the PPMRR will determine which campus individuals would be best suited to manage the various Damage Assessment Branches.

Response Strategies

During the Response and Recovery phase, the Damage Assessment Branch takes direction from the Planning Section Chief who is taking direction from the Executive Policy Group and the UCG in implementing the campus strategies. The Branch Director in consultation with the Section Chief will identify objectives to be accomplished during each Operational Period.

Recovery Strategies

The Damage Assessment Branch Director contributes to the After Action Report all actions pertaining to the function of the Damage Assessment Branch throughout the critical event.

Recovery Branch

The Planning Section may also be involved in developing the Recovery Plan for the event, including emergency and temporary housing for campus residents, and stranded commuter students, faculty, and staff. Planners work in cooperation with other sections in the restoration of campus support services.

Recovery Strategies

The Recovery Branch takes direction from the Planning Section Chief who is taking direction from the Executive Policy Group and the UCG in implementing the campus strategies. The Branch Director continues to work with the Executive Policy Group and the UCG in implementing the campus strategies for Recovery. The Branch Director contributes to the After Action Report all actions pertaining to the function of the Recovery Branch throughout the critical event.

Logistics Section

Logistics is an incident command function activated during the Response and Recovery phases. The Logistics Section takes direction from the Executive Policy Group and the UCG in implementing the campus strategies. The role of the Logistics Section Chief is to procure equipment and materials to support the emergency response. This may include reconstituting current campus facilities for another use, supplying communication and technology services, transporting people and, furniture, housing, and food services to meet the needs of the emergency response team. Select the position at your campus that can best manage this role and responsibility.

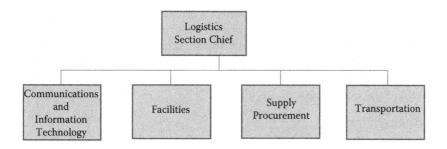

Communications and Information Technology Branch

The Communications and Information Technology Director has the responsibility for managing the continuity of operations, security from threats, and when necessary the recovery of systems of the Communications and

Information Technology systems. The maintenance, purchasing, leasing, renting, and assignment of communications equipment including radios, telephones, cell phones, and computer equipment are all functions of this position. All departments that report to the Communications Director serve as Unit Leaders. Every Unit Leader has an obligation to provide Protection, Prevention, Mitigation, Response, and Recovery strategies for those who report to them.

Prevention, Protection, and Mitigation Strategies

During the Prevention, Protection, and Mitigation phases, the Communications and Information Technology Director coordinates with the PPMRR team on strategies for implementation of efforts for campus wide communications and information technology needs, including phone, and computer network systems backup. This may include using the cloud and/or locating servers at remote locations. Backup decisions and methodology should include random file deletion/error restore, system restore from failed hardware, critical data restore from failed hardware, as well as critical data restore from local disaster. Risk mitigation techniques such as 24 × 7 maintenance support for production systems; RAID disk subsystems; system backups (on-site and off-site); redundant servers (managed by load balancers); uninterruptible power supplies and emergency generators; and data center smoke detection and fire suppression systems should also be incorporated into the plan.

A database of vendors should be in place for maintenance, purchasing, leasing, renting of communications equipment including radios, telephones, cell phones, satellite phones, UHF/VHF radios, and computer equipment. A distribution system of emergency response resources should be developed prior to a critical event, including the construction of a database to track the assignment of all equipment. If there is equipment that necessitates a new user training session, provide such training and document those who have successfully mastered usage of the equipment.

Response Strategies

During the Response and Recovery phase, the Communications and Information Technology Branch Director takes direction from the Logistics Section Chief who is taking direction from the Executive Policy Group and the UCG in implementing the campus Action Plans. The Communications and Information Technology Director serves as the Branch Director. The Branch Director in consultation with the Section

Chief will identify objectives to be accomplished during each Operational Period. The role of the Communications and Information Technology Director during a critical event is to ensure that all communications and information technology needs of the EOC, the PPMRR team, and the campus are met. In the event that resources become damaged as a result of the incident, the Director leads and manages a team focused on emergency repairs and as necessary, activates the computer network systems backup, and the distribution of emergency equipment.

Recovery Strategies

During the Recovery phase, the Branch Director works to restore the campus communications and information technology systems to the pre-critical event status. If data was relocated to a remote server, the data is retrieved and an analysis run to detect deficiencies. Where necessary, the director oversees any repairs to the systems that are needed. The Communications and Information Branch Director contributes to the After Action Report all actions pertaining to the function of the Communications and Information Branch throughout the critical event.

Facilities Branch

The Facilities Director is responsible for the safe operation of the campus for students, staff, faculty, and visitors during nonemergency times, as well as during times of emergency and recovery. He/she is responsible for ensuring continuity of operations for all critical infrastructure operations. This includes ensuring that the buildings and roadways are habitable, and that potable water and sanitation services are available for the campus community. All departments that report to the Facilities Director serve as Unit Leaders. Every Unit Leader has an obligation to provide Protection, Prevention, Mitigation, Response, and Recovery strategies for those who report to them.

Prevention, Protection, and Mitigation Strategies

The Facilities Director plays a critical role in planning during the Prevention, Protection, and Mitigation phases. He/she is responsible to provide a detailed campus map and floor plans for inclusion in the PPMRR. Floor plans must include heating, ventilation, and air conditioning (HVAC), and electrical plans, identify utilities and sprinkler shutoffs, as well as fire extinguishers and fire alarm turnoff locations. Floor plans should also indicate the locations of all communications devices such as telephones, telephone wall jacks, and computer locations. Consideration should be made to use a Global Positioning System (GPS) mapping system for the campus.

During the planning phase, it is imperative for the Facilities Director to ensure that there are master keys for all buildings and doors on campus and that they are tagged for easy identification. There must be written, and easily accessible utility shutoff procedures for fire alarms, and utilities such as gas, water, electricity, sprinkler systems, and cable television. Hard copies of these procedures should be accessible in the event of a power failure.

The Director should conduct a campus asset inventory, including the location of all generators and backup fuel that can be utilized in the event of a power failure. Document the current state of all significant fixed and moveable assets. Photograph buildings and assets as evidence of the existing conditions. This will be critical when assessing damage after a critical event on campus that damages or destroys campus assets.

When looking at ways to mitigate damage from flooding events, especially if the campus is located in a flood zone, consider relocating critical equipment such as mechanical and electrical equipment and irreplaceable research to at least the second floor in each building. Locate back-up power generators and transfer switches well above ground level and ensure that they are protected from wind-borne projectiles. Where indicated dry floodproof buildings and install floodgates.

Training of facilities staff is a critical component of effective prevention, protection, and mitigation planning. They must be included in exercises and drills, not only evacuation and shelter-in-place drills, but also drills that test their knowledge of emergency shutoff procedures and protocols for the relocation/storage of unsecured items on campus prior to an extreme weather event such as an impending tornado or hurricane. Responsibilities must also include a monthly inspection of fire extinguishers; checking that evacuation routes, shelter areas, and emergency procedures are posted; and checking the backup fuel supply. Pre-event planning should also include contingency plans for ensuring that there is a potable water supply and sanitation services available during an emergency.

Response Strategies

During the Response and Recovery phase, the Facilities Branch Director takes direction from the Logistics Section Chief who is taking direction from the Executive Policy Group and the UCG in implementing the campus Action Plans. The Facilities Director serves as the Branch Director.

The Branch Director in consultation with the Section Chief will identify objectives to be accomplished during each Operational Period. During a critical event on campus, facilities personnel play an active role by ensuring that all requests for facilities and facility support are immediately addressed. They may be called upon to provide equipment and personnel to perform shutdown procedures, hazardous area control, barricades, damage assessment, debris clearance, emergency repairs, and equipment protection. The IC will call upon the Facilities Director to provide technical advice about the incident or response activities as they relate to the environment or health and safety of the students, staff, faculty, and visitors. This will include reports that determine the extent of damage to utility systems serving the campus: water, sanitary sewers, wastewater treatment plants, storm drains; electricity, gas, cable television, and telecommunications services.

As emergency responders from outside the campus community arrive on campus, it will be the role of the facilities personnel to provide them with campus maps, indicating the EOC location, incident location, access routes, and as necessary to the event, hazardous materials locations, and any information necessary for a safe and effective response. Additionally, it is the responsibility of the Facilities Director to provide sanitation services and a potable water supply to the EOC.

Recovery Strategies

Critical to returning the campus to its pre-disaster state is restoring its buildings and roadways. During the recovery phase, facilities personnel provide essential services for the maintenance and restoration of critical infrastructure functions and utilities. Responsibilities start with determining the magnitude and impact of an event's damage to the campus infrastructure. Damage assessment reports are conducted for all buildings roadways, sidewalks, parking lots, and so on. Photographing damaged buildings and roadways and any other damaged assets is conducted as evidence of post-disaster damage. When damage includes hazardous materials, it is imperative that the appropriate local, state, and federal authorities are notified. Campuses should consider hiring an independent architectural and engineering firm to assist with the assessment and documentation of damage.

Once the assessment is completed, a plan is created to implement and manage maintenance, repair, and construction projects for critical campus services and facilities. Typically, it will begin with debris removal from buildings, grounds, and roadways. When the debris removal is beyond the scope of campus facilities personnel, contractors may be called in and facilities personnel may oversee the debris removal work. The Facilities Director coordinates with the Procurement Branch to purchase materials to restore the campus facilities and roadways as well as develop contracts for repair work that is beyond the scope of capabilities of the facilities personnel.

For utility systems restoration, the Facilities Director will coordinate with utility companies to determine the restoration schedule. Until full restoration is a viable option, the Facilities Director and personnel work to supply all critical functions with backup power supplies such as the use of generators. The Facilities Branch Director contributes to the After Action Report all actions pertaining to the function of the Facilities Branch throughout the critical event.

Supply/Procurement Branch

The Supply/Procurement Director determines orders, distributes, stores, and maintains accountability of all supplies required by all sections during nonemergency times, Prevention, Protection, and Mitigation, as well as during times of Response and Recovery. All departments that report to the Supply/Procurement Director serve as Unit Leaders. Every Unit Leader has an obligation to provide Protection, Prevention, Mitigation, Response, and Recovery strategies for those who report to them.

Prevention, Protection, and Mitigation Strategies

During the Prevention, Protection, and Mitigation phases, the Supply/ Procurement Director maintains a campus inventory database of supplies and materials. Develop an inventory of all campus-owned equipment such as all motorized transportation, forklifts, and tree-trimming equipment. Maintain a list of rental companies with tools and equipment that might be necessary to restore the campus to its pre-critical state, as well as a list of contractors with heavy equipment that can respond to a critical event on campus expeditiously.

A vendor list, including products, delivery times, purchasing codes, and procurement spending limits, should also be created and maintained. Flexibility should be built in realizing that spending limits may need to be adjusted to reflect the magnitude of the critical event. During the planning phase, define unit costs of supplies and material from suppliers and vendors, and establish payment procedures. For instance, will they accept purchase orders as payment in the event of a critical event on campus? Before a critical event is the time to establish the procedures with the Finance and Administration Section for approval of orders, including orders that may exceed the purchase order limit.

Response Strategies

During the Response and Recovery phase, the Supply/Procurement Branch Director takes direction from the Logistics Section Chief who is taking direction from the Executive Policy Group and the UCG in implementing the campus Action Plans. The Supply/Procurement Director serves as the Branch Director. The Branch Director in consultation with the Section Chief will identify objectives to be accomplished during each Operational Period. As supplies and materials are requested, determine if requested types and quantities of supplies and material are available in campus inventory. Ensure that all resources are tracked and accounted for, as well as resources ordered through mutual aid and new purchases. Coordinate with the Purchasing Unit in the Finance/Administration Section and track deliveries of ordered supplies and material. Work collaboratively with the Finance/Administration Section to ensure that all contracts identify the scope of work and specific site locations, and rental rates are negotiated. A status board to track the progress of all requested supplies and materials should be posted in the EOC. The status board lists the date and time of the request, items requested, the priority designation, the time the request was processed, and the estimated time of arrival or delivery to the requesting party.

During the Response phase, it may be necessary to house and feed those responding to the EOC. When that occurs, the Supply/Procurement Section works in coordination with the Operations Section Chief who coordinates with the Food Services Branch Director, Housing Branch, and Human Resources Branch to provide food and lodging.

Recovery Strategies

During the Recovery phase, the Supply/Procurement Branch Director continues to order, distribute, store, and maintain accountability of all supplies required by all sections. Additionally, documentation of delivery is provided to Finance and Administration. The Supply/Procurement Branch Director contributes to the After Action Report all actions pertaining to the function of the Supply/Procurement Branch throughout the critical event.

Transportation Branch

The Transportation Director prepares transportation plans, provides for fueling, maintenance, repair, and storage of resources and provides the transportation for personnel, food, and supplies. While the Transportation Branch is housed in the Logistics Section, it is critical to integrate the accounting and maintaining of resources with the movement of these resources, which occurs in the Operations Section. All departments that report to the Transportation Branch Director serve as Unit Leaders. Every Unit Leader has an obligation to provide Protection, Prevention, Mitigation, Response, and Recovery strategies for those who report to them.

Prevention, Protection, and Mitigation Strategies

During the planning stage is the time to develop strategies and training for integrating transportation plans with operations strategies for activities such as evacuation, shelter-in-place, search and rescue, debris removal, road restoration, and so on. Road usage outside of the campus may be critical to the response and recovery of an incident on campus. It is in the interest of the campus to include the town/city/state transportation/highway department in the prevention/protection/mitigation stages so they are familiar with the campus should they be called upon during response and recovery stages.

Develop and maintain an inventory of campus transportation vehicles as well as community resources such as local bus companies, school districts with buses, trains, and ambulance companies. Strategize to develop backup systems that include mutual aid agreements with 24-hour contact information. As Edwards & Goodrich (2009) recommends, labor agreements need to be developed that permit drivers and mechanics to work in disaster conditions. When developing these contracts, be sure to ascertain that the vendors also have contracts in place to supply them with the necessary fuel and replacement equipment such as tires. It is also imperative that the transportation outlets and their operators are included in campus disaster training.

Response Strategies

During the Response and Recovery phase, the Transportation Branch takes direction from the Logistics Section Chief who is taking direction from the Executive Policy Group and the UCG in implementing the campus Action Plans. The Transportation Director serves as the Branch Director. The Branch Director in consultation with the Section Chief will identify objectives to be accomplished during each Operational Period. The Transportation Director works under the direction of the IC to ensure that transportation requirements, in support of response operations, are met. In order to meet this obligation, the Transportation Director will manage the campus pool of vehicles, parking operations, and if applicable the campus garage, as well as coordinate the use of transportation outlets such as local bus companies, school districts with buses, trains, and ambulance companies to the campus community. Response strategies for transportation may also include transporting emergency personnel, equipment, and supplies to support emergency operations, as well as transporting students and their personal belongings to temporary or alternative housing facilities.

Having a good traffic management strategy in place will help the Transportation Branch meet its mission. As the Traffic Management Branch falls under the direction of the Public Safety Branch in the Operations Section and the Transportation Branch falls under the direction of the Logistics Section, the coordination will be defined by the Section Chiefs. When road access is hindered by debris, the Operations Section Chief will facilitate coordination with the Transportation Branch Director and the Facilities Branch Director as debris removal is managed by the Facilities Branch.

Recovery

During the Recovery phase, the Transportation Branch Director will inventory resources and where appropriate repair and/or replace as needed. The Transportation Branch Director contributes to the After Action Report all actions pertaining to the function of the Transportation Branch throughout the critical event.

Finance and Administration Section

The role of the Finance and Administration Section Chief is to oversee and manage expenses and to keep the Executive Policy Group and the Command Staff aware of the fiscal situation. In the context of Incident Command, the Finance and Administration Section is one of the four sections that reports to the Executive Policy Group, the UCG, and the IC. This is the one section where in many instances the IC structure mirrors the steady-state organizational structure. In the Finance and Administration Section, you will typically find positions that are responsible for tracking incident costs such as the Vice President of Finance and Administration,

Human Resources, Business Management, as well as the campus attorney. Select as Section Chief the position at your campus that best suits the role of Finance and Administration Section Chief.

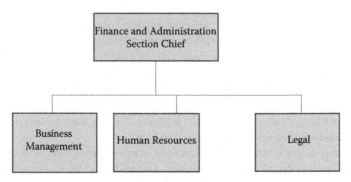

Business Management Branch

The Business Management Director is responsible for all financial transactions during all PPMRR phases. Having standard operating procedures in place is imperative during critical as well as under normal circumstances. All departments that report to the Business Management Branch Director serve as Unit Leaders. Every Unit Leader has an obligation to provide Protection, Prevention, Mitigation, Response, and Recovery strategies for those who report to them.

Protection, Prevention, Mitigation Strategies

Having standard operating procedures (SOPs) in place well before a critical event occurs ensures the ability to oversee and manage expenses and to keep the Executive Policy Group and the Command Staff aware of the fiscal situation. Ensuring that the campus has a methodology for tracking expenses will be critical for reimbursement by insurance carriers, and state and federal entities is of utmost importance.

During the Protection, Prevention, Mitigation phase, policies are examined to ensure that appropriate and up-to-date coverage is maintained on insurance policies. Goods and services as well as mutual aid contracts should also be in place well before an event occurs. These contracts should be reviewed at least annually.

If the campus has contractors with heavy equipment working on-site, it is prudent to include in their contracts a disaster clause that permits the heavy equipment to be used, if needed, during a critical event. "Include a disaster clause in all campus construction contracts that permits the

Logistics Chief to divert the contractor's equipment and personnel to disaster response and recovery operations at the contracted rate, with the understanding that the contract will be extended with no penalty to the contractor to allow adequate time to complete the original work" (Edwards & Goodrich, p. 21).

Response Strategies

During the Response and Recovery phases, the Business Management Director is the Branch Director and takes direction from the Finance and Administration Section Chief who is taking direction from the Executive Policy Group and the UCG in implementing the campus Action Plans. The Branch Director in consultation with the Section Chief will identify objectives to be accomplished during each Operational Period. The Business Management Branch maintains all financial records throughout the emergency, keeping track of expenses incurred as a result of the critical event. Writing contracts and processing purchase orders to ensure that all supplies and equipment needed are obtained in an expeditious, cost-conscious manner and in keeping with state and federal reimbursement standards are a high priority.

Recovery Strategies

During the Recovery phase, the Business Management Branch collects and submits documentation to insurance carriers to support the campus's cost recovery efforts for damage incurred. Such evidence includes pre- and post critical event photographs. When appropriate, applications for state and federal disaster assistance are submitted. The Business Management Branch Director contributes to the After Action Report all actions pertaining to the function of the Business Management Branch throughout the critical event.

Human Resources Branch

The Human Resources Director is responsible for the welfare of all staff during all phases of a critical event. All departments that report to the Human Resources Director serve as Unit Leaders. Every Unit Leader has an obligation to provide Protection, Prevention, Mitigation, Response, and Recovery strategies for those who report to them.

Prevention, Protection, and Mitigation Strategies

Strategies must be devised during the Prevention, Protection, and Mitigation phases to ensure continuity of operations. Employee payroll, tracking vacation, leave time, and sick time should not be interrupted due to a critical event. Not only because employees are entitled and expect their paychecks to be uninterrupted but also if individual employee payroll deductions are not made to their benefit plans, the benefit plans could be suspended.

As the Human Resources Branch is responsible for providing personnel for emergency response, it is imperative to have a system in place to contact personnel. Ensure that there is a system in place to keep track of the time employees are working in response to the critical event so that compensation accurately reflects the hours worked rather than the typical workweek. During the planning phase, develop a staffing plan and backup staffing plan for 24-hour EOC coverage for response and support functions. The plan should indicate special qualifications of the individuals. Create a plan with the Public Safety Officer to ensure access, badging or identification for personnel both internal and external to the campus arriving at the EOC. There may be instances where the IC indicates a need for establishing a pool of campus volunteers. In the planning phase, create a system for the Human Resources Section to establish a volunteer registration system where staff screen and register volunteers, and issue badging/identification cards in cooperation with the Safety Officer.

As training on the procedures, protocols, and strategies is imperative to a successful outcome, all faculty and staff must be included in PPMRR training. The Human Resources Branch and/or the Director of Emergency Management keep training records for all personnel that include communication, evacuation, lock-down, and shelter-in-place strategies.

Response Strategies

During the Response and Recovery phases, the Human Resources Director is the Branch Director and takes direction from the Finance and Administration Section Chief who is taking direction from the Executive Policy Group and the UCG in implementing the campus Action Plans. The Branch Director in consultation with the Section Chief will identify objectives to be accomplished during each Operational Period. The Human Resources Branch will communicate guidance for critical events (pay, leave/time off, staffing, work scheduling, benefits, telework, hiring authorities, and other human resources flexibilities) to managers in an effort to help continue essential functions during a critical event.

The Human Resources Branch processes all incoming requests from the EOC for personnel support, including not only the number of staff needed but also indicating staff with special qualifications. Ensure that a system is put into place for staff members to contact their families to apprise them of their health and welfare.

Work collaboratively with the Planning Section to establish and maintain personnel logs and other necessary files to ensure that all personnel are checking in/out of EOC. It is helpful to have a large poster size EOC organization chart on the wall of the EOC listing each activated position. As people check in, indicate the name of the person occupying each position on the chart. The EOC access/badging/identification plan keeps track of personnel arriving and departing from the EOC. If community volunteers are enlisted, activate the screening and registering mechanism and work with the SO to issue volunteers badging/identification cards. As it may be necessary to enlist the services of a crisis counselor for members of the EOC as well as for the campus community, work with the SO to determine if/when crisis counseling may be needed for emergency responders and the campus at large. As staff and volunteers may become injured as a result of the response and recovery work, it is imperative that a chronological log of injury and illness reports is created and that all injury claims are investigated in a timely manner.

Recovery Strategies

Ensure that Workers' Compensation claims and Disaster Service Worker claims resulting from the response are processed within a reasonable time frame and passed to the appropriate person at the campus within the Finance and Administration Section. In the event that there is a death as a result of the critical event on campus, the Human Resources Branch makes arrangements for the removal of the deceased faculty or staff belongings. Arrangements pertaining to the death or injury of a student are managed by Student Affairs. The Human Resources Branch Director contributes to the After Action Report all actions pertaining to the function of the Human Resources Branch throughout the critical event.

Legal Branch

The Legal Branch provides legal advice, oversees all policies, procedures, and contracts to protect the interest of the campus and in doing so insures campus-wide compliance. All departments that report to the Legal Branch Director serve as Unit Leaders. Every Unit Leader has an obligation to provide Protection, Prevention, Mitigation, Response, and Recovery strategies for those who report to them.

Prevention, Protection, and Mitigation Strategies

It is imperative to include the campus legal entity in all phases of the development and review of the PPMRR strategies. The role of the campus legal advisor is to keep the Executive Policy Group and the PPMRR team up to date on any local, state, or federal emergency management laws and ordinances, updates of standards to NIMS, 34 CFR, the Clery Act, and the National Fire Protection Association (NFPA) 1600, as well as the Occupational Safety and Health Administration (OSHA).

The legal team will advise the campus on immunity from legal liability regarding its roles and responsibilities regarding emergency response. The legal team's responsibility may also include a review of the pros and cons of using the word *procedures* in its documents. Specifically, confirming that if *procedural* steps are specifically described in the PPMRR, would failure to follow the protocols not be considered discretionary action, and therefore there would be no immunity. If protocols are stated as guidelines only, following them could be considered discretionary and therefore immune.

Response Strategies

During the Response and Recovery phase, the Legal Branch takes direction from the Finance and Administration Section Chief who is taking direction from the Executive Policy Group and the UCG in implementing the campus Action Plans. The Legal Director serves as the Branch Director. All departments that report to the Legal Branch Director serve as Unit Leaders. The Branch Director in consultation with the Section Chief will identify objectives to be accomplished during each Operational Period. As a critical situation unfolds on campus the role of the Legal Branch Director is to advice the Executive Policy Group, the UCG and Command and General Staff of the legal obligations of Duty of Care vs. Breach of Duty to ensure that PPMRR team members work within their scope and avoid negligence claims. Duty of Care includes a person's legal obligation to maintain a standard of reasonable care while doing anything that could cause foreseeable harm to others. A person may be found negligent under Breach of Duty if it is found that their actions or lack of action, caused an injury, as compared to the actions of a reasonably prudent person.

The Legal Branch Director may work with the Finance and Administration Branch Director in managing contracts and agreements such as real estate transactions and utility contracts. They may be an integral component working with the Human Resources Branch Director, Student Affairs Branch Director, and/or the Academic Affairs Branch Director in investigating claims, handling mediations, and other critical event-related incidents.

Recovery Strategies

During the Recovery phase, the Legal Branch Director will continue to advise and manage any legal issues pertaining to the incident, including recommendations to change policies and procedures to align with compliance with state and federal regulations. The Legal Branch Director contributes to the After Action Report all actions pertaining to the function of the Legal Branch throughout the critical event.

Sample Executive Policy Group and Command Staff Contact List

Name/Title	Phone	E-Mail	Office Location
Name			
President			
Policy Group			
Name			
EM Director			
Policy Group			
Name			
Liaison Officer			
Command Staff			
Name			
PIO Officer			
Command Staff			
Name			
Safety Officer			
Command Staff			
Name			
Section Chief			
Operations			
Name			
Section Chief			
Planning			
Name			
Section Chief			
Logistics			
Name			
Section Chief			
Finance and Administration			

Sample Community Agency and Vendor Contact List

Local Agencies	Contact Person	Telephone	Address
Community Police Department	Chief John Smith		
Community Fire Department	Chief Bill Hanson		
Community Gas/ Electric	Mary Price		
Community Hospital			
County Sheriff			
County Emergency Management			
Contracted Bus Company			
Contracted Hotel			
Contracted Food Services			

REFERENCES

Edwards, F. L., & Goodrich, D. C. (2009, June). *The role of transportation in campus emergency planning.* San Jose, CA: Mineta Transportation Institute.

FEMA. *FEMA emergency alert system.* Retrieved from http://www.fema.gov/emergency-alert-system

FEMA Emergency Management Institute. *Independent study program.* Retrieved from http://www.training.fema.gov/IS/

FEMA National Integration Center (NIC). NIC recommendations. Retrieved from http://emilms.fema.gov/IS700aNEW/NIMS0106040text.htm

National Incident Management System (NIMS). Readiness and emergency management for schools. Retrieved from http://rems.ed.gov/K12NIMSImplementation.aspx

National Oceanic and Atmospheric Administration. Homepage. Retrieved from www.noaa.gov

U.S. Department of Homeland Security. (2003, February 28). *Homeland Security Presidential Directive 5 (HSPD-5)*. Retrieved from http://www.dhs.gov/ publication/homeland-security-presidential-directive-5

U.S. Department of Homeland Security (2011, March 30). *Presidential Policy Directive 8 (PPD-8)*. Retrieved from http://www.dhs.gov/ presidential-policy-directive-8-national-preparedness

6

Developing Campus PPMRR Strategies

This section helps to organize the layout of the campus emergency prevention, preparedness, mitigation, response, and recovery operations according to FEMA and the Department of Education guidelines.

FEMA and the Department of Education recommend that a campus emergency plan be organized into three sections: Basic Guidelines, Functional Annex, Threat- and Hazard-Specific Annex. Each of the annexes aligns with the NIMS recommendation that for each identified threat and/or hazard a set of Goals, Objectives, and Action Items be constructed for each of the three time frames associated with an incident: before, during, and after.

This resource book replaces the word "before" with the phrase *Prevention, Preparedness, and Mitigation Strategies*; the word "during" is replaced with *Response Strategies*; and the word "after" is replaced with *Recovery Strategies*.

In addition to the three sections—The Basic Guideline, Functional Annex, Threat- and Hazard-Specific Annex—adding a section for Training Compliance Documentation and a section for Campus Policies is recommended. These policies could include

- Emergency Activation Plan Policy for inputting new faculty, staff, student contact information
- Information Technology Security Policy
- Missing Student Policy

- Mutual Aid Policy
- Snow Emergency Closing Policy
- Suspicious Mail Policy

Following the five sections, it is recommended that two appendices be added. Communications Templates for use in activating the mass notification system whether it be by phone, text, or other means, and Safety Message Templates for use in developing emergency preparedness campaigns and training sessions.

The guidelines that follow are never referred to as a plan but always a strategy or guideline. If procedural steps are specifically described in a safety manual, failure to follow the procedures would not be considered discretionary action, and therefore there would be no immunity. If procedures are stated as guidelines, or, as in this resource book, *strategies*, following them could be considered discretionary and therefore immune.

SECTION 1: THE BASIC GUIDELINE

The Basic Guideline sets the stage by defining how the campus has organized itself to protect the campus community. It cites the legal authority for emergency planning and conducting emergency operations, identifies the threats and hazards that the campus should be prepared to address, assigns ICS/NIMS compliant roles and responsibilities to campus staff, as well as provides contact lists for all campus personnel and community partners.

The Basic Guideline begins with a "Statement of Purpose" that provides an overview of why the guideline was created. Following the "Statement of Purpose" is the "Mission Statement," which typically makes a statement regarding the importance of providing a safe environment for learning and working. The next section is called "Authorities," a statement that describes the mandate by which the campus is creating its guidelines or strategies. In the United States, Homeland Security Presidential Directive 5 (HSPD-5) and NIMS are the overarching legal authorities. The strategies should support the U.S. Department of Education (2013), Guide for Developing High-Quality School Emergency Operations Plans for Institutions of Higher Education, and the Clery Act that requires every Title IV institution, without exception, to convey its process for mass notification use in emergencies, and how mass notification tests will be conducted, to have and disclose emergency response and evacuation procedures, and to outline training of response personnel. In addition to following federal mandates, each campus guideline and strategy should support and complement its own state education department regulations.

The primary objective of creating campus guidelines and strategies is to protect the health, safety, and welfare of students, faculty, staff, visitors, and to protect school property. To meet this objective, planning is essential. In order to plan you need to uncover the threats and hazards, a campus might encounter. While it is impossible to cover every possible event that could occur, it is possible to provide a general understanding of activities that should be undertaken no matter what emergency event befalls the school. The "Threat and Hazard Analysis" section follows the "Authorities" section.

Threat and Hazard Analysis

The first step is to examine potential emergencies based on the risk posed by likely hazards; develop and implement programs and actions aimed toward preventing, protecting, and mitigating the campus from the identified hazards; prepare for those risks that cannot be eliminated; and prescribe the possible responses required to deal with the events, and take action to quickly recover from the event and thereby reducing the impact of the event on the campus.

The analysis assesses the probability that a specific threat or hazard will occur; the effects it will likely have, including the severity of the impact; the time the campus will have to warn students, faculty, and staff about the threat or hazard; and how long it may last. It examines environmental, technological, and man-made possibilities that could make the campus vulnerable.

To determine what environmental, technological, and man-made hazards and threats may present themselves at the campus, the first step should be to refer to the community hazard and threat analysis conducted by the town/county/state in which your campus resides. Next examine the campus incident reports to identify historical occurrences. Keeping abreast of what other campuses are reporting as threats and hazards through professional organizations and literature can help thwart a similar event at your campus. Once you have identified the threats and hazards, write a narrative analysis to be inserted into the PPMRR under the title "Threat and Hazard Analysis". The following is a sample narrative analysis.

SAMPLE THREAT AND HAZARD ANALYSIS

(Replace the items in parenthesis with your campus-specific threat and hazard analysis data.)

A threat and hazard analysis for (NAME College/University) was conducted on (Date). A thorough review of the (TOWN/CITY/ COUNTY/STATE) threat and hazard analysis was conducted. It revealed that (NAME College/University), located in the center of this geographic area, is at risk for (seasonal hurricanes, brush fires, tornadoes). The historical incident reports and analysis of probable events that could occur at the college identified the following risks: (flooding of the buildings on the lower campus during significant rain, computer hacking, fire in residential housing, hazmat spill inside a campus building). A review of the literature pertaining to campus emergency management reveals that (active shooter and missing student events) are on the rise. From this threat and hazard analysis, the following Risk Priority table was constructed.

Next enter the data into a table that will ultimately be included in the campus guidelines. For each threat or hazard listed in your analysis table, list one finding for each heading: *Probability, Magnitude, Warning, Duration,* and *Risk Priority:* and include a legend to explain the scales. The purpose is to prioritize the likelihood of the threat or hazard occurring, the length of time needed to warn the campus of the impending danger, how long you estimate that the event will last, which ultimately helps to identify the risk priority. The following table shows two possible threats or hazards; fire and a hazmat spill in a building on campus. *Probability* is presented on a scale of 1 to 4: 4—Very likely, 3—Likely, 2—Possible, 1—Unlikely. *Magnitude* is presented on a scale of 1 to 4: 4—Catastrophic, 3—Critical, 2—Limited, 1—Negligible. *Warning* is represented by the amount of time necessary to warn the campus community of the impending danger; 4 equates to minimal, 3 equates to 6–12 hours, 2 equates to 12–24 hours, and 1 equates to 24 or more hours. *Duration* is the length of time the threat or hazard is expected to last. The *Risk Priority* is what your campus PPMRR team assigns to each threat or hazard, based on the factors of probability, magnitude, warning, and duration.

128

Hazard	Probability	Magnitude	Warning	Duration (hours)	Risk Priority
Fire	4. Very likely	3. Critical	4. Minimal	2. 3–6	High
Hazmat spill inside a campus building	2. Possible	2. Limited	4. Minimal	1. < 3	Low

Legend

Probability	Magnitude	Warning	Duration (hours)	Risk Priority
4. Very likely	4. Catastrophic	4. Minimal	4. 12+	High
3. Likely	3. Critical	3. 6–12 hours	3. 6–12	Medium
2. Possible	2. Limited	2. 12–24 hours	2. 3–6	Low
1. Unlikely	1. Negligible	1. 24+ hours	1. <3	

Emergency Classification Levels (ECLs) can assist in determining threat and hazard risk priorities. Some colleges/universities use three ECLs while others may choose to use four or five levels. The number of ECLs is not as important as the team at your college or university who knows the ECLs used for your campus and what each level indicates. Include the ECLs and your campus's definition of the ECL. This guidebook uses three ECL levels.

Level 1 (Minor Incident): A Level 1 incident is any incident, potential or actual, that will not seriously affect the overall functional capacity of the university. Level 1 incidents could include a medical emergency (cardiac arrest, seizure, drug overdose), severe weather advisory (snow, ice storm), contained fire, chemical spill confined to a single area, loss of electricity or heat, a building flooding from a broken pipe. It may not be necessary for the entire PPMRR team to meet to manage a Level 1 event. The PPMRR team lead will be notified of Level 1 events and make decisions regarding who needs to be contacted based on the individual incident. A Level 1 equates to a Risk Priority of Low.

Level 2 (Emergency/Partial Activation): A Level 2 incident is any incident, potential or actual, that affects an entire building or buildings, and which may disrupt the overall operations of the campus. Level 2 incidents could include a major severe weather event threat (tornado, hurricane), loss of heat/air conditioning, contagious disease

129

outbreak (Ebola, flu), bomb threat, a significant reputation risk to the college/university. These events require a coordinated response with external partners, such as police, Department of Health, local Department of Emergency Management. The PPMRR team will open and man the Emergency Operations Center/Command Post until the event has concluded. A Level 2 equates to a Risk Priority of Medium.

Level 3 (Disaster/Full Activation): A Level 3 incident has the potential to interrupt the continuation of regular campus activities. Level 3 incidents could include: a major severe weather event strike (tornado, hurricane, earthquake), major fire with injuries, structural collapse with injuries, civil unrest in the surrounding community, acts of violence: active shooter, threats involving weapons, hostage and/or kidnapping, terrorist attacks. These critical events require an immediate notification to and response by the PPMRR team. The PPMRR team will open and man the Emergency Operations Center/Command Post until the event has concluded. A Level 3 equates to a Risk Priority of High.

For each incident level, identify the process for activating the mass notification system and the campus response component for threats and hazards. It should include who makes decisions and initiates procedures for any campus emergency event, the procedure for reporting an emergency, when information is released, and how information is provided to the campus community. Be sure to have a procedure in place to send an immediate warning notification to the campus community upon confirmation of a significant emergency or dangerous situation involving an immediate threat to the health or safety of students, staff, or faculty and a timely warning for Clery Act crimes that have already occurred but represent an ongoing threat.

SAMPLE MASS NOTIFICATION AND RESPONSE ACTIVATION PROCESS

A typical campus emergency event is reported to the (Public Safety Office at xxx-xxx-xxxx) from a cell phone or a campus desk phone, on-campus emergency phone, weather radio, weather siren, or other means. The Public Safety staff on duty will contact the (Director of Public Safety) or the assigned duty officer immediately. The Public

Safety Director or duty officer determines the incident level as defined in the PPMRR and immediately contacts the (Director of Emergency Management).

The (Emergency Management Director) will begin the emergency notification procedure to the appropriate Executive Policy Group member, Command Staff, and Section Chiefs via phone/text to assess the situation, and develop recommendations for short- and long-term responses including making notifications to the campus community as appropriate; opening the Emergency Operations Center (EOC), canceling or relocating classes, and so on.

For imminent danger, any member of the PPMRR team can initiate a message through the Emergency Alert System without consultation with other team members.

SECTION 2: FUNCTIONAL ANNEX

Section 2 of the campus guidelines contains the Functional Annexes; critical activities that apply to one or more threats and hazards. This guide places strategies for Accountability, Communication, Evacuation, Shelter-in-Place, and Lock-Down in the Functional Annex. Each activity lists a goal that ties to the Mission Statement and strategies for meeting the goal in all phases: prevention, protection, mitigation, response, and recovery. The goal for each threat and hazard strategy is always to provide direction to the campus community on actions to be taken to keep the community safe. In the prevention, protection, mitigation phases, the objective is to ensure that campus policies consider actions that could prevent or lessen the impact of a threat or hazard.

The strategies listed in this Functional Annex are basic, generic, and meant to be expanded upon with campus-specific strategies. They are not meant to be copied and pasted into any campus guideline. Each campus will develop its own strategies, but where appropriate may use wording from this guide. Use this chapter as a foundation for the layout of your campus Functional Annex.

Accountability

Goals: To ensure that rosters and accountability lists of students, staff, and faculty are available and easily accessible; for staff and faculty to be able to access and utilize rosters and accountability lists in the midst of a critical event; to provide training for staff and faculty that incorporates the use of rosters and accountability lists.

Protection, Prevention, and Mitigation Strategies

Accountability starts with the PPMRR team having access to a campus master list updated each semester. It should include office locations, cell phone numbers of all faculty and staff, faculty office hours, and classroom times and locations, as well as a master student course roster. It is imperative that there is an accurate account of who was in each building before the evacuation order was issued and who was able to safely vacate the premises. In order to accomplish this, faculty and department heads need to know that it is their responsibility to take the attendance rosters with them during evacuation, lock-down, and shelter-in-place events.

Faculty, staff, and students need to be informed of rally points in the event of an evacuation of shelter-in-place events. Designating floor wardens and/or building wardens to assist with accountability has proved to be beneficial. If your campus institutes the floor and/or building warden system, be sure to designate backups for these positions in the event that an evacuation or shelter-in place occurs at a time when the floor and/or building warden is not on campus. Floor wardens are typically assigned to help facilitate a swift evacuation of the floor where they work. Their role is to ensure that everyone evacuates, closes the classroom/ office doors upon exiting, takes the stairs not the elevator, and to relay to Public Safety whether everyone is accounted for or if someone is missing or injured.

Accountability strategies should also be in place for campus groups traveling off-campus whether in campus-owned, leased, or operated vehicles or with a public carrier. Filing a roster with Public Safety before departure is imperative. In the event of an accident or other unscheduled incident, Public Safety should be notified immediately.

Response Strategies

Without delay when an evacuation, shelter-in-place, or lock-down is issued, faculty must lead students, and department heads must lead their staff to the designated rally point and take attendance and inform building or floor warden of any missing or injured students, staff, and faculty. Building wardens contact Public Safety immediately of anyone missing or injured.

In the event of an accident occurring with an off-campus group, assess the situation, activate the accountability strategies, develop recommendations for short- and long-term responses including making notifications to the campus community and families as appropriate.

Recovery Strategies

After the event has concluded, as necessary update rosters, provide training for students, staff, faculty, building and floor wardens. Write an After Action Plan to review what went well and areas for improvement.

Communications

Goals: Create outlets to provide timely and accurate information to the internal and external campus community on the status of any phase of the PPMRR operation; utilize these outlets to effectively communicate with faculty, staff, students, and the general public regarding actions necessary to protect people and property; represent the campus as responsible and caring, and maintain stakeholder confidence.

Prevention, Protection, and Mitigation Strategies

Before a critical event occurs is the time for the campus to devise its communication strategies. Communication strategies should include creating communication templates that are easily updated to reflect the current critical event. Multiple communications modalities should be in place and tested regularly. They could include:

- Mass Notification System for phone calls, text messaging, e-mails
- Website postings
- Electronic bulletin board
- Social media outlets such as Facebook and Twitter
- Speaker systems in buildings
- Bullhorns
- Person to person using campus personnel
- Campus paper notice postings
- Local radio and TV station broadcasts
- Threat- and hazard-specific safety bulletins
- Code Blue emergency phones
- Government Emergency Telephone Systems (GETS)

Create a Timely Notice policy that identifies Emergency Classification Levels (ECLs), and the process that identifies how and who sends notifications to the campus community. Identify types of significant emergencies or dangers for which Timely Notices will be sent to the campus community. Events such as fire, tornado, hurricane, earthquake, gas leak, terrorist incident, armed intruder, bomb threat, and explosion are typically among the types of instances that a message is sent via a Mass Notification System including phone, text messaging, and e-mail. Emergency alert messages can be delivered via the multiple modes as listed earlier. Develop a system that updates the faculty, staff, and student database at least each semester and/or for staff and faculty as they join and separate from the campus.

Create an "All Clear" policy for threats and hazards that have caused the EOC to be activated. Create a strategy for informing the campus community of new policies and to provide training on current systems.

Develop and maintain a database of local and regional media contacts along with telephone and e-mail contact information. Prepare a media kit on CD or in USB format: campus fact sheet, campus map, list of key contacts. Identify a location to be designated as a media center, equipped with Internet connections, telephone lines, and located away from the EOC.

Create a database of support agencies: local police department, fire department, hospital, local emergency management, utility companies along with a contact person and their phone number, e-mail and physical address. Include town, county, and state representatives, as well as the Red Cross, Salvation Army, and other voluntary agencies. These databases should be ready and available in print, online, and on a USB for use by the Liaison Officer at the start of a campus critical event.

Develop strategies to enhance the skills of the communication staff. Enroll staff in training courses such as Basic Public Information Officers (G290); Advanced Public Information Officers (E388); Public Information Awareness (IS-29) all provided by FEMA. Information regarding content and availability of these courses can be obtained at the National Preparedness Directorate at: http://www.training.fema.gov.

SAMPLE EMERGENCY TELEPHONE HOTLINE MESSAGE

Due to (name event), (campus name) will be closed on (day of week), (date or dates). Day and evening classes have been canceled.
Please check (website) and stay tuned to area television and radio stations for further information.

SAMPLE TEXT MESSAGE ALERTS

Shelter-in-Place

Emergency at (location)—Go indoors immediately and shelter-in-place until further notice.
Check (website) for updates.

Shooting on Campus—Lock-Down

Shooting at (location)—Go to a secure location and deny entry (lock-down) now!
Check (website) for updates.

Weather Emergency

(Name weather event) approaching—Seek indoor shelter immediately until further notice.
Check (website) for updates.

SAMPLE POTENTIAL EVENT COMMUNICATION TEMPLATE

(Campus name) received a serious threat of a potentially violent incident on campus. At (time, date), the (local) Police Department received a (name the threat). In order to ensure the safety of the campus community, the campus will be closed (day) and all classes have been canceled.

SAMPLE GENERIC COMMUNICATION TEMPLATE

At approximately (time) today, an (name the event) occurred (at/struck the) (locality/campus). (Campus Police/Public Safety) were immediately dispatched to assess injuries and damage. (Indicate injuries, deaths, property damage, fires, etc., reported to date.) Response personnel from community police/fire agencies were called into action, and the staff of the (Campus Police/Public Safety) and the PPMRR team, under the direction of the President, opened the Emergency Operations Center. Classes are (in session/canceled) until (date). Further information will be provided as it becomes available. Check the campus (website) for detailed information.

Response Strategies

Activate the Timely Notice system. Take the lead in utilizing and monitoring social media to counter misinformation and rumors that may negatively impact the campus as the crisis progresses. Develop prepared statements to be made by the PIO. Provide a dedicated phone number for telephone inquiries from parents and the media. Change the Safety Hotline recording to indicate the campus situation and status.

Recovery Strategies

Activate the "All Clear" directive when appropriate via the mass communication system. Encourage faculty, staff, and students to call their families to let them know their status. This will help to minimize overload of the campus telephone system with incoming calls.

Review data on messages, delivery, and effects from

- Letters from the community
- News articles
- Letters to editors

Update templates and databases as necessary. Contribute to the After Action Report all actions pertaining to the function of communications throughout the critical event.

Evacuation

Goals: To provide the campus community an opportunity to become familiar with the sound of the fire alarm, the location of exits, practice timely evacuation drill procedures; during a critical event to be able to use this tested knowledge to make an expeditious evacuation; to make recommendations for improving evacuation time.

Prevention, Protection, and Mitigation Strategies

At the first meeting of each semester at the respective meetings of the faculty, staff, students, an agenda item will be the evacuation safety and accountability strategies. Relay the location of exits and rally points to be used during an evacuation of each campus facility. Assign building and

136

floor wardens to assist with evacuation. Provide strategies for evacuating people with mobility challenges.

Schedule and conduct evacuation drills at least once in the beginning of each semester in residence halls, and all office and academic buildings. Coordinate with facilities to ensure that evacuation route schematics are posted in every room on campus; that every exit sign is lit; that a policy is in place to keep stairwells and exits clear. When determining shelter locations consider including an engineer to determine the use of campus facilities as shelter points.

SAMPLE EVACUATION POLICY FOR STUDENTS, STAFF, AND FACULTY

- Secure hazardous operations if possible.
- Take only important personal items. Leave nonessential items.
- Close doors behind the last person out of the room.
- Walk quickly and orderly to the nearest safe exit.
- Do not exit using elevators unless authorized emergency personnel tell you to do so.
- Do not re-enter the building until authorized emergency personnel give the "All Clear" signal.
- Report any missing or trapped persons to authorized emergency personnel.
- Move away from the building to an established evacuation area.
- If you are unable to do so due to a physical disability, injury, or obstruction, go to the nearest location where there are no hazards, such as a hazard-free stairwell and call Public Safety at xxx-xxx-xxxx or call 911 from a safe location.
  - Signal out the window to emergency responders, if possible.
  - Remain calm, responders will arrive.

SAMPLE RALLY POINT COMMUNICATION

Administration Building

- Evacuation: Assemble in north parking lot
- Shelter: Assemble in the hallway of the basement, interior offices, or in the restrooms

Student Center

- Evacuation: Assemble in the open area of the quad by the athletic field
- Shelter: Assemble on the first floor away from windows in the hallway or bathrooms

Academic Commons North Building

- Evacuation: Assemble at the south side of the building near the quad fountain
- Shelter: Assemble on the first floor in interior rooms or faculty/staff restrooms

Scheduling Evacuation Drills

Develop a strategy to conduct announced and unannounced evacuation drills each semester to test the emergency response and evacuation procedures, and to assess and evaluate the emergency evacuation plans and capabilities. Assign responsibilities for monitoring, evaluating, and making recommendations for improvements. What follows is a suggested evacuation drill frequency table. Consider publishing drill results and scheduling training where necessary.

Facility Type	Minimum Drill Frequency
Residence halls	Once per semester
Facilities used for educational purposes, containing notable amounts of hazardous materials, exceeding three stories in height	Once per semester
Academic buildings	Once per semester
Office buildings	Annually
Daycare	Monthly

Response Strategies

For imminent danger such as a fire, any member of the campus community can initiate an evacuation by pulling a fire alarm. Evacuate all classes, offices, and campus facilities as safely and expeditiously as possible. Activate accountability strategies. Include here the process in place at your campus for contacting the local fire department and emergency response personnel such as EMS.

Refer to communication strategies for initiating an evacuation directive through the Mass Notification System, and for informing PPMRR team members to check into the EOC. The Executive Policy Group will assess the situation and make recommendations for short- and long-term responses including making notifications to campus community as appropriate; cancellation of classes, relocating classes, and so on.

The following scale is used in classifying successful evacuation drill times. Follow-up drills are required for buildings classified as Needs Improvement.

Evacuation Time (minutes)	Rating	Cooperation
<5–10	Excellent	Prompt and orderly evacuation
<10–15	Average	Minor objections to leaving
>15	Needs improvement	Notable delays and opposition

SAMPLE EVACUATION INSTRUCTIONS FOR FACULTY, STAFF, AND STUDENTS WITH PHYSICAL CHALLENGES

Mobility Impairment (use crutches, cane, wheelchair, or walker)

- If evacuation is ordered, proceed to the nearest designated exit.
- If in a building with more than one story, exit to the nearest stairwell and call Public Safety at xxx-xxx-xxxx.

Deaf or Hearing Impaired

- If evacuation is ordered, proceed to the nearest designated exit.
- Look for the visual fire alarm in the hallway.
- Ask for assistance by writing a note or using hand gestures.

Blind or Visually Impaired

- If evacuation is ordered, proceed to the nearest designated area.
- Listen for the audio fire alarm or other warning signal.
- Ask for assistance and tell the person how to best assist you.

Recovery Strategies

The safety of the campus community is paramount. After the fire has been extinguished and all community members have been accounted for, the process of determining the extent of the damage and repairing or rebuilding the structures begins. An After Action Report is written for actual events as well as for drills.

Lock-Down

Goals: To keep the campus community safe from all acts of violence, including the active shooter, by providing lock-down training to minimize assaults and deaths; to put steps in place to initiate a timely notice lock-down; to provide appropriate aftercare to the campus community.

Prevention, Preparation, and Mitigation Strategies

At least once a year, a lock-down training and drill should be conducted to provide strategies to the campus community on how to properly respond to a directive to lock-down. Typically, a lock-down is called in response to a campus intruder. A lock-down directive is not the same as a shelter-in-place directive.

Provide training for all faculty, staff, and students to include guidance for what to do if they observe an individual on campus with a weapon or a potential weapon. Empower faculty, staff, and students through training to say something by calling Public Safety and 911 and to protect themselves by locking themselves in a classroom and/or office, turn off the lights and cell phones. And as a last resort, fight off a campus intruder rather than becoming a statistic. Strategies such as Run, Hide, Fight are recommended by the Department of Homeland Security. The ALICE Institute, an acronym for Alert, Lock-Down, Inform, Counter, Evacuate, uses the same principles to instruct faculty, staff, and students on how to keep safe during an act of violence event.

Mitigation strategies also include installing deadbolts on all classroom doors and safe area locations, and arming the Public Safety personnel with tools to assist in responding to an intruder on campus. Include guidelines for when and how to contact the local police force.

To assist in identifying persons of concern before an event occurs, it is recommended that all campuses create a Behavior Intervention Team (BIT) and a reporting system to review incidents and/or behaviors involving employees, students, or visitors with regard to potential threats of violence or harm.

Response Strategies

Activate communication strategies to initiate the campus lock-down directive through the Mass Notification System. Activate the EOC. All PPMRR

140

team members if able to safely do so should go to the EOC, or contact the PPMRR team via phone/text to assess the situation and develop recommendations for short- and long-term responses including making notifications to the campus community as appropriate; cancellation of classes, relocating classes, and so on. Follow the directions of the responding police force as they take over the role of Incident Commander.

SAMPLE LOCK-DOWN POLICY FOR STUDENTS, STAFF, AND FACULTY

- Immediately go to the nearest available classroom or office
- Close and lock all windows and doors
- Move away from all windows and doors
- Turn off classroom lights
- Turn cell phones off
- Use ALICE strategies (Alert, Lock-Down, Inform, Counter, Evacuate)
- Do not leave the classroom or office until instructed to do so by appropriate authorities

Recovery Strategies

Develop a strategy for issuing the "All Clear" when appropriate via the mass communication system. Violations of the law will be managed by the law enforcement agency. Provide access to counseling services for all persons affected by this incident. Review the BIT team records and prepare the After Action Report.

Shelter-in-Place

Goal: To provide training for the campus community to keep safe from chemical, biological, or radiological contaminants that may be released accidentally or intentionally into the environment or an imminent weather event such as a tornado or hurricane; to put steps in place to initiate a shelter-in-place; to provide appropriate aftercare to the campus community.

Preventive, Protective, and Mitigation Strategies

At least once a year, a shelter-in-place training and drill should be conducted to provide strategies to the campus community on how to properly respond to a directive to shelter-in-place. Typically a shelter-in-place directive is initiated to protect the community from an impending weather emergency or an impending or actual unsafe air quality event. A shelter-in-place directive is not the same as a lock-down directive.

> "Shelter-in-place" means to take immediate shelter where you are. It may also mean "seal the room"; in other words, take steps to prevent outside air from coming in.

Provide strategies for keeping the campus community safe. Provide training for all faculty, staff, and students that includes identifying a safe location in each building. Typically, this is the lowest level, inner hallways or inner rooms, preferably without windows. These Safe Areas should be posted on the floor plans, in classrooms, and office areas. In order to keep safe from a chemical, biological, or radiological contaminant, this may also include methods for ensuring that no outside air permeates into the building.

Training for the facilities staff should incorporate a periodic inspection of windows and doors to ascertain that there are no cracks, seals are tight, and locks are in working order. Upon receiving notification of a toxic release, the facilities staff should immediately shut down the HVAC system. For classrooms and/or offices with window A/C units, the responsibility to shutoff the unit may reside with individual staff and faculty members. Develop guidelines for the types of events that require the HVAC systems to be shut down.

Determine who at the campus has responsibility for monitoring the U.S. Department of Commerce, National Oceanic and Atmospheric Administration (NOAA) Weather Alert Systems, local news and weather stations around-the-clock, every day of the year. Develop a process to relay threats as determined by these monitoring agencies. To maintain a higher level of awareness for weather-related events, campuses may choose to participate in the Storm Ready Program for colleges and universities. Over 150 campuses nationwide are registered with this National Weather Service program, which is designed to help communities better prepare for and mitigate effects of extreme weather-related events. Information is available about this program at: http://www.stormready. noaa.gov/university.htm.

Response Strategies

Activate communication strategies to initiate the campus Shelter-in-Place directive through the Mass Notification System. Activate the guidelines as determined by the impending event for protecting the campus from weather or toxic releases. Activate the EOC. All PPMRR team members if able to safely do so should go to the EOC, or contact the PPMRR team via phone/text to assess the situation, and develop recommendations for short- and long-term responses including making notifications to the campus community as appropriate; cancellation of classes, relocating classes, and so on. Follow the directions of the Incident Commander.

Recovery Strategies

Develop a strategy for issuing the "All Clear" when appropriate via the mass communication system. The physical and emotional safety of the campus community is paramount. Provide access to counseling services for all persons affected by this incident. After the event has concluded and all community members have been accounted for, the process of determining the extent of the damage and repairing or rebuilding the structures begins. An After Action Report is written for actual events as well as for drills.

SAMPLE SHELTER-IN-PLACE POLICY FOR STUDENTS, STAFF, AND FACULTY

- Take immediate cover in the closest building.
- Locate an interior room; without windows or with the least number of windows.
- Shut and lock all windows and close exterior doors.
- Stay away from windows.
- Turn off air conditioners, heaters, and fans.
- Close vents to ventilation systems.
- Write down the names of everyone in the room, and call the Building Coordinator to report who is in the room with you.

SECTION 3: THREAT- AND HAZARD-SPECIFIC ANNEX

Section 3 of the campus PPMRR provides a goal statement and strategies for prevention, protection, mitigation, response, and recovery actions for threats and hazards identified and assigned a Risk Priority rating in the Threat and Hazard Analysis.

While the threats and hazards found in this section of the PPMRR template may be the same as those identified by your campus Threat and Hazard Assessment, the strategies listed are not meant to be copied and pasted into any campus PPMRR guideline. Each campus will develop its own strategies based on its threat and hazard analysis. This PPMRR template does not specifically address the limitless, diverse threats that confront colleges and universities; instead, it provides general operating goals, and strategies for managing critical events before, during, and after they occur. Nothing in this guide shall limit the use of experience, good judgment, common sense, discretion, flexibility, and ingenuity to adapt to any type of critical event, emergency, and the complexities that exist under emergency conditions.

Cyber Attacks

Goals: To create strategies that ensure the campus can provide a secure open network that protects the integrity and confidentiality of information while maintaining its accessibility; to employ immediate strategies that block posing threats and update when necessary security systems and strategies.

Protection, Prevention, and Mitigation Strategies

Create a campus information technology security policy that holds each member of the campus community responsible for the security and protection of electronic information resources over which he or she has control. Create strategies to protect networks, computers, software, and data; unauthorized intrusions, malicious misuse, or inadvertent compromise. Monitor for areas of vulnerability 24/7. Develop a plan that addresses computer network systems backup both before, and during a critical event.

Response Strategies

Block computer(s) posing a threat from network access, make repairs to system as dictated by the invasion. Assess the situation, and develop recommendations for short- and long-term responses particularly when Protected Personal Information may have been compromised.

Recovery Strategies

During the Recovery phase, the Communication and Information Technology Branch Director works to restore the campus communications and information technology systems to the pre-critical event status.

If data was relocated to a remote server, the data is retrieved and an analysis should be run to detect deficiencies. Where necessary, the director oversees any repairs to the systems that are needed.

After the cyber event has concluded, install methods to elevate the security capabilities. It is imperative that the campus community know that the campus takes violations seriously and enforces its legal sanctions on violators, including expulsion if the violator was a student. Create a communication strategy that emphasizes a renewed commitment to protecting personal information from cyber threats. An After Action Report is written for actual events as well as for drills.

Bomb Threats

(*Portions of the information contained below have been adapted from materials provided by the U.S. Department of Homeland Security, Office of Bombing Prevention, Bomb Threat Call Procedures, and Bomb Prevention Training.*)

Goals: Develop strategies to keep the campus community safe from acts of violence, in particular a bomb threat or incident to put steps in place to ensure that timely notice is made to the campus community; to provide appropriate aftercare to the campus community.

A *bomb threat* is defined as the communication through the use of written message, telephone call, e-mail, social media, or other instrument of commerce; the willful making of any threat; or the malicious conveyance of false information knowing the same to be false which concerns an attempt being made, or to be made; to kill, injure, intimidate any individual; or unlawfully to damage or destroy any building, vehicle, or other real or personal property by means of an explosive.

Protection, Prevention, and Mitigation Strategies

As a bomb threat call may be answered by anyone on campus, it is imperative to develop guidance with a script and a form with prompts and distribute it campus wide.

SAMPLE GUIDANCE FOR RECEIVERS OF BOMB THREATS

- DO NOT use two-way radios or cellular phones; radio signals can cause a detonation.
- DO NOT evacuate the building until police arrive and evaluate the threat.

- DO NOT activate the fire alarm.
- DO NOT touch or move a suspicious package.
- Gain as much information as possible about the caller and the credibility of the threat.
- Use the Bomb Threat Report to guide conversations and record details for police.
- If you can, determine the location of the bomb and the time of detonation.
- If you have a digital phone, look for, and record the caller's phone number.
- If possible, do not hang up the phone. Have a coworker call Public Safety at xxx-xxx-xxxx or 911. If you are alone, call immediately after hanging up.

Response Strategies

The receiver of the bomb threat message contacts Public Safety who then notifies 911 and initiates the Mass Notification System. Depending on the situation, the directive may be to stay clear, evacuate, or shelter-in-place.

Activate the EOC. All PPMRR team members if able to safely do so should go to the EOC, or contact the PPMRR team via phone/text to assess the situation, and develop recommendations for short- and long-term responses including making notifications to campus community as appropriate; cancellation of classes, relocating classes, and so on. Follow the directions of the Incident Commander.

Public Safety takes immediate actions to restrict access to the building or area of the campus and to coordinate internal and external response up to and including evacuation of area affected by the bomb threat. The Facilities Director will contact the applicable utilities for shut down of electric, gas, and water. Activate communication strategies to initiate Evacuation or Shelter-in-Place directives as is indicated by the location of the bomb. As necessary initiate the Accountability plan.

Recovery Strategies

Issue the "All Clear" when directed by the IC. The physical and emotional safety of the campus community is paramount. Provide access to counseling services for all persons affected by this incident. In the event that a bomb was detonated, then begins determining the extent of the damage and repairing or rebuilding the affected structures. Collect data to develop the After Action Report.

Death on the Campus of Student/Staff/Faculty

Goals: To provide guidelines to be followed immediately upon notification of the death of a student, staff, or faculty member; and action steps to follow during the days that follow.

Response Strategies

In the event of a death on campus of a student, staff, or faculty member, develop a strategy that directs an immediate notification call to be made to the Department of Public Safety. The Public Safety Director investigates the claim and calls 911. Public Safety takes immediate actions to restrict access to the room where the deceased is located to preserve any forensic evidence, in case it is needed. The Executive Policy Group with assistance from the Command Staff assesses the situation, and develops recommendations for short- and long-term responses including making notifications to the campus community as appropriate.

Contact with the parents or family members should take place only after it can be clearly demonstrated that the authorities have already done so. Develop a policy that states who shall contact the parents or family members of the deceased. Depending upon the circumstances and the category of the individual involved, it may be the President, the Provost, the Vice President for Student Affairs, or the Director of Human Resources.

Recovery Strategies

Develop a recovery strategy that might include the President writing to the campus community about the death. Depending on the situation, it may include information about funeral and viewing arrangements. Again, depending on the situation, the family may be invited to the come to the campus to meet with the President, or other administrators. If the campus chooses to host the family, designate someone who will make arrangements for overnight stays for the family and who will assist the family in removing belongings from rooms, offices, and so forth. In the case of a student death, consider tuition and fees refunds after a review by the Vice President of Student Affairs, in consultation with the Vice President for Finance/Treasurer. Remove the deceased person's name from campus mailing database so the family does not receive any unsolicited mail. Before conducting a memorial service, or establishing a memorial

147

scholarship, consult with the family. Provide access to counseling services for all persons affected by the incident and as appropriate write an incident and/or After Action Report.

Displaced Students

Goals: To prepare beforehand for an unexpected housing displacement of significant numbers of the campus community from on and off-campus residences due to a fire, building collapse, flood, fire, tornado, and so on; to respond in a timely manner to the displacements; and action steps for the days that follow.

Protection, Prevention, and Mitigation Strategies

Develop strategies to assist displaced students. This should include maintaining a database of short- and long-term housing options in the event that the campus housing becomes compromised. Include strategies for transporting students to and from the alternate housing locations to campus. Develop strategies to maintain contact with students in the event that a "Katrina-like" event should occur where no housing is available, nor is the campus open for an extended period of time.

Response Strategies

The PPMRR team assembles to assess the situation and develop recommendations for short- and long-term responses to place students in safe and secure temporary housing and to provide board. If no housing options are available in on- or off-campus housing, call upon mutual aid resources such as hotels, motels, other colleges, or other housing options in the area. Contact the families of students to inform them of the occurrence.

Recovery Strategies

If personal property of an academic nature is destroyed, the campus may choose to make appropriate arrangements to replace those items. If personal property (clothes, toiletries, etc.) were destroyed, voluntary agencies such as Red Cross may be able to assist.

Develop contact strategies with displaced students to keep them abreast of any developments in restoring the on campus residence. Provide access to counseling services for all persons affected by this incident. Collect information and contribute to the writing of the After Action Report.

Extreme Weather Emergencies

Goals: To put strategies in place to reduce injuries, deaths, and facility damage that could occur as a result of an extreme weather emergency, such as an earthquake, hurricane, tornado, snow/ice, or any other severe weather situation; to put steps in place to ensure that timely notice is made to the campus community; to provide appropriate aftercare to the campus community.

Prevention, Protection, and Mitigation Strategies

As indicated in the Shelter-in-Place strategy, delegate the monitoring of the Emergency Alert System, and the U.S. Department of Commerce, National Oceanic and Atmospheric Administration (NOAA) Weather Alert System, as well as local news and weather stations, 24/7.

Develop a process to relay threats as determined by these monitoring agencies. To maintain a higher level of awareness for weather-related events, campuses may choose to participate in the Storm Ready Program for colleges and universities. Over 150 campuses nationwide are registered with this National Weather Service program, which is designed to help communities better prepare for and mitigate effects of extreme weather-related events. Information is available about this program at: http://www.stormready.noaa.gov/university.htm.

Other strategies that a campus may consider include installing safe rooms in school buildings, stocking sandbags for flood prevention and salt for snow and ice, inspecting and cleaning drains on a regular basis, elevating files and vulnerable equipment. Create messaging for faculty, staff, and students on methods for keeping safe during extreme weather events. Do not attempt to send students home ahead of storms; this may result in injury or death for which schools may be held liable.

SAMPLE STUDENT, STAFF, AND FACULTY GUIDELINES FOR EARTHQUAKE AND TORNADO SAFETY

During an Earthquake or Tornado

- Immediately take cover; Drop, Cover, Go, and Hold On
  - DROP down on your knees and make yourself as small a target as possible.
  - COVER your head, neck, and face.

149

- GO under a sturdy desk or table to protect your head and body.
- HOLD ON to your cover.
- If you are indoors, stay there. Find an interior hallway or classroom/office without windows. Get under a desk or table. Stay clear of windows, bookcases, mirrors, and fireplaces. Move away from windows, tall shelves, or cabinets.
- Do not use elevators!
- If you are outside, get into an open area away from trees, buildings, walls, and power lines.

After the Earthquake or Tornado

- Do not move seriously injured individuals unless they are in immediate danger.
- Call Public Safety if you suspect or know that someone is trapped in the building.
- Do not touch downed power lines or damaged building equipment.
- If building is damaged, evacuate, contact Public Safety. Do not re-enter damaged buildings.
- If you evacuate, post a message in clear view stating where you can be found.

Natural Gas Leak

If you smell the odor of gas, or if you discover a gas leak, leave the area immediately and contact Public Safety at xxx-xxx-xxxx or 911.

Response Strategies

Activate the EOC. All PPMRR team members if able to safely do so should go to the EOC, or contact the PPMRR team via phone/text to assess the situation, and develop recommendations for short- and long-term responses including making notifications to the campus community as appropriate; cancellation of classes, relocating classes, and so forth. Follow the directions of the Incident Commander.

Timely Notice: For imminent danger, any member of the PPMRR team can initiate a message through the Mass Notification System. For notice events, prepare messaging in advance and distribute to the campus community as appropriate. Strategies might include providing a dedicated phone number for telephone inquiries from parents and the media and changing the Safety Hotline recording to indicate the campus situation and status.

The Facilities Department directives should include taking immediate action to control the infiltration of water into buildings to prevent damage to property and ensure the safety of occupants. Actions could include the following:

- Close all windows and doors
- Control and capture water entering a building
- Turn off appropriate circuit breakers if water appears to be infiltrating electrical devices
- Take appropriate action to remove water from all areas
- Assess damage and submit reports to campus insurance representative

Recovery Strategies

As the event concludes, update the campus community via the Mass Notification System. Encourage students, staff, and faculty to call their families to let them know their status. This will help to minimize overload of the campus telephone system with incoming calls. Public Safety strategies should include responding to calls from injured and blocking off damaged areas to keep people away from hazards.

The facilities staff checklist should include check buildings for cracks and damage, check for gas and water leaks, broken electrical wiring, and broken sewage lines. Determine whether buildings are safe to return to; whether classes can be resumed in such and/or students can continue to reside in residence halls. If buildings are compromised, recovery strategies should include developing relocation plans for classes as well as for housing. Short- and long-term plans may include restoring facilities to pre-disaster functionality as well as upgrading buildings, where necessary, to current codes and standards.

For extreme weather events that cause extensive damage and/or deaths, consider providing access to counseling services. Collect information and contribute to the writing of the After Action Report.

Fires

Goals: To put strategies in place to reduce and/or eliminate fires on campus; to put steps in place to ensure that timely notice is made to the campus community; to provide appropriate aftercare to the campus community.

Prevention, Protection, and Mitigation Strategies

Develop campus-wide fire prevention programs. This may include fire safety in the dorms for students, the use of storing combustible materials in fireproof containers, as well as fire safety for kitchen staff. Consider adding YouTube videos: *Graduation Fatally Denied* and/or *9 Fires Documentary*, which detail fire events at colleges across the United States. Use the website: www.CampusFireWatch.com, as a resource to develop effective campus prevention program.

Provide training for faculty staff and students that includes:

- How to call for assistance in the event of fire
- How to contain a fire
- How to use a fire extinguisher for small fires
- Following evacuation routes and meeting places
- Evacuating safely in a fire
- Student, staff, faculty accountability

Consider installing a sprinkler system throughout the campus.

Response Strategies

Ensure that guidelines are in place for notification of local fire and police departments, and ambulances as needed. Provide assistance in guiding local emergency responders to the building(s) on fire. Direct the fire chief to the EOC. Public Safety takes immediate actions to restrict access to the building or area of the campus and to coordinate internal and external response up to and including evacuation of area(s) affected by the fire.

Activate the EOC. All PPMRR team members if able to safely do so should go to the EOC, or contact the PPMRR team via phone/text to assess the situation, and develop recommendations for short- and long-term responses including making notifications to campus community as appropriate; cancellation of classes, relocating classes, and so on. Activate communication strategies to initiate campus closures, evacuation, or shelter-in-place and accountability directives as is indicated by the location, magnitude, and duration of the fire.

Recovery Strategies

Public Safety strategies should include responding to calls from the injured and blocking off damaged areas to keep people away from hazards. For fire events that cause extensive damage and/or deaths, consider providing access to counseling services. As the event concludes, update the campus community via the Mass Notification System. Encourage students, staff, and faculty to call their families to let them know their status. This will help to minimize overload of the campus telephone system with incoming calls.

The facilities staff determines whether buildings are safe to return to; whether classes can be resumed in such and/or students can continue to reside in residence halls. If buildings are compromised, recovery strategies should include developing relocation plans for classes as well as for housing. Short- and long-term plans may include restoring facilities to pre-disaster functionality as well as upgrading buildings, where necessary, to current codes and standards.

Manage arrangements pertaining to the death or injury of faculty or staff. As needed, activate strategies for displaced students. Collect information and contribute to the writing of the After Action Report.

Hate Crimes

Goals: To promote an environment where crimes motivated by racial, sexual, or other prejudice, are not tolerated; and to put actions in place to quickly respond should such a crime occur.

Prevention, Protection, and Mitigation Strategies

Establish violence prevention measures, support systems, resources, and strategies through the integration of campus policies and procedures regarding crimes motivated by racial, sexual, or other prejudice.

Response Strategies

Develop a strategy such as this: If the incident is reported directly to Public Safety, then the responding officer takes a verbal or written report from the complaining party including contact information: address and/or telephone number of complaining party. If the incident is reported to another campus department, Public Safety should be notified as soon as possible for action.

Public Safety will gather and/or document all available evidence. Public Safety contacts the VP of Student Affairs or the Human Resources Director. The VP of Student Affairs or the Director of Human Resources will make immediate contact by phone or in person with the individual reporting the incident. During this contact, the VP of Student Affairs or the Human Resources Director will seek to arrange a meeting with the reporting individual and will offer counseling via the Counseling Center or through a referral to other qualified resources both on and off campus.

Every attempt will be made to assist in resolving concerns faced as a result of having been a victim of such hate crimes. The VP of Student Affairs or the Human Resources Director will meet with the complaining party as soon as possible to address concerns. Reports will be kept anonymous unless the complaining party or witness wishes to have her/his name used. The VP of Student Affairs or the Human Resources Director will be authorized to call in all other offices (e.g., Network Resources, Public Safety, etc.) as needed to review events and investigate circumstances. The VP of Student Affairs or the Human Resources Director should maintain ongoing contact with the complaining party to indicate what steps have been taken and/or what has been learned about the possible perpetrator.

Recovery Strategies

The strategy is to provide access to counseling services for all persons affected by this incident and to provide training of employees and students with regard to nondiscrimination. In doing so creates a positive messaging campaign. It is also recommended that a Behavior Intervention Team be created in order to review incidents and/or behaviors involving employees, students, or visitors with regard to potential threats of violence or harm. Collect information and contribute to the writing of the After Action Report.

Hazardous Materials Release

Goals: To provide strategies in the event an on-campus chemical spill threatens the health and safety of the campus community; to put steps in place to ensure that timely notice is made to the campus community; to provide appropriate aftercare to the campus community.

Protection, Prevention, and Mitigation Strategies

Identify and create a database of all areas of the campus where chemicals are located that could create a physical hazard (a combustible liquid, a compressed gas, explosive, flammable, an organic peroxide, an oxidizer, an unstable, reactive, or water-reactive chemical). Obtain Material Safety Data Sheets (MSDSs) for all hazardous chemicals used across the campus. Institute training programs for safe use and storage of hazardous chemicals for all employees who use such chemicals and ensure warning labels are prominently displayed on the hazardous chemical containers.

Response Strategies

Any hazardous spill must be reported immediately to Public Safety. For imminent danger, any member of the campus community can initiate an evacuation of a building by pulling a fire alarm. Public Safety will respond, call 911 and the PPMRR team. PPMRR team will check into the EOC, or contact PPMRR team via phone/text to assess the situation, and develop recommendations for short- and long-term responses including making notifications to the campus community as appropriate; cancellation of classes, relocating classes, and so on. For toxic releases, all fans, heating, and air conditioning systems must be shutoff.

Recovery

Collect information and contribute to the writing of the After Action Report.

Missing Persons

Goals: To provide safety training for students; training for timely notice actions; training protocol for all when an enrolled student, who resides in campus housing has been deemed missing for at least 24 hours; to provide appropriate aftercare to the campus community.

Protection, Prevention, and Mitigation Strategies

Create Public Safety seminars for students on staying safe in a campus environment. Provide training for faculty, staff, and students to notify Public Safety if a residential student has been missing for more than 24 hours. Encourage all students to register a confidential contact (an individual who will be contacted by police in the event that the student is reported missing) with Public Safety.

Response

Develop a response strategy such as reporting the missing person claim to Public Safety. Public Safety is responsible for checking the resident's room, the resident's class schedule, locating the resident's vehicle, calling the resident's cell phone, and contacting the resident's friends and/or roommate. After investigating a missing person report and the Public Safety Director determines that the student has been missing for 24 hours, Public Safety will

155

- Notify the individual identified by the student as the missing person's contact.
- If the student is under 18 years old, the college will notify a parent or guardian.
- If the student is over 18 and has not identified a person to be contacted, Public Safety will notify appropriate law enforcement officials.

Recovery

Develop Recovery strategies for when a student is located, Public Safety will notify the PPMRR team. If the student is not found, the PPMRR will meet to make decisions regarding the student. Actions could include

- Informing the campus community about the missing student.
- Make arrangements for the family to come to campus to meet the (President, Provost, Vice President for Student Affairs) and other individuals (groups) requested by the family.
- Assist the family in removing belongings from the residence hall.
- Make decisions regarding refunding of tuition in consultation with the Vice President for Finance/Treasurer.
- Notify registrar.
- Remove the student's name from the campus mailing database so the family does not receive any unsolicited mail.
- Provide grief counseling for the campus community through the Counseling Center.

Pandemic/Ebola or Other Public Health Emergency

Goals: To provide strategies for staff and faculty before an event occurs; to provide guidelines to be followed in response to confirmed or alleged cases of communicable diseases such as pandemic flu or Ebola virus contracted by a member of the campus community when the disease poses a threat to the campus community; to provide appropriate aftercare to the campus community.

Protection, Prevention, and Mitigation Strategies

Provide training for the PPMRR team to define roles and responsibilities should there be a pandemic health event affecting the operation of the campus. Devise measures to ensure that key staff will be able to execute key functions such as continuation of classes, facilities operation, payroll, and public safety. Consult with local health-care authorities for guidance in preparing for the execution of infection control measures. Provide training to the campus community regarding health and safety precautionary measures.

Devise strategies for alternative procedures to assure continuity of instruction (e.g., web-based distance instruction, telephone trees, mailed lessons and assignments, instruction via local radio or television stations) in the event of campus closure. Develop policies for employee and student sick leave absences unique to highly contagious communicable pandemic influenza, or Ebola virus (e.g., nonpunitive, liberal leave). Establish policies that address faculty, staff, and students suspected to be ill or who become ill on campus.

Response

Activate the EOC. The PPMRR team assembles to assess the situation, and develop recommendations for short- and long-term responses including making notifications to the campus community as appropriate; cancellation of classes, relocating classes, use of sick/vacation time by faculty and staff, modifying campus policies to accommodate the communicable disease event. Strategies are implemented for continuation of education with alternative methods. Activate policies for employee and student sick leave absences unique to highly contagious communicable pandemic influenza, or Ebola virus (e.g., nonpunitive, liberal leave). Activate policies that address faculty, staff, and students suspected to be ill or who become ill on campus. Continue to seek guidance from local health-care authorities for the execution of infection control measures, reporting information about ill students and employees, and provision of healthcare. Respond to media inquiries and make all public comments via the PIO in consultation with the PPMRR team and the Department of Health or other medical consultants.

Recovery

Institute procedures for previously ill faculty, staff, and students to return to campus. Restore and/or modify the campus academic schedule as needed. Provide information and assistance to the Department of Health as requested.

REFERENCES

Department of Homeland Security. *Bomb threat call procedures.* Retrieved from http://emilms.fema.gov/is906/assets/ocso-bomb_threat_samepage-brochure.pdf

Department of Homeland Security. *Bomb prevention training*. Retrieved from http://www.dhs.gov/bombing-prevention-training

National Preparedness Directorate (NPD). Retrieved from http:www.training.fema.gov

Nine Fires. (2012). Retrieved from http://www.youtube.com/watch?v=ketJsMBeB1M

U.S. Department of Education. (2013). *Guide for developing high-quality emergency operations plans for Institutions of Higher Education*. Retrieved from http://www.fema.gov/media-library/assets/documents/33597

7

Ongoing Management and Maintenance

This chapter defines training requirements for faculty and staff, and details methods of testing the functionality of the PPMRR strategies through seminars, workshops, games, tabletop exercises, drills, functional, and full-scale exercises.

Training is a critical component that ensures compliance with all applicable federal, state, and local laws pertaining to National Incident Management System (NIMS) and provides guidance to the faculty, staff, and students regarding their role in the PPMRR strategy. The scheduling and coordinating of training is an important function of the PPMRR team. Typically, it falls under duties of the person who holds the lead PPMRR position, such as the Emergency Manager. But as the composition of the teams vary from campus to campus so will the position whose task it is to schedule and track training.

In addition to identifying who will be scheduling and tracking training, a timeline too must be set. For example, stating in the PPMRR that all personnel will complete their annual training by October 15 each year, and that all new hires will complete the level of NIMS training commensurate with their position within 30 days of their start date of employment. The Emergency Manager ensures that a system is in place to notify employees of their upcoming training events and notifies new hires when they come on board of their PPMRR role and ensures that they receive training. At some campuses, it might be the Human Resources Director that takes on the tracking of training responsibilities.

Each campus will coordinate these activities as it best fits into the campus PPMRR organizational structure.

SAMPLE PPMRR TRAINING POLICY

The PPMRR team oversees and ensures compliance with all applicable federal, state, and local laws pertaining to National Incident Management System (NIMS) requirements. All personnel will complete their annual training by October 15 each year, and all new hires will complete the level of NIMS training commensurate with their position within 30 days of their start date of employment. The training tracking database is maintained by the Director of Emergency Management.

The Department of Homeland Security (DHS), the NIMS Integration Center (NIC), and the U.S. Department of Education (ED) recommend that all key personnel involved in school emergency management and incident response to take the National Incident Management System (NIMS), incident command system (ICS), and National Response Framework (NRF) training courses.

When making determinations for training, based on the ICS format, staff can be organized into two levels: Leadership, which includes the Incident Commander, the Public Information Officer (PIO), Safety Officer (SO), Liaison Officer (LNO), and Section Chiefs; General Staff, which consists of personnel who represent the five functional areas.

Training Courses

Course #	Course Title	Leadership	General
100.HE	An Introduction to ICS for Higher Education	X	X
200.b	ICS for Single Resources and Initial Action Incidents	X	X
300	Intermediate ICS for Expanding Incidents	X	
400	Advanced Incident Command	X	
700.a	An Introduction to NIMS	X	X
800.b	An Introduction to the National Response Framework (NRF)	X	X

COURSE DESCRIPTIONS

IS-100.HE: Introduction to Incident Command System for Higher Education

This course introduces the incident command system (ICS) and provides the foundation for higher level ICS training. This course describes the history, features, and principles, and organizational structure of the ICS. It also explains the relationship between ICS and the National Incident Management System.

IS-200.b: ICS for Single Resource and Initial Action Incidents

This course is designed to enable personnel to operate efficiently during an incident or event within the incident command system. ICS-200 provides training on and resources for personnel who are likely to assume a supervisory position within the ICS.

ICS-300: Intermediate ICS for Expanding Incidents

ICS-300 is designed for responders and personnel who will be in leadership positions during a major incident. Topics include unified command, assessment and objectives, incident action planning process, incident resource management, demobilization, transfer of command, and closeout. *Prerequisites: I-100, 200, 700, 800.*

ICS-400: Advanced ICS, Command, and General Staff for Complex Incidents

ICS-400 is designed for personnel who will be directing emergency response during a major incident. Topics include major/complex incident or event management, area command, complexes, and multiagency coordination. *Prerequisites: I-100, 200, 300, 700, 800.*

IS-700.a: National Incident Management System (NIMS)—An Introduction

This course introduces and overviews the National Incident Management System (NIMS). The NIMS provides a consistent nationwide template to enable all government, private-sector, and nongovernment organizations to work together during domestic incidents.

IS-800.b: National Response Framework—An Introduction

This course introduces participants to the concepts and principles for the National Response Framework. This course is intended for government executives, private sector and nongovernmental organization (NGO) leaders, and emergency management practitioners. This includes senior elected and appointed leaders, such as Federal department or agency heads, State governors, mayors, tribal leaders, and city or county officials—those who have a responsibility to provide for effective response.

The FEMA Emergency Management Institute offers no cost online training for the following courses at: www.training.fema.gov/IS/crslist.

IS-100.HE: Introduction to the Incident Command System for Higher Education
IS-200.b: ICS for Single Resource and Initial Action Incidents
IS-700.a: National Incident Management System (NIMS)—An Introduction
IS-800.b: National Response Framework—An Introduction

The following courses are available via classroom delivery only:

ICS-300: Intermediate ICS for Expanding Incidents
ICS-400: Advanced ICS, Command and General Staff for Complex Incidents

DISCUSSION-BASED AND OPERATIONAL EXERCISES

It is critically important that every college and university exercise its emergency preparedness plans. It is not enough to have a written plan on the shelf that is unknown to anyone except the PPMRR team. Reading the words, whether from a circulated document or from a website, pales in comparison to exercising. Exercising brings life to the written strategies, providing an opportunity to see what works and where vulnerabilities still exist. Well-developed and implemented exercises will enable the campus to take corrective actions to the PPMRR.

While the PPMRR strategies are developed for campus-specific identified threats and hazards, this does not mean that a college or university has a scripted response for every possible event that could occur at the campus. Because that is an impossibility, the PPMRR must have flexibility built into it. This means that the campus community must know that while there are policies in place and recommended strategies to be followed, it allows for individual decision making when faced with an adverse situation. Training and exercising result in an increase in individual capabilities to make those decisions with confidence.

EXERCISE DESIGN

Now that you recognize the benefits of incorporating exercising into your campus preparedness plan, how do you create the exercises? There are a multitude of resources and consultants available for assistance in developing college and university emergency preparedness exercises. However, the scope of this chapter is to assist the campus emergency preparedness team in the creation of its own exercises or at least recognizing a well-developed exercise. When designing or evaluating exercise plans, take into account all four phases of the campus emergency preparedness plan: preparedness, response, recovery, and mitigation. Each exercise can focus on the individual components of the plan or incorporate multiple phases.

The Federal Emergency Management Agency (2003) organizes the development of an emergency exercise into eight steps:

1. *Needs Assessment* focuses on determining which emergency events or hazards the campus has a likely probability of encountering, such as natural hazards: floods, tornadoes, fires, or manmade hazards: an active shooter or a power outage.
2. *Scope* sets the stage with the type of exercise being conducted, the type of emergency, where it is occurring, functions to be exercised, and who will be participating in the exercise.
3. *Purpose Statement* defines what the campus is looking to achieve by conducting this particular exercise.
4. *Narrative* is the story provided to the players to provide general context, technical details, and conditions for assessing the situation.
5. *Objectives* should directly link to the needs assessment, scope, and purpose as well as be SMART: Simple to understand, Measurable, Achievable, Realistic, and Task-oriented.

6. *Major and Detailed Events* refers to the list of predetermined actions and details that the players need to achieve in order for the exercise to be considered to have met its objectives.
7. *Expected Actions* are the anticipated results of the exercise objective. For instance, raising elevators to a higher floor will contribute to saving it from the effects of floodwaters.
8. *Prepare Messages* is achieved by the compilation of the seven previous steps.

FEMA recommends that organizations use a 2-year progressive series of exercises, starting with a discussion-based tabletop and culminating with a full-scale exercise. The Multiyear Training and Exercise Plan, a series of multiple connected exercises with a continuous theme, is the premise of the FEMA building block approach to exercising using *seminars, workshops, tabletops, games, drills, functional,* and *full-scale* exercises in a progressive order over time. External partners, such as the police, fire, and utility company, should participate in exercises as appropriate and the campus should also participate, as appropriate, in all community (city, regional, and state) exercises.

Most institutions begin with discussion-based exercises such as *seminars* and *workshops,* then move into *tabletops* and sometimes *games.* Discussion-based exercises focus on policies and procedures incorporated in the campus emergency plan. They are led by a facilitator whose role is to set the stage for the team, identify the objective of the exercise, explain the process that will be followed, and keep the conversation on track. No resources are deployed in discussion-based exercises.

A *seminar* is typically used to provide the campus with information regarding policies, plans, or procedures.

A *workshop* typically provides an opportunity for two-way communication. It could be a meeting of the PPMRR team and a community partner group where both parties are working out processes and procedures that will be incorporated into a working mutual aid plan. It is led by a facilitator, to keep the group on track. The parties share and collect information, obtain consensus, and develop a written procedural guide.

A *tabletop* provides an opportunity for the campus to test a policy, plan, or procedure. It provides the PPMRR team an opportunity to react to a situation presented to them by a facilitator in scenario format with injects at specific intervals. The scenarios are typically a probable event that may affect the campus community. The "players," which could be the PPMRR team, all sit together and talk through the scenario and injects taking guidance for their actions from the already developed PPMRR strategies. There may be an evaluator/recorder who observes the activities, takes minutes, and then reports his/her observations back to the group. As the exercise focuses on the roles, procedures, and responsibilities of the PPMRR team and the campus community, the end result could be a revision of policies and procedures to improve the PPMRR policy, plan, procedure, and strategy tested.

> For an active shooter *tabletop,* the players are provided with a scenario by the facilitator. The players react to the situation from their job titles. The exercise could have multiple identifiable attainable exercise objectives such as testing response time of the campus and/or local police, and testing the campus communications system to alert campus members to shelter-in-place through an "All Clear" message.

A *game* is a simulation of operations using the PPMRR strategies to work through a potential threat or hazardous situation. Differing from a *tabletop* where the players work as one team, in a *game* the players are divided into two or more groups where each group works together to resolve the scenario with a "what-if" analysis. Like the *tabletop,* the end result could be a revision of policies and procedures to improve the PPMRR policy, plan, procedure, and strategy tested.

> What-if
>
> - The active shooter was engaged in conversation by a faculty member/student/staff
> - Campus police stormed the building where the shooting was taking place
> - Tear gas was used to subdue shooter
> - Classrooms were able to be locked from inside and shooter was unable to access classrooms

Once the campus has exercised its policies, plans, procedures, and strategies using discussion-based methods, it may choose to move to operations-based exercises such as *drill, functional,* and *full-scale exercises.*

Operations-based exercises require a coordination of resources deployed from either other campus units and/or off-campus organizations such as fire, police, and hospitals.

A *drill* is used to measure the capabilities of the campus resources: people, facilities, and equipment focused on a specific task of the PPMRR. The *drill* uses a scenario relayed by an evaluator. It requires the player(s) to react at their duty station. The player is expected to react in accordance with what they learned in a training venue such as a seminar or workshop.

Drill Example: An evaluator approaches unannounced to the front desk of a residence hall and informs the security person sitting at the entrance desk that they have been selected to participate in this unannounced drill. The evaluator tells the residence hall security person, who depending on your campus, may be a student worker, an unarmed guard, or an armed police officer, to imagine that they just heard what he/she believes to be gunshots. The evaluator asks the "player" to think out loud as to what steps he or she would take in reaction to hearing what they think are gunshots.

Other items that a campus may consider when drilling include: communications systems, evacuation plans, or shelter-in place for individual buildings.

Functional exercises are designed to test capabilities of an event that requires problem solving, typically of the Command Staff. It involves players, simulators, a controller, and an evaluator. As the players, responding in their PPMRR role, receive the exercise message, they try to figure out what is happening and what needs to be done to remedy the situation.

Building on previous exercise's capacity, the functional exercise is put into play with the addition of the Command Staff. Using the active shooter scenario for the *functional* exercise, additional "players" would be included in the exercise. The Director of Campus Police, the college President, the Communications Department Director, and Residence Life Director could all be components of the Command Staff.

Full-scale exercises are real-time events that deploy resources, and test reactions by the campus to a probable threat or hazard. This is the culminating event in the Multi-Year Training and Exercise Program. There are no scripts. The decisions made by the players are driven by the action that is taking place around them.

To efficiently execute the delivery of these operational-based exercises requires the use of a facilitator, controller, and evaluator. FEMA lists the duties of the facilitator, controller, and evaluator as follows.

Facilitator	Controller	Evaluator
• Introduces the discussion topic or narrative	• Ensures that the simulators and evaluators are properly trained before the exercise	• Tracks action relative to the evaluation objectives
• Facilitates problem solving	• Orients the participants to the exercise and presents the narrative	• Identifies any resolved and unresolved issues
• Controls the pace and flow of the exercise	• Monitors the sequence of events and supervises the input of messages	• Helps analyze the exercise results
• Distributes the messages or injects	• Makes decisions in the event of unanticipated actions or resource requirements	• Participates in postexercise meetings and critiques
• Draws answers and solutions from the players	• Adjusts the pace of the exercise when needed— inserting more messages when it drags and discarding messages when the pace is too frantic	• Does not interfere with the exercise flow

EXERCISE MATERIALS

The Department of Homeland Security (DHS) recommends the following documents to be used to assist with the implementation of exercises.

A *Situation Manual* (*SITMAN*) is the participant handbook for discussion-based exercises. It provides background information on the scope, schedule, and objectives of the exercise. It also presents the scenario narrative for participant discussions during the exercise.

The *Exercise Plan* (*EXPLAN*) is the participant handbook for operations-based exercises. The *EXPLAN* provides controllers, evaluators, players, and observers with information such as the purpose, scope, objectives, and logistical information of the exercise.

Controller Evaluator (*C/E*) *Handbooks* supplement *EXPLANs* for operations-based exercises. The *C/E Handbook* contains more detailed information about the exercise scenario and guides controllers and evaluators in their roles and responsibilities.

The *Master Scenario Events List* (*MSEL*) contains a chronological listing of the events and injects that drive operations-based exercise play.

Exercise Evaluation Guides (*EEGs*) provide evaluators with a checklist of critical tasks to be completed by participants during an exercise. *EEGs* contain the information to be discussed by participants, space to record evaluator observations, and questions to consider after the exercise, such as: Was the exercise a success?

After each exercise, a *Hot Wash* is completed to detail the strengths and weaknesses revealed by the exercise. These findings are incorporated into an *After Action Plan* that details what happened during the exercise as well as recommendations for modifications of the PPMRR policies, plans, procedures, and strategies.

RECOMMENDED HSEEP AFTER ACTION PLAN (AAP) FORMAT

EXECUTIVE SUMMARY

EXERCISE OVERVIEW

Includes background information: Participating organizations; the date, time, and location of the exercise that was conducted; the type of exercise; the hazard, and the evaluation methodology.

EXERCISE GOALS AND OBJECTIVES

Exercise Events Synopsis: A chronological synopsis of major events and actions.

Analysis of Mission Outcomes: Summarizes how the performance or nonperformance of tasks and interactions affected the achievement of the mission outcomes.

Analysis of Critical Task Performance: Summarizes and addresses issues regarding each task in terms of consequences, analysis, recommendations, and improvement actions.

CONCLUSION

Appendix: Improvement Plan Matrix: Provides a task list of recommendations, due dates, and responsible organizations.

Information in this chapter comes directly from the Homeland Security Exercise and Evaluation Program (HSEEP). Exercise evaluation templates and customizable job aids are available at https://www.Fema.gov/exercise.

REFERENCES

FEMA. (2003). *Building a disaster-resistant university*. Retrieved from http://www.fema.gov/institution/dru.shtm

FEMA. (2015). National exercise program. Retrieved from https://www.fema.gov/exercise.

FEMA Emergency Management Institute. (2015). Online course catalog. Retrieved from https://www.training.fema.gov.

National Incident Management System (NIMS). (2015). NIMS implementation. Retrieved from http://rems.ed.gov/K12NIMSImplementation.aspx

8

Creating a Campus-Based Community Emergency Response Team

Creating a campus CERT (C-CERT) provides guidance for a campus interested in developing an on-campus community emergency response team.

While college public safety departments are efficient entities in ordinary times, recent events at campuses across the country have shown that there have been situations where their capabilities have been stretched. Additionally, in the early stages of a widespread disaster, it is extremely probable that not only the campus but also the larger community in which it resides will be on its own and will need to call upon the assistance of its citizens. Communities need to be trained in order to provide an effective supplementary response team to reduce the number of casualties. Campus-community emergency response teams (C-CERT) and student emergency response teams (SERT) have been forming across the country to prepare campus communities to assist themselves in the event of an emergency that depletes the resources of local first responders.

In the early stages of a disaster, it is extremely probable that campus personnel, families, and community members will be on their own. There is a need for a faster and more effective response to reduce the number of casualties. Breeding (2007) states that increasing the citizen's ability to "prepare, prevent, and respond to terrorist attacks and other emergencies" is a goal of the Department of Homeland Security. This increase on the focus on education and emergency management training of the American people is evidenced by voluntary programs such as CERT, a federally funded program available in most states through Citizens Corp. In 2002, President George W. Bush established the USA Freedom Corps. The Citizens Corps is one group within the USA Freedom Corps, and CERT and SERT are entities of Citizens Corps. President Bush (2004) proclaimed that it was necessary for the future of our country that we "encourage and support the character development of our young people and support institutions that give direction and purpose: our families, our schools, and our faith-based and community organizations." He appealed to all citizens to commit to 2 years of volunteer service for the betterment of our society.

But, as Harris (2005) states, perhaps the overarching reason that emergency management planning is important is that disaster management has become a "national priority in the post-9/11 era" (p. 24). On January 21, 2009, (DHS, 2009) the secretary of the Department of Homeland Security (DHS), Janet Napolitano, issued her action directives for DHS, which included focusing on the missions critical to the department: preparedness, response, recovery, and mitigation. She has been an advocate of the CERT program and a host of other partnerships, which bring together the resources of the federal, state, and local governments in meeting this mission.

The recommendation is for community members to receive first aid training in order to develop a community's capability to provide basic medical assistance during the immediate post-disaster phase until professional assistance becomes available. The premise is that trained individuals can help themselves and their neighbors before emergency personnel are able to get to them (Angus, Pretto, & Abrams, 1993; Crippen, 2001; Kano, Siegel, & Bourque, 2005). The Association for Supervision and Curriculum Development has already begun to train its members in CERT and encourages learning institutions to integrate CERT training programs (Community in Action, 2004).

Hart (2004) suggests that campus-based CERT programs can provide opportunities for students to become empowered by the knowledge they receive, which will enable them to not only help themselves but also their neighbors. Through active participation in CERT, students increase the chances of their survival and those around them. In addition to learning a skill set that will enable students to participate in activities that will prove beneficial if the campus community should find itself in a state of emergency, through participation in CERT students benefit from service learning in their communities and this in turn increases our "social capital" (Bush, 2004; Sanders, 2003). Service learning provides a platform for "education and intellectual achievement as necessary aspects of public education, equally important is a focus on community and civic participation" (Ruggenberg, 1993, p. 13).

In order for a campus to be able to successfully form a campus-based CERT, the following will need to be addressed:

- Support from campus administration
- Support from student participants
- Support from CERT trainers

How will this be accomplished? Who will advocate for the program and the necessary support, including resources? Some college-based CERTs are a subset of the local county CERTs, others provide training independent of the local groups, but all work together in serving their communities when a disaster strikes. CERTs can participate in all phases of disaster management: mitigation, preparedness, response, and recovery.

ORGANIZING A CERT ON YOUR CAMPUS

Such a partnership requires time to develop from a great idea to presenting it to upper administration, to planning, and to logistics. The director of emergency management and director of public safety on your campus need to be behind this initiative in order for it to be successful. The collaborative program requires a dedicated "resource coordinator" acting on behalf of the campus and a coordinator from the CERT. The resource coordinators for this and any campus/community collaborative project need to be flexible, possess excellent interpersonal skills and high energy, and sustain a strong motivation for the program to succeed. It is a good idea to have formal agreements written and signed to define the responsibilities of each partner. This is simply to define the expectations up-front so that there are no surprises later.

LOGISTICS

After the resource coordinator on your campus and the CERT coordinator have committed to working together, decisions need to be made regarding training. Ideally, the training will be conducted on the campus at a time most convenient for students. After training dates are confirmed with the local CERT and the campus resource coordinators, an announcement of the program must take place to notify the students of the initiative in order to secure student volunteers. Working with the campus public relations committee will ensure that an effective message is created and delivered. Suggested venues are as follows: provide a web presence with the capability to capture names, addresses, phone numbers, and e-mails of interested students (potential CERT members); use social media outlets to do the same; create an e-mail message to be sent out through campus e-mail that announces the new CERT program and directs potential volunteers to the web page where they can enter their contact information; create a paper brochure that can be distributed to students who attend other campus events such as student activity sessions; hold a public information meeting led cooperatively by the campus resource coordinator, emergency management director, and/or public safety representative, as well as the CERT representative, to articulate the vision to potential volunteers. If the CERT training program is to begin in September, the web presence, the message coming from the office of public relations, and the paper brochures need to be in place by mid-summer at the latest; the student information session should be held at least a week or two prior to the intended start of the CERT training but after the e-mail announcement is delivered by public relations. The likelihood of participation of college students is high if consistent with the research (Larsson, Martensson, & Alexanderson, 2002) that shows participation in first aid training correlates with a young age and higher levels of education.

TRAINING

You may consider starting with a team of 20 student volunteers for each September. The standard CERT format utilizing FEMA materials typically covers disaster preparedness, basic first aid, light search and rescue, small fire suppression, disaster psychology, mass sheltering, and disaster scene organization. A classroom will be needed for lectures and hands-on exercises. Fire suppression exercises will be conducted outdoors. Once the 8-week training is completed, the team might meet monthly for training reviews or organizational meetings. CERT is a federally funded program through Citizen Corps. All classes are free of charge.

EVALUATION

As with most campus programs, an assessment will be required to review the program. The campus and CERT coordinators will evaluate and make decisions for the future of your CERT based on the number of volunteers for the CERT program, participation throughout the semester, availability of CERT trainers, funding, and other variables.

HOW THE PROJECT RELATES TO STUDENT LEARNING

Berg, Melaville, and Blank (2006) found that "community engagement, together with school efforts, promotes a school climate that is safe, supportive, and respectful and that connects students to a broader learning community" (p. 2). The student volunteers will learn firsthand how their efforts can provide a safer environment. Through their work with CERT, they will understand the importance of having an effective strategy in place for the activation of citizens in the event of a widespread crisis. They will learn how their local, state, and federal government agencies work together to provide for the safety of the citizens of the United States and its visitors. Volunteering in this capacity for the good of the community will help to develop strong personal character and a compassion for their community. Through CERT, neighborhoods and community colleges may create citizens who are engaged and committed to the success of their communities. Students develop a sense of empowerment, a can-do attitude that becomes omnipresent in all that they do—work, school, increased satisfaction in themselves and in their surroundings. This hands-on volunteer program can initiate an opportunity for lifetime citizenry. Becoming involved, in a program such as CERT, encourages students to connect as citizens to the larger local community and, therefore, increases social capital. For additional information on campus-based CERT, contact a local CERT or find a host of resources at: http://www.c-cert.msu.edu/resources.htm.

REFERENCES

Angus, D., Pretto, E., & Abrams, P. S. (1993). Recommendations for life-supporting first aid training of the lay public for disaster preparedness. *Prehospital and Disaster Medicine, 8,* 157–160.

Berg, A. C., Melaville, A., & Blank, M. (2006). *Community and family engagement: Principals share what works.* Washington, DC: Coalition for Community Schools.

Breeding, D. C. (2007). Defining the role of the environmental health profession in Homeland Security. *Journal of Environmental Health, 69*(6), 41–45.

Bush, G. W. (2002). Remarks on the citizens corps in Knoxville. *Weekly Compilation of Presidential Documents, 38*(15), 582–586.

Bush, G. W. (2004). Proclamation 7834—National character counts week, 2004. *Weekly Compilation of Presidential Documents, 40*(43), 2455–2455.

Crippen, D. (2001). The World Trade Center attack—Similarities to the 1988 earthquake in Armenia: Time to teach the public life-supporting first aid? *Critical Care, 5*(6), 312–314.

Department of Homeland Security. (2009). *Secretary Napolitano issues first in a series of action directives.* Press Release. Retrieved from http://www.dhs.gov/xnews/releases/pr_1232576802004.shtm

Harris, P. (2005). Emergency training takes CENTER STAGE. *TD Magazine, 59*(11), 24–31.

Hart, A. (2004). Student emergency response training program. *Officer Review Magazine, 43*(9), 13–14.

Kano, M., Siegel, J. M., & Bourque, L. B. (2005). First-aid training and capabilities of the lay public: A potential alternative source of emergency medical assistance following a natural disaster. *Disasters, 29*(1), 58–74.

Larsson, E., Martensson, M., & Alexanderson, K. (2002). First-aid training could improve risk behavior and enhance bystander actions. *Prehospital and Disaster Medicine, 17,* 134–141.

Ruggenberg, J. (1993). *Community service learning: A vital component of secondary school education* (p. 13). New York: Moral Education Forum.

Sanders, M. G. (2003). Community involvement in schools: From concept to practice. *Education and Urban Society, 35*(2), 161–180.

APPENDIX A: PREVENTION, PROTECTION, MITIGATION, RESPONSE, AND RECOVERY TEMPLATE[*]

Template for

(Name College/University)

(Address of School/Date Plan Was Written)

- Use this template as a guide in the organization of your campus strategies for emergency preparedness, protection, mitigation, response, and recovery. Enter campus-specific details where you find the information in parenthesis. They are placed throughout the template as placeholders. Each campus should create campus-specific processes and strategies. Directions to assist you in using this template are placed throughout.
- For each role and the responsibility, list the campus-specific job titles along with the responsibilities in place, for before (Prevention, Protection, and Mitigation), during (Response), and after (Recovery).
- For each threat and hazard, list the campus-specific strategies in place, for before (Prevention, Protection, Mitigation), during (Response), and after (Recovery). This guide has a suggested goal; replace it with your actual goal.
- The campus PPMRR should be available online, as a hard copy, and saved on an external drive, making it accessible in the event that the campus network experiences problems or no electrical power is available during an incident.

---

[*] This template is also available online at: http://www.crpglobal.org.

RECORD OF REVISIONS

Date	Action	Entered by

RECORD OF DISTRIBUTION

Date	Name	Position

EXECUTIVE POLICY GROUP AND COMMAND STAFF CONTACT LIST
(Use during Response and Recovery Phase)

NAME/TITLE	PHONE	E-MAIL	OFFICE LOCATION
(NAME) PRESIDENT POLICY GROUP			
(NAME) EM DIRECTOR POLICY GROUP			
(NAME) LIAISON OFFICER COMMAND STAFF			
(NAME) PIO OFFICER COMMAND STAFF			
(NAME) SAFETY OFFICER COMMAND STAFF			
(NAME) SECTION CHIEF OPERATIONS			
(NAME) SECTION CHIEF PLANNING			
(NAME) SECTION CHIEF LOGISTICS			
(NAME) SECTION CHIEF FINANCE & ADMIN			

DEPARTMENT HEAD AND ACADEMIC CHAIR CONTACT LIST

(Enter contact information for all department heads and academic chairs, as well as contact information for each employee, by department as well as alphabetically. It can be entered in any readable format: Word table, Excel spreadsheet, the campus database system, etc.). This contact list is updated annually by (September 10). It is available here in hard copy, electronically, and on USB held by the (Director of Emergency Management).

NAME/TITLE	PHONE	E-MAIL	OFFICE LOCATION

COMMUNITY AGENCY AND VENDOR CONTACT LIST

AGENCY NAME/ TITLE	PHONE	E-MAIL	OFFICE LOCATION
(My Town) Police Department Chief John Smith			
(My Town) Fire Department Chief Bill Hanson			
(My Town) Gas/ Electric Mary Price, Supervisor			
Hospital Emergency			
County Sheriff			
County Emergency Management			
Contracted Bus Company			
Contracted Hotel			
Contracted Food Services			

INTRODUCTION

Federal and state laws require that colleges and universities develop a written emergency operations and response plan. Additionally, these plans need to be exercised, tested, and rewritten where necessary. The guidelines for (Name College/University) that follow not only focus on operations and response but also incorporate a more holistic approach to managing emergency and crisis events that could befall a campus community. It incorporates Prevention, Protection, Mitigation, Response, and Recovery guidelines for possible threats and hazards that were identified in a Hazard Analysis that was conducted on (Month, xx, 20XX). From this point forward, this guide will be referred to as *PPMRR Strategies*.

Prevention, Protection, Mitigation, Response, and Recovery (PPMRR) planning is essential in preparing for a multitude of hazards that can adversely affect the safety of this institution and the health and general welfare of students, faculty, staff, visitors, and individuals with disabilities and special needs.

The PPMRR will be reviewed and updated annually to ensure the safety of students, faculty, staff, and visitors and the continuity of operations of (Name College/University).

This PPMRR is organized into five sections, with four appendices.

Section 1 contains the Basic Guideline, which defines how (Name College/University) has organized itself to protect the campus community. It begins with a *Statement of Purpose* and a *Mission Statement.* Also cited is the legal authority under which this plan was created, a threat and hazard analysis, and a listing of ICS/NIMS compliant roles and responsibilities for the PPMRR team.

Section 2 contains the Functional Annexes, which are strategies that apply to one or more threats and hazards. This guide places accountability procedures, communication strategies, evacuation, shelter-in-place, and lock-down in the Functional Annexes. Each activity lists a goal that ties to the Mission Statement and strategies for meeting the goal in all phases: Prevention, Protection, Mitigation, Response, and Recovery.

Section 3 is the Threat- and Hazard-Specific Annex. It provides guidance for Prevention, Protection, Mitigation, Response, and Recovery actions for vulnerabilities that were assigned a risk priority rating from the campus threat and hazard analysis. For each vulnerability, a goal that ties to the Mission Statement is defined and strategies for meeting the goal in all phases: Prevention, Protection, Mitigation, Response, and Recovery.

These PPMRR Strategies do not specifically address the limitless, diverse threats, and hazards that may confront this campus; instead, it provides general operating goals and strategies for managing critical events and emergencies . Nothing in this guide shall limit the use of experience, good judgment, common sense, discretion, flexibility, and ingenuity to adapt to any type of critical event, emergency, and the complexities, which exist under emergency conditions.

Section 4 contains the training compliance documentation and schedule for this academic year for (Name College/University) employees. Scheduling, coordinating, and tracking is a critical component that ensures compliance with all applicable federal, state, and local laws pertaining to the National Incident Management System (NIMS) and provides guidance to the faculty, staff, and students regarding their role in the PPMRR Strategy.

Section 5 contains (Name College/University) policies that guide the operation of the campus as it pertains to emergency preparedness. The policies found in this section are (Emergency Alert Activation Policy, Process for Inputting New Students, Staff, and Faculty in the Emergency Alert System, Emergency Operations Center Operational Plan, Flexible Leave in the Event of a Highly Contagious Communicable Disease, Information Technology Security Policy, Mutual Aid Policy, Missing Student Policy).

- Appendix A contains the (Campus Map)
- Appendix B contains the (Communication Templates)
- Appendix C contains the (Safety Message Templates)
- Appendix D contains the (Bomb Threat Report)

SECTION 1: THE BASIC GUIDELINE

(Use this as a framework. Replace with your campus-specific Statement of Purpose, Mission Statement, and Authorities.)

STATEMENT OF PURPOSE: (To establish capabilities for protecting students, faculty, staff, and the campus itself from the effects of threats and disasters.)

MISSION STATEMENT: (To prevent, protect, and mitigate against events that could compromise the safety of any person in a classroom, residence hall, office, or any other campus facility as well as any event that could jeopardize the continuation of use of any campus facility.)

AUTHORITIES:

HSPD-5

On February 28, 2003, with the issuance of the Homeland Security Presidential Directive 5(HSPD-5) by President George W. Bush, the National Incident Management System (NIMS), developed by the U.S. Department of Homeland Security (DHS), became the overarching legal authority for emergency and crisis planning in the United States. It is designed to structure the framework used nationwide for both governmental and nongovernmental agencies to respond to natural disasters and/or terrorist attacks at the local, state, and federal levels of government.

PPD-8

Presidential Policy Directive* (PPD-8), issued on March 30, 2011, by President Barack Obama, provides guidance that further strengthens the nation's ability to respond to threats and hazards.

Presidential Policy Directive 8 (PPD-8) defines preparedness around five mission areas: Prevention, Protection, Mitigation, Response, and Recovery.

Prevention, for the purposes of this PPMRR plan, means the action colleges/universities take to avoid or deter an emergency event from occurring.

Protection focuses on ongoing actions that protect the campus community: students, teachers, staff, visitors, networks, and property from a threat or hazard.

Mitigation means reducing the likelihood that threats and hazards will happen.

Response means the actions taken to stabilize the campus from an event that has occurred or is about to happen in an unpreventable way.

Recovery means the actions taken to return the college/university to its pre-event status.

CLERY ACT

The Clery Act requires that every Title IV institution, without exception, to convey its process for mass notification use in emergencies, and how mass notification tests will be conducted, to have and disclose emergency response and evacuation procedures, and to outline training of response personnel.

U.S. Department of Education (2013)—*Guide for Developing High-Quality School Emergency Operations Plans for Institutions of Higher Education.*

In addition to following federal mandates, the PPMRR supports and complements the (state name) education department regulations).

These PPMRR Strategies meet NIMS and PPD-8 requirements. It incorporates Clery Act regulations; includes strategies for the five core mission areas; aligns with NIMS recommendation that for each threat and hazard identified, goals, objectives, and action items be constructed for each of the three time frames associated with an incident: before, during, and after; and meets the NIMS requirement that the campus organizational structure for the response and recovery phases implement the incident command system (ICS).

The majority of Prevention, Protection, and Mitigation activities occur before an incident, although these three mission areas do have ongoing activities that can occur throughout an incident. Response activities occur during an incident, and Recovery activities can begin during an incident and continue to occur after an incident has been resolved.

In the Prevention, Protection, and Mitigation phases, the objective is to ensure that campus policies consider actions that could lessen the impact of a threat or hazard. In the Response phase, the objective includes suggested actions that members of the campus community should take to minimize the impact and in the Recovery phase suggested courses of actions that will bring the campus to its pre-event status and an After Action Plan to review what went well and areas for improvement.

THREAT AND HAZARD ANALYSIS

A threat and hazard analysis for (Name College/University) was conducted on (Date). A thorough review of the (Town/City/County/State) threat and hazard analysis was conducted. It revealed that (Name College/University), located in the center of this geographic area, is at risk for seasonal hurricanes, brush fires, and tornadoes. The historical incident reports and an analysis of probable events that could occur at the college identified the following risks: flooding of the buildings on the lower campus during significant rain, computer hacking, fire in residential housing, hazmat spill inside a campus building. A review of the literature pertaining to campus emergency management reveals that active shooter and missing student events are on the rise. From this threat and hazard analysis, the following Risk Priority table was constructed.

Threat and Hazard Analysis

Hazard	Probability	Magnitude	Warning	Duration	Risk Priority

Legend

Probability	Magnitude	Warning	Duration	Risk Priority
4. Very likely	4. Catastrophic	4. Minimal	4. 12+ hours	High
3. Likely	3. Critical	3. 6–12 hours	3. 6–12 hours	Medium
2. Possible	2. Limited	2. 12–24 hours	2. 3–6 hours	Low
1. Unlikely	1. Negligible	1. 24+ hours	1. <3 hours	

EMERGENCY CLASSIFICATION LEVELS

(Emergency Classification Levels [ECLs] can assist in determining threat and hazard risk priorities. Some colleges/universities use three ECLs, while others may choose to use four or five levels. The number of ECLs is not as important as the team at your college or university who knows the ECLs used at your campus and what each level indicates. Include the ECLs and your campus's definition of the ECL. This template uses three ECL levels.)

(Name College/University) uses Emergency Classification Levels (ECLs) to determine threats and hazards risk priorities. The ECLs are:

Level 1 (Minor Incident): A Level 1 incident is any incident, potential or actual, that will not seriously affect the overall functional capacity of the campus. It may not be necessary for the entire PPMRR team to meet to manage a Level 1 event. A Level 1 equates to a Risk Priority of Low.

(List examples of a Level 1 incident. Examples: Broken pipe, small contained fire.)

Level 2 (Emergency/Partial Activation): A Level 2 incident is any incident, potential or actual, that affects an entire building or buildings, and which may disrupt the overall operations of the campus. The PPMRR team will open and man the Emergency Operations Center until the event has concluded. A Level 2 equates to a Risk Priority of Medium.

(List examples of a Level 2 incident. Examples: Bomb threat, fire affecting residence halls or classroom building.)

Level 3 (Disaster/Full Activation): A Level 3 incident has the potential to halt the continuation of regular campus activities. In all cases, the PPMRR team will open and man the Emergency Operations Center/ Command Post until the event has concluded. A Level 3 equates to a Risk Priority of High.

(List examples of a Level 3 incident. Examples: Hurricane, tornado, earthquake; fire affecting residence halls or classroom building.)

EMERGENCY PLAN ACTIVATION AND NOTIFICATION PROCESS

(Replace with your campus-specific process.)

A typical campus emergency event is reported to the (Public Safety Office at xxx-xxx-xxxx) from a cell phone or a campus desk phone, on-campus emergency phones, weather radios, weather siren, or other means. The (Public Safety staff on duty) will contact the (Director of Public Safety) or (the assigned duty officer) immediately. The (Public Safety Director or duty officer) determines the incident level as defined in the PPMRR, and immediately contacts the (Director of Emergency Management).

The (Emergency Management Director) will begin the emergency notification procedure to the appropriate Executive Policy Group member, Command Staff, and Section Chiefs via phone/text to assess the situation and develop recommendations for short- and long-term responses, including making notifications to the campus community as appropriate—opening the Emergency Operations Center (EOC), canceling or relocating classes, and so on.

For imminent danger, any member of the PPMRR team can initiate a Timely Notice message through the (Emergency Alert System) without consultation with other team members.

Timely Notice: Immediate warning notifications to the campus community upon confirmation of a significant emergency or dangerous situation involving an immediate threat to the health or safety of students or employees occurring on the campus such as: fire, tornado, hurricane, earthquake, gas leak, terrorist incident, armed intruder, bomb threat, and explosion.

When the threat or hazard is not immediately imminent, the PPMRR team confers, and the VP for Communications drafts an approved message, and depending on the situation uses the most appropriate communications messaging system to relay the information to the campus community, including any or all listed above.

ORGANIZATION AND ASSIGNMENT OF DUTIES

The following Organization and Assignment of Duties is meant to provide a suggested functional description of responsibilities for ICS/NIMS positions. Draw from this information to help identify the assignment of duties for a campus-specific ICS/NIMS compliant organizational chart. Replace the titles in parenthesis with the title of the person who has been delegated this responsibility at your campus. Identify and categorize all campus departments and the names of the personnel and enter them into a table by department. Place these contact lists in the front of the campus PPMRR guide.

(Name College/University) is organized for disaster response and recovery actions using the NIMS structure. The goal of the ICS system is to ensure the safety of responders and others, to achieve tactical objectives and use resources efficiently. Its characteristics include: common terminology; correct terminology for organizations, positions, resources, facilities; clear plain language; chain of command; and a three- to seven-person span of control.

The Organizational Chart that follows is used during the Response and Recovery phases of a critical event. In many instances, it will not resemble the steady-state organizational chart of the campus. During the Response and Recovery phases, each Section is tasked with specific responsibilities to meet the incident objectives based on goals set by the Executive Policy Group and the UCG to meet incident objectives. The Section Chiefs of each functional section: Operations, Planning, Logistics, and Finance and Administration advise the Executive Policy Group and the UCG and execute their responsibilities with the cooperation of the various Branch Directors that report to each Section Chief, all supporting the incident objectives. Based on the situation, the Section Chiefs will activate branches/units within their section and designate Branch Directors and Unit Leaders.

The following pages describe how (Name College/University) organizes itself using the ICS system, details the assignment of duties of each ICS position, and the assignment of duties for each section and department head. While ICS is a Response and Recovery function, for ease of use of this component of the PPMRR Strategies listed next each Role, you will also find the Responsibilities of each Role during the Prevention, Protection, and Mitigation phases.

During an event, the campus takes its lead from the Unified Coordination Group (UCG), with policy input from the Executive Policy Group, comprised of (the president, provost, chancellor, board of directors). The UCG is comprised of (a representative to the Executive Policy Group), the (Director of Emergency Management), and depending on the severity of the event outside agencies such as local police, fire, EMS, utility company representatives, town, county, state, and even federal representatives. One of these individuals, or a Section Chief, all depending on the situation, is the Incident Commander (IC). The incident commander is a representative from any of the organizations represented in the UCG, based on the incident itself and who is most qualified to lead. Reporting directly to the UCG is the Command Staff, consisting of a Safety Officer (SO), Public Information Officer (PIO), Liaison Officer (LO), and Section Chiefs.

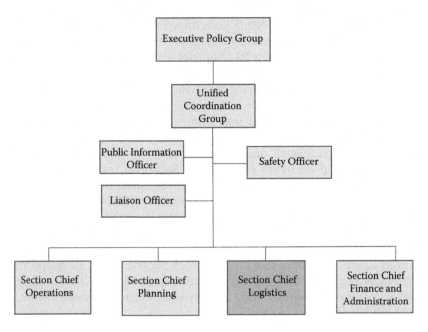

Not every threat or hazardous event at the campus will require the mobilization of all positions and sections. Mobilization is dependent on the incident itself and the incident planning objectives. The incident command structured is flexible and expanding and contracting as needed. However, if a Section is not mobilized the IC will typically manage those functions.

EXECUTIVE POLICY GROUP

Consists of the (President, Director of Emergency Management, Provost) and is accountable for any threat or hazard that affects the campus community. This group provides guidance on priorities and objectives of such threats and hazards. They have the authority to make and change policy decisions, commit resources, obligate funds, and delegate authority to the Incident Commander.

(Later you will find a framework to get you started in creating the Roles and Responsibilities for the Executive Policy Group and the Command Staff for each phase. One or two possible strategies for each are listed for Prevention, Protection, Mitigation, Response, and Recovery. Add specific strategies that have been developed for your campus. Refer back to Chapter 5 for suggestions.)

The (President) is responsible for the safe operation of the campus day-to-day operations.

- The (Director of Emergency Management) is responsible for the overall direction and control of the implementation of the PPMRR operations.
- The (Provost) has the delegated responsibility of ensuring continuity of operations for all academic activity during times of emergency and during recovery efforts and assumes the President's responsibilities when not available.

Line of succession for leading the team is:

1. (President)
2. (Director of Emergency Management)
3. (Provost)

DIRECTOR OF EMERGENCY MANAGEMENT

The (Director of Emergency Management) chairs the Executive Policy Group and leads the initiative to implement PPMRR strategies for all phases: Prevention, Protection, Mitigation, Response, and Recovery.

Prevention, Protection, and Mitigation Strategies

- Ensure that all campus departments are included in the PPMRR.
- Ensure that the PPMRR is available to campus community electronically as well as in hard copy.
- Develop strategy to ensure that all new faculty and staff receive a copy of the campus policies and procedures, and PPMRR Strategies at the new employee orientation.

Response Strategies

- Provide copy of the campus PPMRR Strategies, including the campus map, as needed to any internal and external units and/or agencies responding to an emergency or crisis event.
- Activate Response component of the PPMRR Plan, establish the Incident Command Post, open the EOC, and coordinate on-site response.

Recovery Strategies

- Be prepared to provide input to the After Action Report.
- Deactivate the EOC when appropriate.
- Notify appropriate faculty and the Registrar if the incident will affect class attendance of any students.

PUBLIC INFORMATION OFFICER

The (Director of Communications) serves as the official spokesperson, Public Information Officer (PIO), for the campus; the "one voice" of the campus to the public and the media. The PIO has responsibility for disseminating information that has been approved by the Executive Policy Group and the Command Staff, through all communication channels during emergencies, major disasters, or matters that have potential to impact the reputation of the college/university.

Response Strategies

- Serve as backup to President as the campus spokesperson.

- Coordinate all crisis communications with the media, including prepared statements, talking points, fact sheets, and press releases. These items should contain standardized items such as: name of the school, point of contact—name, phone, e-mail, and should be numbered consecutively as they are issued, include a date and time, and be approved before release.

Recovery Strategies
- Contribute to the After Action Report.
- Distribute the After Action Report to the campus community as well as to its external partners.

SAFETY OFFICER

The (Director of Public Safety) serves as the Safety Officer (SO). He/she is responsible for the front-line management of emergencies, for tactical planning and execution, for determining whether assistance is required, and for relaying requests for outside assistance. The SO monitors incident operations and offers advice on all matters related to operational safety, including the health and safety of emergency responder personnel. The SO has emergency authority to stop or prevent unsafe acts during incident operations.

Response Strategies
- Exercise authority to immediately stop or prevent unsafe acts or conditions when appropriate.
- Provide technical advice to the IC about the incident or response activities as they relate to the safety of the students, staff, faculty, and visitors.

Recovery Strategies
- Collaborate with (Director of Communications) on creating awareness and education programs to promote safety.
- Notify the appropriate local, state, and federal authorities of all hazardous materials emergencies that require such notification.

LIAISON OFFICER

The Liaison Officer (LO) serves as the primary contact for agencies responding to the campus emergency situation.

Response Strategies

- Work collaboratively with the Director of Communications.
- Obtain the external agency database ready and available in print, online, and on USB for use by the PPMRR team.
- When appropriate, correspond and collaborate with outside agencies on behalf of the campus.

Recovery Strategies

- Update, as necessary, the agency database.
- Invite agency contacts to contribute to the campus After Action Report.

OPERATIONS SECTION

Operations is an incident command function. The Operations Section Chief takes direction from the Executive Policy Group and the UCG in implementing the campus Action Plans. The Operations Section Chief position will vary depending on the actual incident. If it is a safety or criminal event, a likely choice for Operations Section Chief is the Public Safety Director; if the threat is a pandemic health event, a likely choice for Operations Section Chief is the Health Services Director.

In the Operations Section, you will find roles and responsibilities for taking actions and carrying out specific actions to meet incident objectives. Typical branches of the Operations Section that might be utilized in the campus environment include Public Safety, Communications/ Public Relations, Academic Affairs, Student Affairs, Health Services, Food Services, Housing, and Enrollment Services. Not all branches are activated for every critical event. The IC and the actual critical event will determine which branches need to be activated. Listed next are all the campus departments that might be activated under Operations. A goal is listed that you can adopt or modify. Add specific strategies that have been developed for your campus for Prevention, Protection, Mitigation, Response, and Recovery.

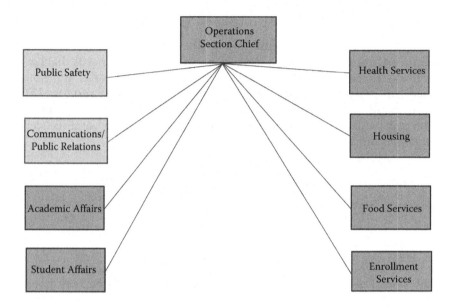

PUBLIC SAFETY BRANCH

The (Public Safety Director), as Branch Director, is responsible for managing the personal safety students, staff, faculty, and visitors to the campus. He/she may also be the initiator of campus wide timely notices.

Prevention, Protection, and Mitigation Strategies

Response Strategies

Recovery Strategies

COMMUNICATIONS/PUBLIC RELATIONS

The (Director of Communications/Public Relations), as Branch Director, is responsible for gathering, sharing, and managing incident-related information for constituents internal and external to the campus.

Prevention, Protection, and Mitigation Strategies

Response Strategies

Recovery Strategies

ACADEMIC AFFAIRS BRANCH

The (Provost or VP of Academic Affairs), as Branch Director, is responsible for ensuring that teaching schedules and other faculty needs that have been disrupted due to the critical event are being addressed and managed. All campus department heads and academic chairs serve as Unit Leaders, all reporting to the (Provost). Every Unit Leader has an obligation to provide protection, prevention, mitigation, response, and recovery strategies for those who report to them.

Prevention, Protection, and Mitigation Strategies

Response Strategies

Recovery Strategies

STUDENT AFFAIRS BRANCH

The (Vice President of Student Affairs), as Branch Director, is responsible for making sure that student housing, food services, transportation, class schedules, and counseling needs due to the critical event are being managed. All departments that report to the (Vice President of Student Affairs) serve as Unit Leaders. Every Unit Leader has an obligation to provide protection, prevention, mitigation, response, and recovery strategies for those who report to them.

HEALTH SERVICES BRANCH

The (XXX Director) serves as the Branch Director.
Health Services as it pertains to critical events is an entity that pertains to all campuses, even those campuses that do not provide any medical services to students, staff, or faculty. Areas of concern include personnel safety and health issues. Guidance for Occupational Health and Safety is provided from the Health and Hospital Services (HHS), the Department of Labor (DOL), Department of Homeland Security (DHS), and the Department of State Health Services (DSHS).

Prevention, Protection, and Mitigation Strategies

Response Strategies

Recovery Strategies

FOOD SERVICES BRANCH

The (Food Services Director), as Branch Director, is responsible for managing all kitchen facilities and food distribution locations across the campus during nonemergency times as well as during times of emergency and recovery. All departments that report to the Food Services Director serve as Unit Leaders. Every Unit Leader has an obligation to provide protection, prevention, mitigation, response, and recovery strategies for those who report to them.

Prevention, Protection, and Mitigation Strategies

Response Strategies

Recovery Strategies

HOUSING BRANCH

The (Housing Director), as Branch Director, is responsible for the management of residential locations both on and off campus during nonemergency times as well as during times of Response and Recovery. All departments that report to the Housing Director serve as Unit Leaders. Every Unit Leader has an obligation to provide protection, prevention, mitigation, response, and recovery strategies for those who report to them.

Prevention, Protection, and Mitigation Strategies

Response Strategies

Recovery Strategies

ENROLLMENT SERVICES BRANCH

The (VP of Enrollment Services), as Branch Director, is responsible for the management of all units that comprise Enrollment Services: (Admissions, Academic Advising, and Financial Aid). All departments that report to the Housing Director serve as Unit Leaders. Every Unit Leader has an obligation to provide protection, prevention, mitigation, response, and recovery strategies for those who report to them.

Prevention, Protection, and Mitigation Strategies

Response Strategies

Recovery Strategies

PLANNING SECTION

The Planning Section of the ICS is an incident command function activated during the Response and Recovery phases, not to be confused with the planning that every department is involved with during the Prevention, Protection, and Mitigation phases. The Planning Section takes direction from the Executive Policy Group and the UCG in implementing the campus Action Plans. Those in the Planning Section collect, evaluate, and disseminate information within the emergency operations center (EOC). During an incident, the Planning Section collects information from the Executive Policy Group, UCG, Operations, Logistics, and Finance and Administration Sections to enter into the Incident Action Plan (IAP), which at a minimum includes an accurate and current description of the incident and the resources available, probable course of events, and strategies to achieve incident objectives set for the operational period. The Planning Section holds the responsibility of maintaining status boards and maps, performing data analysis, and preparing reports. At the end of each operational period, the IC, Command Staff, and appropriate Section Chiefs review the incident objectives to see if they have been met or need to be redefined. This information is recorded in the Situation Report for that operational period, and it provides the necessary information to develop objectives for the next operational period and IAP.

Branches that fall under the Planning Section Chief are the Situation Analysis Branch; Damage Assessment Branch; and Recovery Branch. Depending on the scope of the campus critical event, these responsibilities may be managed by separate individuals or all fall under the responsibility of one person. Select the position at your campus that can best manage these roles and responsibilities.

SITUATION ANALYSIS BRANCH

During the Response and Recovery phase, the Situation Analysis Branch takes direction from the Planning Section Chief who is taking direction from the Executive Policy Group and the UCG in implementing the campus Action Plans. The (xxx Director) serves as the Branch Director and is responsible for collecting, evaluating, and analyzing all critical incident information and providing updated status reports to the Executive Policy Group and Command Staff.

Prevention, Protection, and Mitigation Strategies

Prevention, Protection, and Mitigation are not IC functions. However, during the Prevention, Protection, and Mitigation phases the PPMRR team will identify which campus personnel will be delegated to work in the Situation Analysis Branch. Mechanisms for collecting, evaluating, and analyzing critical incident information from the Sections and their Branches will be determined as will the process and the individual(s) tasked with writing briefings, the Incident Action Plan (IAP), and Situation Reports (SITREPs). This individual will work cooperatively with the Communications/Public Relations Branch Director who will manage the dissemination of the reports, briefings, IAPs, and SITREPs under the direction of the Operations Section Chief, the Executive Policy Group, and the UCG. As the Situation Analysis Branch is also responsible for tracking personnel deployed to the EOC, working cooperatively with Human Resources is imperative as is developing a system for tracking personnel.

Response Strategies

The Branch Director in consultation with the Section Chief will identify objectives to be accomplished during each Operational Period. The Situation Analysis Branch Director will activate the strategies developed during the Prevention, Protection, and Mitigation phases: receive, evaluate, and analyze all critical incident information and provide updated status reports to the Executive Policy Group and Command Staff in the form of oral reports, briefings, IAPs, and SITREPs. The Branch Director will work cooperatively with the Communications/ Public Relations Branch Director who will manage the dissemination of briefings, IAPs, and SITREPs, as well as issue news releases, and disseminate information through appropriate communication channels.

It is the responsibility of the Situation Analysis Branch to keep records and documentation of all EOC activities including the tracking system for personnel deployed to the EOC.

Recovery Strategies

During the Recovery phase, the Situation Analysis Branch continues to collect, evaluate, and analyze critical incident information from the Sections and their Branches. All actions pertaining to the function of all Sections and Branches from throughout the critical event are collected by, and are included in, the After Action Report and written by the Situation Analysis Branch.

DAMAGE ASSESSMENT BRANCH

The Damage Assessment Branch Director is responsible for assessing damage at the campus. Damage may be physical damage of structures and facilities, injuries and fatalities, as well as damage to the reputation of the institution. It may also include damage to the reputation of an individual, such as a faculty member, which could affect the reputation of the institution. The position of Damage Assessment Branch Director will be assigned by the Executive Policy Group and the UCG as it is dependent on the critical event.

Prevention, Protection, and Mitigation Strategies

Prevention, Protection, and Mitigation are not IC functions. However, during the Prevention, Protection, and Mitigation phases, the PPMRR will determine which campus individuals would be best suited to manage the various Damage Assessment Branches.

Response Strategies

During the Response and Recovery phase, the Damage Assessment Branch takes direction from the Planning Section Chief who is taking direction from the Executive Policy Group and the UCG in implementing the campus strategies. The Branch Director in consultation with the Section Chief will identify objectives to be accomplished during each Operational Period.

Recovery Strategies

The Damage Assessment Branch Director continues to work as needed with the Executive Policy Group and the UCG in implementing the campus strategies for Recovery. The Branch contributes to the After Action Report all actions pertaining to the function of the Damage Assessment Branch throughout the critical event.

RECOVERY BRANCH

The Planning Section may also be involved in developing the Recovery Plan for the event, including emergency and temporary housing for campus residents, and stranded commuter students, faculty, and staff. Planners work in cooperation with other sections in the restoration of campus support services. The position of Recovery Branch Director will be assigned by the Executive Policy Group and the UCG after an event has occurred and will be dependent on the actual incident.

Recovery Strategies

The Recovery Branch takes direction from the Planning Section Chief who is taking direction from the Executive Policy Group and the UCG in implementing the campus Action Plans. The Branch Director in consultation with the Section Chief will identify objectives to be accomplished during each Operational Period. The Recovery Branch Director contributes to the After Action Report all actions pertaining to the function of the Recovery Branch throughout the critical event.

LOGISTICS SECTION

Logistics is an incident command function activated during the Response and Recovery phases. The Logistics Section takes direction from the Executive Policy Group and the UCG in implementing the campus strategies. The role of the Logistics Section Chief is to procure equipment and materials to support the emergency response. This may include reconstituting current campus facilities for another use, supplying communication and technology services, transporting people, furniture, housing, and food services to meet the needs of the emergency response.

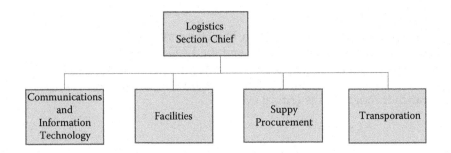

COMMUNICATIONS AND INFORMATION TECHNOLOGY BRANCH

The (Communications and Information Technology Director) as Branch Director has the responsibility for managing the continuity of operations, security from threats, and when necessary the recovery of systems of the Communications and Information Technology systems. The maintenance, purchasing, leasing, renting, and assignment of communications equipment, including radios, telephones, cell phones, and computer equipment, are all functions of this position. All departments that report to the Communications Director serve as Unit Leaders. Every Unit Leader has an obligation to provide protection, prevention, mitigation, response, and recovery strategies for those who report to them.

Protection, Prevention, and Mitigation Strategies

Response Strategies

Recovery Strategies

FACILITIES BRANCH

The (Facilities Director) as Branch Director is responsible for the safe operation of the campus for students, staff, faculty, and visitors during nonemergency times as well as during times of emergency and recovery. He/she is responsible for ensuring continuity of operations for all critical infrastructure operations. This includes ensuring that the buildings and roadways are habitable, and that potable water and sanitation services are available for the campus community. All departments that report to the Facilities Director serve as Unit Leaders. Every Unit Leader has an obligation to provide protection, prevention, mitigation, response, and recovery strategies for those who report to them.

Protection, Prevention, and Mitigation Strategies

Response Strategies

Recovery Strategies

SUPPLY/PROCUREMENT BRANCH

The (Director of XXX) serves as the Supply/Procurement Branch Director whose responsibilities include ordering, distributing, storing, and maintaining accountability of all supplies required by all Sections during non-emergency times, Prevention, Protection and Mitigation, as well as during times of Response and Recovery. All departments that report to the Supply/Procurement Director serve as Unit Leaders. Every Unit Leader has an obligation to provide protection, prevention, mitigation, response, and recovery strategies for those who report to them.

Protection, Prevention, and Mitigation Strategies

Response Strategies

Recovery Strategies

TRANSPORTATION BRANCH

The (Director or xxx) serves as the Branch Director with responsibilities for preparing transportation plans, providing for fueling, maintenance, repairing, and storage of resources and providing the transportation for personnel, food, and supplies. While the Transportation Branch is housed in the Logistics Section, it is critical to integrate the accounting and maintaining of resources with the movement of these resources, which occurs in the Operations Section. All departments that report to the Transportation Branch Director serve as Unit Leaders. Every Unit Leader has an obligation to provide protection, prevention, mitigation, response, and recovery strategies for those who report to them.

Protection, Prevention, and Mitigation Strategies

Response Strategies

Recovery Strategies

FINANCE AND ADMINISTRATION SECTION

The (VP of Finance and Administration) is the Finance and Administration Section Chief responsible for overseeing and managing expenses and keeping the Command Staff aware of the fiscal situation. The Finance and Administration Section positions are responsible for tracking incident costs: the Vice President of Finance and Administration, Human Resources, Business Management, the campus attorney. Select a Section Chief the position at your campus that best suits the role of Finance and Administration Section Chief.

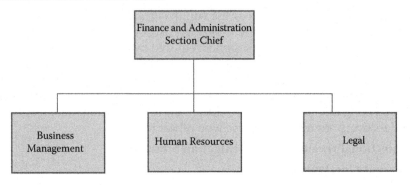

BUSINESS MANAGEMENT BRANCH

The (Vice President for Business) as Branch Director is responsible for all financial transactions during all PPMRR phases. During the Response and Recovery phases serves as the Business Management Branch Director. All departments that report to the Business Management Branch Director serve as Unit Leaders. Every Unit Leader has an obligation to provide protection, prevention, mitigation, response, and recovery strategies for those who report to them.

Protection, Prevention, and Mitigation Strategies

Response Strategies

Recovery Strategies

HUMAN RESOURCES BRANCH

The (Human Resources Director) as Branch Director is responsible for the welfare of all staff during all phases of a critical event. All departments that report to the Human Resources Director serve as Unit Leaders. Every Unit Leader has an obligation to provide protection, prevention, mitigation, response, and recovery strategies for those who report to them.

Prevention, Protection, and Mitigation Strategies

Response Strategies

Recovery Strategies

LEGAL BRANCH

The (General Counsel) as Branch Director provides legal advice, oversees all policies, procedures, and contracts to protect the interest of the campus and in doing so insures campus-wide compliance. All departments that report to the Branch Director serve as Unit Leaders. Every Unit Leader has an obligation to provide protection, prevention, mitigation, response, and recovery strategies for those who report to them.

Prevention, Protection, and Mitigation Strategies

Response Strategies

Recovery Strategies

SECTION 2: FUNCTIONAL ANNEX

Functional Annexes are critical activities that can apply to one or more threats and hazards. Listed below are strategies for Accountability, Communication, Evacuation, Shelter-in-Place, and Lock-Down. Any one, or all, of these activities may be used in conjunction with strategies for specific threats, hazards, or actual campus incidents. Each takes into account Prevention, Protection, Mitigation, Response, and Recovery phases of an incident.

(Below you will find a framework to help get you started creating Accountability, Communication, Evacuation, Shelter-in-Place, and Lock-Down strategies for each phase. It lists a goal that you can adopt or modify. Add specific strategies that have been developed for your campus for Prevention, Protection, Mitigation, Response, and Recovery.)

ACCOUNTABILITY

Goals: To ensure that rosters and accountability lists of students, staff, and faculty are available and easily accessible; for staff and faculty to be able to access and utilize rosters and accountability lists in the midst of a critical event; and to provide training for staff and faculty that incorporates the use of rosters and accountability lists.

Prevention, Protection, and Mitigation Strategies

Response Strategies

Recovery Strategies

COMMUNICATIONS STRATEGIES

Goals: Create outlets to provide timely and accurate information to the internal and external campus community on the status of any phase of the PPMRR operation; utilize these outlets to effectively communicate with faculty, staff, students, and the general public regarding actions necessary to protect people and property; represent the campus as responsible and caring, and maintain stakeholder confidence.

Prevention, Protection, and Mitigation Strategies

Response

Recovery

EVACUATION DRILLS/ACTUAL EVENTS

Goals: To provide the campus community an opportunity to become familiar with the sound of the fire alarm, the location of exits, practice timely evacuation drill procedures; during a critical event to be able to use this tested knowledge to make an expeditious evacuation; and to make recommendations for improving evacuation time.

Prevention, Protection, and Mitigation Strategies

Scheduling Evacuation Drills

The PPMRR team coordinates announced and unannounced evacuation drills each semester, to assess and evaluate the emergency evacuation procedures and capabilities. The (Director of Emergency Management) monitors, evaluates, and makes recommendations for improvement.

Emergency evacuation drills will be conducted at the frequency listed in the following table. The campus will publish a summary of its Emergency Response and Evacuation Procedures in conjunction with at least one drill or exercise each calendar year.

Facility Type	Minimum Drill Frequency
Residence Halls	Once per semester
Facilities used for educational purposes, containing notable amounts of hazardous materials, exceeds 3 stories in height	Once per semester
Academic Buildings	Once per semester
Office Buildings	Annually
Daycare	Monthly

Response

This campus uses the following scale in classifying successful evacuation drill times. Follow-up drills are required for buildings classified as Needs Improvement.

Evacuation Time	Rating	Cooperation
< 5–10 minutes	Excellent	Prompt and orderly evacuation
< 10–15 minutes	Average	Minor objections to leaving
> 15 minutes	Needs Improvement	Notable delays and opposition

Recovery

LOCK-DOWN STRATEGIES

Goals: To keep the campus community safe by providing training for the campus community to minimize assaults and deaths by an on-campus intruder; to put steps in place to initiate a lock-down; to provide appropriate aftercare to the campus community.

Prevention, Preparation, and Mitigation

Response

Recovery

SHELTER-IN-PLACE STRATEGIES

Goals: To provide training for the campus community to keep safe from chemical, biological, or radiological contaminants that may be released accidentally or intentionally into the environment or an imminent weather event such as a tornado or hurricane; to put steps in place to initiate a shelter-in-place; and to provide appropriate aftercare to the campus community.

Preventive, Protective, and Mitigation Strategies

Response

Recovery

SECTION 3: THREAT- AND HAZARD-SPECIFIC ANNEX

ACTIVE SHOOTER

Goals: Develop strategies to keep the campus community safe from acts of violence; to put steps in place to ensure that timely notice is made to the campus community; to provide appropriate aftercare to the campus community.

Prevention, Protection, and Mitigation Strategies

Response Strategies

Recovery Strategies

CYBER ATTACKS

Goals: To create strategies that ensure that the campus can provide a secure open network that protects the integrity and confidentiality of information while maintaining its accessibility; to employ immediate strategies that block posing threats, when necessary update security systems and strategies.

Prevention, Protection, and Mitigation Strategies

Response Strategies

Recovery Strategies

BOMB THREATS

Goals: Develop strategies to keep the campus community safe from acts of violence; to put steps in place to ensure that timely notice is made to the campus community; and to provide appropriate aftercare to the campus community.

A bomb threat is defined as the communication through the use of a written message, telephone call, e-mail, social media, or other instrument of communication; the willful making of any threat; or the malicious conveyance of false information knowing the same to be false, which concerns an attempt being made, or to be made; to kill, injure, intimidate any individual; or unlawfully to damage or destroy any building, vehicle, or other real or personal property by means of an explosive.

Prevention, Protection, and Mitigation Strategies

Response Strategies

Recovery Strategies

DEATH ON THE CAMPUS OF STUDENT/STAFF/FACULTY

Goals: To provide guidelines to be followed immediately upon notification of the death of a student, staff, or faculty member; and action steps to follow during the days following.

Response Strategies

Recovery Strategies

DISPLACED STUDENTS

Goals: To prepare beforehand for an unexpected housing displacement of significant numbers of campus community from on- and off-campus residences due to a fire, building collapse, flood, fire, tornado and so forth; to respond in a timely manner to the displacements and action steps for the days following.

Protection, Prevention, and Mitigation Strategies

Response Strategies

Recovery Strategies

EXTREME WEATHER EMERGENCY

Goals: To put strategies in place to reduce injuries, deaths, and facility damage that could occur as a result of an extreme weather emergency, such as an earthquake, hurricane, tornado, snow/ice, or any other severe weather situation; to put steps in place to ensure that timely notice is made to the campus community; and to provide appropriate aftercare to the campus community.

Prevention, Protection, and Mitigation Strategies

Response Strategies

Recovery

FIRES

Goals: To put strategies in place to reduce and/or eliminate fires on campus; to put steps in place to ensure that timely notice is made to the campus community; to provide appropriate aftercare to the campus community.

Prevention, Protection, and Mitigation Strategies

Response Strategies

Recovery Strategies

HATE CRIMES

Goals: To promote an environment where crimes motivated by racial, sexual, or other prejudice are not tolerated; and to put actions in place to quickly respond should such a crime occur.

Prevention, Protection, and Mitigation Strategies

Response Strategies

Recovery Strategies

HAZARDOUS MATERIALS RELEASE

Goals: To provide strategies in the event an on- or off-campus chemical spill threatening the health and safety of the campus community; to put steps in place to ensure that timely notice is made to the campus community; and to provide appropriate aftercare to the campus community.

Prevention, Protection, and Mitigation Strategies

Response Strategies

Recovery Strategies

MISSING PERSONS

Goals: To provide safety training for students; provide training for timely notice actions; for when an enrolled missing student, who resides in campus housing has been deemed missing for at least 24 hours; to provide appropriate aftercare to the campus community.

Prevention, Protection, and Mitigation Strategies

Response Strategies

Recovery Strategies

PANDEMIC/EBOLA OR OTHER PUBLIC HEALTH EMERGENCY

Goals: To provide strategies for staff and faculty before an event occurs; to provide guidelines to be followed in response to confirmed or alleged cases of communicable diseases such as a pandemic flu or Ebola virus contracted by a member of the campus community when the disease poses a threat to the campus community; to provide appropriate aftercare to the campus community.

Prevention, Protection, and Mitigation Strategies

Response Strategies

Recovery Strategies

SECTION 4: TRAINING AND EXERCISING

The Department of Homeland Security (DHS), the NIMS Integration Center (NIC), and the U.S. Department of Education (ED) recommend that all key personnel involved in school emergency management and incident response take the National Incident Management System (NIMS), incident command system (ICS), and National Response Framework (NRF) training courses.

The (Director of Emergency Management) oversees and ensures compliance with all applicable federal, state, and local laws pertaining to National Incident Management System (NIMS) requirements. All personnel will complete their annual training by (October 15) each year, and all new hires will complete the level of NIMS training commensurate with their position within (30 days) of start date of employment. The training tracking database is maintained by the (Director of Emergency Management).

Determinations for training are based on the ICS format with staff organized into two levels: Leadership, which includes the Incident Commander, the Public Information Officer (PIO), Safety Officer (SO), Liaison Officer (LNO), and Section Chiefs; General Staff, which consists of personnel who represent the five functional areas.

COURSE #	COURSE TITLE	LEADERSHIP	GENERAL
100.HE	An Introduction to ICS for Higher Education	X	X
200.b	ICS for Single Resources and Initial Action Incidents	X	X
300	Intermediate ICS for Expanding Incidents	X	
400	Advanced Incident Command	X	
700.a	An Introduction to NIMS	X	X
800.b	An Introduction to the National Response Framework (NRF)	X	X

Course Descriptions:

IS-100.HE: Intro to Incident Command System and I-100: For Higher Education
This course introduces the incident command system (ICS) and provides the foundation for higher level ICS training. This course describes the history, features, and principles, and organizational structure of the incident command system. It also explains the relationship between ICS and the National Incident Management System.

IS-200.b: ICS for Single Resource and Initial Action Incidents
This course is designed to enable personnel to operate efficiently during an incident or event within the incident command system (ICS). ICS-200 provides training on and resources for personnel who are likely to assume a supervisory position within the ICS.

ICS-300: Intermediate ICS for Expanding Incidents
ICS-300 is designed for responders and personnel who will be in leadership positions during a major incident. Topics include: unified command, assessment and objectives, incident action planning process, incident resource management, demobilization, transfer of command, and closeout. *Prerequisites: I-100, 200, 700, 800*

ICS-400: Advanced ICS, Command and General Staff for Complex Incidents
ICS-400 is designed for personnel who will be directing an emergency response during a major incident. Topics include: major/complex incident or event management, area command, complexes, and multiagency coordination. *Prerequisites: I-100, 200, 300, 700, 800*

IS-700.a: National Incident Management System (NIMS)—An Introduction
This course introduces and overviews the National Incident Management System (NIMS). NIMS provides a consistent nationwide template to enable all government, private-sector, and nongovernment organizations to work together during domestic incidents.

IS- 800.b: National Response Framework—An Introduction
This course introduces participants to the concepts and principles for the National Response Framework. This course is intended for government executives, private-sector, and nongovernmental organization (NGO) leaders, and emergency management practitioners. This includes senior elected and appointed leaders, such as Federal department or agency heads, State governors, mayors, tribal leaders, and city, or county officials—those who have a responsibility to provide for effective response.

The FEMA Emergency Management Institute offers no cost online training for the following courses at www.training.fema.gov.

IS-100.HE: Introduction to the Incident Command System for Higher Education
IS-200.b: ICS for Single Resource and Initial Action Incidents
IS-700.a: National Incident Management System (NIMS)—An Introduction
IS-800.b: National Response Framework—An Introduction

The following courses are available via classroom delivery only.

ICS-300 Intermediate ICS for Expanding Incidents
ICS-400 Advanced ICS, Command and General Staff for Complex Incidents

TRAINING SCHEDULE

In addition to the individual courses, the PPMRR team will participate in at least one exercise on the campus annually to test the PPMRR policies and procedures. The exercise may be a tabletop, functional, or full-scale exercise. External partners, such as the police, fire, utility company will be invited to participate as appropriate. The (Director of Emergency Management) participates as appropriate, in all community (city, regional, State) exercises.

This academic year (20XX–20XX), the (NAME COLLEGE/UNIVERSITY) PPMRR team will exercise the (response time and process for activation of the emergency alert system in October) with an active shooter tabletop exercise. To be followed in (March with an active shooter drill to be conducted in the residence halls). Plans for the spring semester include a tabletop in (January to prepare the campus PPMRR team for a public health emergency such as Ebola or pandemic flu).

CAMPUS-WIDE FIRE DRILL SCHEDULE:	
(location)	(date)
CAMPUS-WIDE SHELTER-IN-PLACE SCHEDULE:	
(location)	(date)

SECTION 5: CAMPUS POLICIES

(In Section 5, place details of your college or university policies such as):

- Emergency Alert Activation Policy
- Process for Inputting New Students, Staff, and Faculty in the Emergency Alert System
- Emergency Operations Center Operational Plan

- Flexible Leave in the Event of a Highly Contagious Communicable Disease
- Information Technology Security Policy
- Mutual Aid Policy
- Missing Student Policy

(Place the policies in alphabetical order and include them in the index.)

CAMPUS MAP
(INSERT CAMPUS MAP HERE)

COMMUNICATIONS TEMPLATES
(Create a database of communication templates and place them here. Below you will find a few samples that can be modified based on the campus need.)

Emergency alert messages that can be modified and used for emergency telephone, text, website alerts.

EXTREME WEATHER EVENT
Due to (name weather event), (campus name) will be closed on (day of week), (date or dates). Day and evening classes have been canceled. Please check (website) and stay tuned to area television and radio stations for further information.

SHELTER-IN-PLACE
Emergency Message—Shelter-in-Place. Go indoors immediately and shelter-in-place until further notice. Check (website) for updates.

ACTIVE SHOOTER
Emergency Message—Shooting on Campus—Lock-Down. Shooting at (location). Go to a secure location and deny entry (lock-down) now! Check (website) for updates.

POTENTIAL EVENT
(Campus name) received a threat of a potentially violent incident on campus. At (time, date), the (local) Police Department received a (name the threat). In order to ensure the safety of all students, faculty, staff, and campus visitor, all campus locations will be closed (day) and all classes have been canceled.

215

SAFETY MESSAGE TEMPLATES FOR
THE CAMPUS COMMUNITY

(Each campus should create its own campus-specific safety messages for students, staff, and faculty. The messages below contain basic safety information that can be edited for your campus. The safety messages can be postthe campus website, printed in brochures, or used anyway that the PPMRR team in collaboration with the Marketing and Communications Department at your campus sees fit. Insert your campus-specific safety message templates here.)

1. Evacuation

EVACUATION POLICY FOR STUDENTS, STAFF, AND FACULTY

- Secure hazardous operations if possible.
- Take only important personal items. Leave nonessential items.
- Close doors behind the last person out of the room.
- Walk quickly and orderly to the nearest safe exit.
- Do not exit using elevators unless authorized emergency personnel tell you to do so.
- Do not re-enter the building until authorized emergency personnel give the "All Clear" signal.
- Report any missing or trapped persons to authorized emergency personnel.
- Move away from the building to an established evacuation area.
- If you are unable to do so due to a physical disability, injury, or obstruction, go to the nearest location where there are no hazards, such as a hazard-free stairwell and:
  - Call 911 from a safe location.
  - Signal out the window to emergency responders, if possible.
  - Remain calm, responders will arrive.

EVACUATION INSTRUCTIONS FOR FACULTY, STAFF, AND STUDENTS WITH PHYSICAL CHALLENGES

MOBILITY IMPAIRMENT (use crutches, cane, wheelchair, or walker)

- If an evacuation is ordered, proceed to the nearest designated exit.
- If in a building with more than one story, exit to the nearest stairwell and call Public Safety at xxx-xxx-xxxx.

216

Deaf or Hearing Impaired

- If an evacuation is ordered, proceed to the nearest designated exit.
- Look for the visual fire alarm in the hallway.
- Ask for assistance by writing a note or using hand gestures.

Blind or Visually Impaired

- If an evacuation is ordered, proceed to the nearest designated area.
- Listen for the audio fire alarm or other warning signal.
- Ask for assistance and tell the person how to best assist you.

2. Rally Points

RALLY POINTS NOTICE

Administration Building

Evacuation: Assemble in north parking lot

Shelter: Assemble in the hallway of the basement, interior offices or in the restrooms

Student Center

Evacuation: Assemble in the south parking lot

Shelter: Assemble in the hallway of the basement, interior offices, or in the restrooms

Academic Commons North Building

Evacuation: Assemble at the south side of the building near the quad fountain

Shelter: Assemble on the first floor in interior rooms in the restrooms

3. Lock-Down

LOCK-DOWN POLICY FOR STUDENTS, STAFF, AND FACULTY

- Immediately go to the nearest available classroom or office.
- Close and lock all windows and doors.
- Move away from all windows and doors.
- Turn off classroom lights.
- Turn cell phones off.

- Use ALICE strategies (Alert, Lock-Down, Inform, Counter, Evacuate).
- Do not leave the classroom or office until instructed to do so by appropriate authorities.

4. Shelter-in-Place

SHELTER-IN-PLACE POLICY FOR FACULTY, STAFF, AND STUDENTS

- Take immediate cover in the closest building.
- Locate an interior room; without windows or with the least number of windows.
- Shut and lock all windows and close exterior doors.
- Stay away from windows.
- Turn off air conditioners, heaters, and fans.
- Close vents to ventilation systems.
- Write down the names of everyone in the room, and call the Building Warden to report who is in the room with you.

5. Guidance for Receivers of Bomb Threats

GUIDANCE FOR RECEIVERS OF BOMB THREATS

- DO NOT use two-way radios or cellular phones; radio signals can cause a detonation.
- DO NOT evacuate the building until police arrive and evaluate the threat.
- DO NOT activate the fire alarm.
- DO NOT touch or move a suspicious package.
- Gain as much information as possible about the caller and the credibility of the threat.
- Use the Bomb Threat Report to guide the conversation and record details for police.
- If you can, determine the location of the bomb and the time of detonation.
- If you have a digital phone, look for and record the caller's phone number.
- If possible, do not hang up the phone. Have a coworker call (Public Safety at xxx-xxx-xxxx) or 911. If you are alone, call immediately after hanging up.

BOMB THREAT REPORT	COLLEGE NAME	
DO NOT HANG UP ON THE CALLER	Date:	Time:
Call Public Safety at xxx-xxx-xxxx to report the bomb threat as soon as possible.	Phone number where call received:	Time caller hung up:

EXACT WORDS OF CALLER

QUESTIONS TO ASK

Where is the bomb located? (building, floor, room, etc.)

When will it go off?

What does it look like?

What kind of bomb is it?

What will cause it to explode?

Did you place the bomb?

Why did you place the bomb?

Where are you calling from?

What is your name?

INFORMATION ABOUT THE CALLER

Sex: Male   Female

Accent:

Is voice familiar? If so, who does it sound like?

Back-ground Noise	• Children	• Street noise	• Airport noise	• Office noise	• Motor
	• Clear	• Static	• Music	• Conver-sation	• Other
Caller's Voice	• Loud	• Nasal	• Raspy	• Crying	• Cough
	• Soft	• Normal	• Rapid	• Slurred	• Angry
	• Disguised	• Slow	• Calm	• Lisp	• Squeaky
	• Excited	• Deep Breathing	• Laughing	• Stutter	• Other
Threat Language	• Incoherent	• Message Read	• Taped		
	• Irrational	• Well-spoken	• Profane		

Remarks:

Name of Person Taking Report:

Contact Telephone Number:

APPENDIX B: MUTUAL AID AGREEMENTS

Through mutual aid agreements (MAAs), the campus lines up resources to be employed as needed. Agreements could be constructed with emergency response professionals, food service industries, transportation, and housing, to name a few. When MAAs are integrated in a campus PPMRR strategy, the better equipped the campus will be to manage a critical event.

The National Incident Management System (NIMS) defines an MAA as a written or oral agreement between and among agencies/organizations and/or jurisdictions that provides a mechanism to quickly obtain emergency assistance in the form of personnel, equipment, materials, and other associated services. The primary objective is to facilitate rapid, short-term deployment of emergency support prior to, during, and/or after an incident. To clarify the expectations and reduce misunderstandings, it is recommended that the agreements be written to define the request, the agreed upon procedures, liability, reimbursement, and worker's compensation procedures.

An MAA should include the following components:

Purpose and Scope: Sometimes called a *Preamble*, the Purpose and Scope section sets the tone for the agreement. This section should include:
- The need for an agreement
- The range of incidents in which it is applicable
- The member organizations

References and Authorities: References and Authorities refer to existing statutes or regulations that authorize mutual aid contracts or compacts. This section also includes a listing of any prior agreements that are mentioned in the MAA, such as those that will be superseded or will in some way affect the new agreement. By including a References and Authorities section, applicable statutes can be quickly accessed by interested parties.

Definitions: Defining key terms helps avoid differences in interpretation. For example, words like "emergency" can have different meanings for different organizations. Defining terms is especially important for complex agreements that go into small levels of detail. If levels of aid are to be determined by the agreement itself, then clear definitions must be in place.

Effect on Existing Agreements: Comprehensive legal review should determine if any serious conflicts exist with existing agreements. A clause should be included that states what effect the new agreement has on existing agreements. New agreements should replace older agreements in order to avoid conflict and potential disputes between parties. In general, new agreements should not prohibit future supplemental agreements between all or some of the parties to the agreement.

Roles and Responsibilities: The Roles and Responsibilities section should include the roles and responsibilities of each party. This section usually contains information about who can activate the agreement.

Mediation/Dispute Resolution: The Mediation/Dispute Resolution section should include information on how disputes will be resolved. This may include the use of mediation, arbitration, and/or court of jurisdiction.

Training and Exercises: MAAs should include language on training and exercises, including how often training and exercises will be conducted. The agreement should mandate joint planning, training, and exercises with the same liability immunity as if it were a real emergency.

Liability and Insurance: The Liability and Insurance section of an MAA should spell out the liability of all parties and provide guidance for arbitration or resolution of any claims. Legal counsel should play a lead role to draft and review all issues related to language in the agreement.

In most cases, agreements should indemnify mutual aid partners from any liability from alleged negligence, except for cases of gross negligence and/or willful misconduct, occurring during a mutual aid response. Insurance, including workers' compensation insurance, should be required of all parties, and insurers must be made aware of mutual aid requirements. Some tribal governments may request or even require resolution of legal disputes within a Tribal Court System, particularly if the event leading to the dispute occurs within the tribe's jurisdiction.

Limitations: The Limitations section of an MAA specifies the conditions under which a participating jurisdiction's obligation to provide assistance and resources may or may not be limited.

License, Certificate, and Permit Portability: The License, Certificate, and Permit Portability section specifies the conditions under which a person or entity who holds a license, certificate, or other permit is deemed to be licensed, certified, or permitted in the jurisdiction requesting assistance.

In general, it is best to allow for a responder's license, certificate, or permit to be valid in the requesting jurisdiction. For example, a lawenforcement official from County X should have the same arrest powers in County Y that he or she has in County X.

Terms and Conditions: The purpose of this section is to specify the duration or the life expectancy of the agreement. It is important to clarify expectations of all signatories about the lifespan of the agreement and how it will be renewed.

It is recommended that the agreement have a beginning and an end date. In addition, if it is necessary to renew the agreement, there should be stipulations as to what actions need to take place to renew it or there should be indications that the renewal is automatic.

Reimbursement: The goal of this section is to clarify issues over reimbursement such as:

- Who is responsible for paying for specific resources
- What expenses are eligible for reimbursement
- What triggers the reimbursement provision of the agreement (e.g., some agreements are written in such a way that for the first 24 hours of aid provided, there is no cost to the requesting jurisdiction); reimbursement becomes an issue only following that initial period

Severability: The "Severability" section of an MAA addresses how one or more of the signatories can leave the agreement while the rest of the agreement is intact. This section can also make provisions for cases in which an article of the agreement is found invalid. In this case, the "Severability" section will include language which ensures that the rest of the agreement remains binding for the rest of the parties.

Information regarding mutual aid agreements was extracted from FEMA's Legal Issues in Emergency Management.

APPENDIX C: EMERGENCY OPERATIONS CENTER SETUP PROCEDURES

A location designated as a fully capable Emergency Operations Center (EOC) is an essential element of a campus PPMRR strategy. It can be a dedicated location or one designated to be converted to an EOC as needed. It should be large enough to hold the PPMRR team as well as outside agency representatives in order to centralize incident management.

Benefits

- Provides a central point where all information related to the incident is received and analyzed, incident priorities are determined, strategies are developed, and critical resources are assigned to tactical operations.
- Provides for operations during extended periods of time.
- Enhances coordination between involved agencies and provides for the efficient and effective use of all modes of communications available for the incident.
- Minimizes disruption to campus departments not directly affected.
- Provides a centralized location to conduct planning meetings, tactics meetings, shift briefings, media briefings, press conferences, public information releases, and other information dissemination.

Assumptions

- Field operations will be controlled from one or more Incident Command Post(s), which will be located near the emergency/disaster scene.
- The EOC has the capability to communicate with the field operations, as well as local, state, and federal agencies.

Sample statements to be included in the PPMRR guide.

ACTIVATION OF THE EOC

The EOC will be activated when necessary to facilitate response and subsequent recovery from any emergency. The Emergency Classification Levels are used to classify the significance of the event. The following individuals are authorized to activate the EOC:

- President
- Director of Emergency Management
- Provost

SAMPLE TO BE INCLUDED IN YOUR CAMPUS PPMRR

The primary Campus EOC is located in (Room XXX of XXX Hall, Building XX on the Campus map). The facility is a designated, but not a dedicated, EOC facility. Supplies are maintained in a state of readiness for conversion and activation when needed. The EOC serves as the centralized location in which campus staff will report for duty and assume their PPMRR roles. In the event that the primary EOC cannot be used, an alternate EOC will be established in (Room XXX of XXX Hall, Building XX on the Campus map).

EOC SETUP

Upon notification of EOC activation, the Logistics Staff will initiate the setup of equipment. General setup responsibilities include

- Ensure that the EOC is accessible.
- Ensure that adequate furniture, fixtures, telephones, and space are available.
- Locate EOC supplies in supply room.
- Set up and test telephones, fax machines, and other logistical supplies.
- Set up prepositioned management aids and tools including:
  - General message board
  - Whiteboards
  - Flip charts
- Set up an area to post communications information (incoming telephone numbers, incoming fax machine numbers, Media Briefing Center number, etc.).

226

- Establish a "quiet space" where EOC staff can take a break and make private calls.

Depending on the operation of your campus EOC, PPMRR team members may be asked to bring their own laptops into the EOC.

SAMPLE EMERGENCY OPERATIONS CENTER FLOOR PLAN

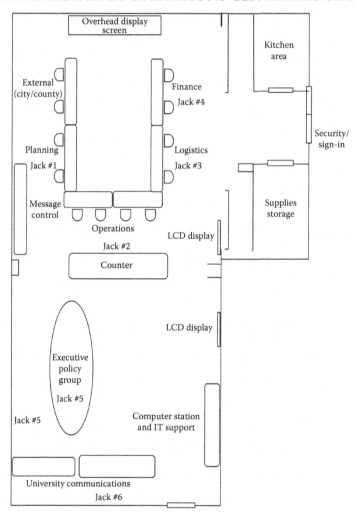

Sample EOC Supply List

Qty	Unit	Item
1	Each	Analog clock, battery powered (min 11″)
6	Each	Personal or laptop computers; Building has wireless capability; Staff to bring their own laptops
1	Each	Copier/Fax
1	Each	Printer
5	Pad	Easel chart pads
5	Box	Easel chart markers
2	Each	Easel chart stand
1	Each	Campus maps—Large hard copy in addition to GIS based
1	Each	Individual building maps—Hard copy in addition to GIS based
3	Roll	Masking tape
24	Each	Writing pads (legal or letter)
24	Each	Pens
24	Each	Pencils
5	Box	Paper clips
2	Box	File folders
1	Box	Labels
5	Each	Flashlights with extra batteries
6	Each	Telephones
1	Each	Large whiteboard
2	Each	LCDs for data projection and commercial TV/media display
1	Each	Handheld radio 800 MHz

INCIDENT DOCUMENTATION

It is imperative that all activities involving the event be properly documented from the beginning through the recovery phase. Provide Activity Logs for each UCG, Command, and Section Chief to record the following:

- Time and information for telephone calls made and received
- Time and information for actions requested and taken
- Other general notes and information

As available, the Planning Section Chief collects the Activity Logs and collates information to be entered into Incident Action Reports and Situation Reports.

SHIFT CHANGES

In incidents where response and recovery efforts span multiple days, the Director of Emergency Management will evaluate the situation and define necessary shift changes (e.g., 8 or 12 hours). At every shift change, outgoing PPMRR team members will brief the incoming staff. This briefing should include a review of the most recent operational period action plan, significant changes in the response strategy.

DEACTIVATION AND DEMOBILIZATION OF THE EOC

The university President or designee, advised by the IC, will determine when to deactivate the EOC and transition to normal campus operations. The process of demobilizing includes demobilizing all units, and documenting the incident in preparation for the After Action Report, and updating the campus plans and procedures. To accomplish this:

- The IC will notify sections when they are no longer required in the EOC.
- All staff must ensure that any open actions not yet completed will be handled after the deactivation.
- All staff must ensure that all required forms or reports are completed prior to deactivation and have copies made of all logs, reports, messages, and any other documents used and received in the EOC. Leave originals in the position folder.
- The Emergency Management Director will return and secure supplies and equipment to the storage location.
- An official notification will be sent to all involved internal and external participants that the EOC is deactivated.

This action signifies the transition from the response phase to the recovery phase. Prior to deactivation, the IC will assign staff to a Disaster Recovery Group (DRG) to establish the short-term recovery goals that facilitate long-term recovery. The recovery plan should address the following if necessary:

- The recovery effort's goals
- Short-term recovery operations, such as debris removal and volunteer and donation management
- Temporary shelter and housing, permanent housing if on-campus housing has been compromised
- Economic recovery

- Environmental recovery
- Infrastructure and lifelines
- Financial and community resources
- Social and psychological aspects of recovery

RESPONSE CAPABILITY PERFORMANCE OBJECTIVES

The campus should develop measurable response capability performance objectives for the capability to activate and manage EOC operations, collect information and conduct situation assessments, develop priorities and strategies for incident management, manage resources, coordinate with other agencies, and implement executive directions. The following table provides targets that can be used in assessing performance in the activation and operation of the EOC.

	Performance Objective	Performance Measure	Metric (minutes)
1	Activate and manage EOC operations	Activate EOC for an incident within 1 hour from determination of need.	<60
2	Collect information and conduct situation assessment	Ensure the ability to have a planning function capability at the EOC and to establish information linkages with incident command and field assets, university departments, and other governmental entities within 2 hours of determination of need.	<120
3	Support development of priorities and strategies for EOC management	Coordinate operations at the EOC within 2 hours of notification and establish procedures for developing an Incident Action Plan within 2 hours of determination of need.	<120
4	Manage resources	Ensure the ability to coordinate logistics within the EOC by receiving, staging, and distributing resources to meet identified needs within 2 hours of determination of need.	<120

(Continued)

	Performance Objective	Performance Measure	Metric (minutes)
5	Coordination with other agencies	Ensure the ability to maintain 24/7 coordination with multiple agencies at an EOC within 2 hours of determination of need.	<120
6	Support executive decision making	Ensure the ability to establish a Common Operating Picture necessary for decision making within 2 hours of determination of need.	<120

EOC information was extracted from the University of the Rockies Emergency Operations Plan.

APPENDIX D: UNIVERSITY CRISIS ACTION TEAM DECOMPRESSED TRAINING MODEL

Andrew Rendon, Jeremy Baham, and William L. Kibler

Mississippi State University

This article demonstrates how one higher education institution, Mississippi State University, has embraced the emergency management principles of the Federal Emergency Management Agency (FEMA), the National Response Framework (NRF), and the Department of Education (DOE) in the creation of its campus emergency strategies.

A CULTURE OF PREPAREDNESS

The Mississippi State University (MSU) leadership has a successful track record of responding to and managing crises. Whether due to the harsh effects of a Category 5 Tornado or the maligned behavior of a distraught student, key leaders have developed and implemented programs, procedures, and policies to respond to crises while insuring the utmost safety of the university students, faculty, and staff. A good example of the university's culture of emergency preparedness can be illustrated in a recent shooting incident at an on-campus resident hall, resulting in what some may refer to as a textbook response. Within minutes of the incident, a police officer was on the scene and the University Police Department Dispatch had notified the on-call Crisis Action Team Leader. Notifying respective key leaders, implementing the *Maroon Alert Message System,*

233

and making the decision to set up the university's command center were all immediate actions taken by the on-call leader resulting in the quick identification and apprehension of the suspect and the restoration of stability to the campus. A handful of success stories such as the shooting incident provide key evidence that the university's approach to emergency management is working. In this appendix, the authors attempt to define the framework that has led to the university's reputable *culture of emergency preparedness*. A discussion will include the established foundation for emergency preparedness, the composition, and background of the university's emergency management team (referred to as the Crisis Action Team) and the applied multiapproach training plan, which includes a unique training model designed to comprehensively train for most contingencies associated with a crisis. Finally, the authors identify successful techniques and procedures employed by the university's emergency management team including effective communication systems, resource management surveys, and external relationship building with local, state, and federal agencies.

PREPAREDNESS FOUNDATION

Focusing on a foundation of education and training, the university establishes the basis for emergency preparedness in a Presidential Policy (Emergency Operations 01.04, 2009) and ties the policy to a framework for preparedness in an *Incident Preparedness Plan* (both of these documents can be found in the Mississippi State University's *Operating Policies* website under Presidential Matters). Policy implementation through the incident preparedness plan calls for organizations at all levels to play a role in emergency preparedness including a basic understanding of response to common emergencies. Due to this focus, expected responses to common scenarios including severe weather, active shooter, and fire are consistent outcomes during real and scenario-based situations. Similar in format to emergency management plans developed by the Federal Emergency Management Agency (FEMA) and defined in the National Response Framework (NRF), the university's incident preparedness plan identifies the organizational structure for major incidences, functional area roles and responsibilities, and a framework for responding to common emergencies including weather, fire, civil disorder, and bomb threats. Finally, protocols are established to assist leaders in determining at what level the Incident Command Center will be activated and the crisis action team assembled.

COMPOSITION OF THE TEAM

With the policy and procedure foundation in place, the university weaves a web of people, resources, and relationships at the local, state, and federal levels designed to comprehensively prepare for emergencies. At the center of this success is the creation of the University's Crisis Action Team (CAT). While the MSU Crisis Action Team formally organized its membership in 2005, the principles in which it operates were in place before then. Essential to the success of the team is its homogenous composition of leaders from across campus coupled with the importance the team places on emergency management education and training. Meeting on a monthly basis, the MSU Crisis Action Team divides their time into reviewing policies and procedures associated with campus emergency management and conducting scenario-based training exercises, including tabletop and full-scale drills.

The CAT is based upon the FEMA's incident command system structure for Higher Education as outlined in FEMA's Emergency Management Institute's course IS-100.HE (http://training.fema.gov). CAT members are designated by the Divisional Vice Presidents of the university with the Incident Commanders designated by the President. CAT members provide support during an incident through five major functions directly outlined by FEMA: (1) Incident Command which has overall responsibility for resolving the incident; (2) Operations which directs the operational resources responding to the incident; (3) Planning which collects and analyzes information regarding the incident as well as maintaining the incident documentation critical for reviewing the incident response at the conclusion of incident operations; (4) Logistics that provides the resources and services necessary to meet the goals set by the Incident Commander (IC); and (5) Administration and Finance which provides procurement and monitors costs of the incident response. Depending on the particular needs during an incident, the IC is empowered to determine who, of the trained pool of CAT members, is needed to respond to a crisis. Consisting of approximately 20 individuals, typically the CAT consists of the IC, the CAT support team which monitors information coming to the Command Center and provides any other needed support within the Command Center, representatives from Campus Services and Physical Plant, a representative from the Provost Office, a representative from the University Relations Office to function as a liaison with the media, a representative from Information Technology Services, the Chief of Police for the university or her representative, and a representative from the University

Housing Office. Other members of the CAT may be called in at the discretion of the Incident IC. An important aspect of the CAT is the 3 Deep Contact List. This list is maintained by the CAT Coordinator and contains the emergency contact phone numbers for every department on campus that might be involved in incident response as well as the emergency contact numbers of agencies outside the university that may be involved in incident response. This list has the names and emergency contact numbers for not only department heads but also for at least two additional people who can be contacted and have the authority to make decisions for their department in the absence of the department head. This 3 Deep list reduces significantly the chances that a department or agency becomes unreachable during an emergency.

Three roles that have been added to the standard Incident Command Structure by the university are the CAT Coordinator, On-Call Specialists (all of which are on the CAT support team), and the Training Coordinator. The CAT Coordinator takes the lead in monitoring and maintaining the physical space and equipment used by CAT as well as providing budgetary oversight for the funds set aside by the university for CAT. This includes periodic inspections of the Command Center and the Alternate Command Center. While conducting these inspections, the coordinator is tasked with ensuring that equipment is in working order and that there are no issues that would hinder command operations from functioning. The coordinator is also tasked with maintaining the CAT manual, which contains the policies and protocols that govern CAT. This manual is updated whenever a change is made to these policies and procedures, but is reviewed annually regardless of changes made during the previous academic year. The updated CAT Manual is provided each year to the CAT members.

The On-Call Specialists are six professional staff members who rotate the on-call duty. One of these specialists is on call 24 hours/day 365 days/year. These specialists are tied in to the University Police Dispatch and are notified when an incident occurs on campus. While first responders, such as the University Police, meet the immediate needs of the incident, the on-call specialist makes the initial decisions for the university response. When warranted, the specialist notifies an IC and begins the process of assembling the CAT. These specialists also coordinate the initial communication with the university community by e-mail, text message, and website when such a response is appropriate.

The Training Coordinator is tasked with ensuring that the CAT is ready to respond at any given time to incidents that affect the university.

While most incidents cannot be predicted specifically, these incidents can be trained for by identifying the most likely emergencies and training for similar types of incidents. For example, the university knows that the most likely incident to affect the entire campus is dangerous weather such as a tornado. Extremely beneficial to the CAT is the affiliation the university shares with the State of Mississippi Climatology Office. Housed here at Mississippi State University, the State Climatologist (also a professor of Meteorology and Climatology) works with the team to provide timely around-the-clock weather information including forecasts and briefings specifically tailored for CAT team decisions. Where most universities rely on national weather reports, the university is privileged to have its own built-in emergency weather service. Therefore, the Training Coordinator can build scenarios that test the university's ability to respond in case a tornado touches down on campus or in the community where it would affect students. Utilizing these training scenarios and the review of these exercises, the Training Coordinator helps the CAT and the university to refine their ability to respond to any type of crisis. The Training Coordinator also liaises with agencies and individuals outside the university that may be involved in incident response to provide for complimentary training and outside involvement in university training exercises.

INDIVIDUAL TRAINING REQUIREMENTS

Every member of the CAT is responsible for individual training as well as being expected to participate in training exercises as designed by the Training Coordinator. The individual training is provided through the Emergency Management Institute provided by FEMA. Every CAT member is required to take courses 100.HE (Introduction to the Incident Command System for Higher Education), 200.b (ICS for Single Resources and Initial Action Incidents), 700.a (National Incident Management System, an Introduction, 2011), and 800.b (National Response Framework). Some CAT members then have additional courses, which are required based on their team function, for example, the staff that will function as Public Information Officers are required to take IS-704 (Communications and Information Management). Completion of these courses is monitored by the CAT Coordinator in cooperation with the Human Resources Management office of the university.

COLLECTIVE TRAINING

Focused on a high expectation for effective response to an emergency situation, the CAT incorporates a comprehensive approach to training including identifying individual and team/collective training requirements. Meeting on a monthly basis, the MSU Crisis Action Team divides their time into reviewing policies and procedures associated with campus emergency management and conducting scenario-based training exercises, including tabletop and full-scale drills. Because the composition of the CAT team includes extremely busy top-level university administrators, training and meeting times are limited to an hour. Hence, maximizing the time available for a myriad of objectives can pose significant challenges when developing a training plan. Always mindful of this fact, purposeful/effective training is at the core of the training plan. Development of the CAT meeting agenda starts with dividing the period into two 30-minute sessions. The first half hour is reserved for administrative "house cleaning" which can include a number of items. Reviewing and correcting contact rosters/policies/support documents, identifying individual training shortfalls, reviewing and discussing recent emergency responses, in-service training from external agencies (including our host county emergency management director and Mississippi Emergency Management Agency training coordinators), and general discussions are but a few of the tasks accomplished during the first session of the meeting. In the second session, the CAT team focuses on a scenario-based drill applying different methods of execution including tabletop, functional, and full-scale exercises. The training plan also includes no-notice and unscheduled drills aimed at evaluating and ultimately developing the team's responsiveness and decision-making capabilities. While this approach has been successful for the team, the university is continuously striving to improve its emergency management capabilities—*because you can never be too prepared*. Finally, at the center of improving emergency management capabilities is a twofold challenge: refresher training and new team member training. This can be accomplished through the application of what the authors refer to as the *Decompressed Training Model*.

DECOMPRESSED TRAINING

Understanding and applying sound, effective emergency management techniques is a proven perishable skill. In addition, team members are often replaced or substituted, which requires new training. These factors can hamper the overall capability of a team attempting to respond to crisis. A new, yet untrained, team member with substantial institutional authority can prove to be hazardous. In an effort to mitigate some of the challenges to maintaining a high degree of team emergency management capability is by the application of what the authors refer to as *Decompressed Training*.

At the center of this concept is the application of a scenario-based drill/exercise spread over a year time frame. Conceptually, the training would consist of a weeklong scenario, for instance, a weather incident that results in shutting down the campus, spread out over the duration of a training year. Meeting once a month, the team can extensively discuss the first day of the event, including possible scenarios, contingencies, outcomes, branches, and sequels. As the training year progresses, team members can continue to develop the scenario, hopefully giving it some thought even while not in session. Slowing down the clock and allowing the exercise to be drawn out accommodates several training objectives. First, setting up a quality, effective scenario takes work and practice and often can confuse more than train. Human nature tends to shy away from "notional ideas" so emplacing a base scenario in which teammates can continue to draw from can be helpful. Finally, decompressing or slowing the timeline also provides for comprehensive discussion and thought on certain events allowing for vetting of planned responses for future real events.

Under a compressed, stressful real-world scenario, drawing from a wealth of comprehensive and planned responses can be helpful when formulating a decision or plan of action. Conversely, executing real-time scenario-based training may result in rushed and inadequate learned responses that are then mirrored in a real scenario. Finally, because of its unique design of building upon previous sessions, the decompression concept accommodates new team members and those needing refresher training. Using MSU's system of recording and tracking an incident (discussed later in this appendix), a team member would simply go into the MSU E-CATS module and quickly "get up to speed" with the situation. He or she is then ready to participate in the scenario.

While this training concept does not focus on the ability to develop decision-making skills in a compressed, stressful, and hazardous environment, those skills are addressed by including smaller unscheduled drills throughout the year. The importance of this training concept is it exceeds expectations for other critical training objectives, such as contingency planning, collective team building, and comprehensive resourcing.

TOOLS FOR SUCCESS

Identifying the tools for success is critically important both in the development of training objectives and plans and during an actual emergency response. The old adage of *having and not needing versus needing and not having* comes sharply into focus when building a comprehensive list of tools and resources needed in support of crisis management. For the MSU Crisis Action Team, these tools are divided into several different categories including communication, resources, and relationships. Most likely at the top of the list of essential tools needed in an emergency response scenario is the ability to communicate and for MSU, the leadership has developed a broad and comprehensive communication plan designed to provide immediate information to the university's population. Referred to as the *Maroon Alert System*, the concept simply employs all available modes of communication to relay information to the university's population. Vetted by an appointed university Public Information Officer (PIO), information is then delivered through e-mail, web posting, text, radio and TV broadcasting, and instant messaging. Additionally, the university can also make use of a campus-wide siren and loudspeaker system that can be employed to communicate with students, faculty, and staff that may not have access to other means of communication. Finally, the university has started to employ the use of social media sites on Facebook and Twitter to relay emergency messages. Analysis and discussion between the PIO and the Crisis Action Team members will determine the specific usage of the Maroon Alert System including the language and message used and the delivery method. The level or urgency of the message is also considered. For example, Advisories (nonemergencies) are posted to the MSU website using a blue banner. Emergencies requiring immediate action are highlighted with a yellow banner and ultimately should the university declare a campus emergency, the yellow banner will appear on the top of the MSU website. Describing the significance of the banner colors to our students, faculty, and staff is done through educational programs including in-service faculty sessions, student orientations, flyers, and e-mail. Text messaging plays a significant role in emergency response as it is typically only used if there is imminent danger to campus requiring immediate action. Finally, as a means to organize information that can be made readily available to decision makers, the crisis action team has developed a web-based information tracking system referred to as the Emergency Crisis Action Team System (E-CATS). Developed by the university's

Information Technology and University Relations Office, the E-CATS allows team members the ability to open an event, categorize the event, and start posting information regarding the event including times, location, reports, and status. Key leaders needing a quick update on the event can simply go to the E-CATS and review the postings by functional area. A more basic understanding of the event can be determined by looking at the summary page. Restricted to CAT members, E-CATS provides the team the ability to electronically store records of all activities for actual events and exercises while also providing a site for CAT members to communicate. Critically important for noise levels to remain low in the command center, the E-CATS provides for exchange of information with a minimal amount of "cross-talk."

Identifying resources and capabilities throughout the campus and in the surrounding communities is also an extremely important tool that should be considered when planning for contingencies. Having a good grasp as to the number, location, and operational status of all the generators on campus becomes critical during a severe weather scenario. The middle of an electrical campus-wide outage is probably not the best time to attempt to understand the complexities of a power generator. Resource identification, status, and location can be determined during exercises and drills. More importantly though, it is critical to keep a running estimate of this information and assign someone with the additional duty of maintaining an accurate and accessible record. MSU's crisis action team has assigned this responsibility to the Vice President of Campus Services and ultimately the Director of Facilities Management as they typically manage a large bulk of the rolling stock equipment and machinery typically needed during an emergency scenario (both of these individuals are members of the CAT). Collaboration between Facility Management and the VP of Student Affairs Office has allowed the CAT to identify specific equipment to be used in times of emergency. Efforts are currently underway to map current locations of emergency equipment for use during an emergency response. Finally, the establishment and development of formal and informal external relationships provides strong bonds that will be needed during a real-world emergency. For most university employees, a background in emergency preparedness training does not exist and while a comprehensive training plan can strengthen crisis management skills for CAT members and key leaders on campus, strong relationships with external agencies can fill the expertise gap associated with emergency management. For the university, reliance on several different agencies and programs can provide realistic training guidance associated with emergency and crisis management in a university setting. At the tip of the spear is the critically important relationship the university has with its host county Emergency Management Agency (EMA) Director. Initiated by the catastrophic events of the September 11, 2001 terrorist attacks and coupled with the 2005 Katrina natural disaster response, the Department of Homeland Security and ultimately FEMA's National Response Framework is *the guiding principle that enables all response partners to prepare for and provide a unified national response to disasters and emergencies—from the smallest incident to the largest disaster* (NRF Publication, January 2008). Conceptually, the university plugs into the National Response Framework through its relationship with the County EMA (which then has a direct link to the state's emergency management agency, then FEMA, etc.). The MSU/Host County EMA relationship is formalized through the university's endorsement of the County's Comprehensive Emergency Management Plan, but the strength of the relationship is its ongoing collaboration during real-world emergencies and monthly training sessions. In a real emergency requiring state and federal funding/support, the university will work through and with the host county emergency management agency to ensure real needs are met. Another source of support and assistance comes from the Institution of Higher Learning and their Risk Management section. And while the university sits within the boundaries of a county and therefore will work closely with the host county during an emergency response, there is also the requirement to work with the university's governing body—The State of Mississippi Institution of Higher Learning. Developing emergency management relationships with the university's governing agency and its associated risk management office provides yet another source of resources and expertise in support of training and real-world emergency response scenarios. Finally, tapping into academic scholarship in support of developing incident preparedness training plans, policies, and procedures provides a wealth of current and cutting-edge information. Fortunately, the university has developed an emergency management training program backed by academic scholarship and real-world experience. Housed within the Mississippi State University Extension Service, the Center for Government and Community Development provides development and implementation of technical assistance and education programs, including emergency management training, for local government officials. As one of several key relationships, the university CAT relies on this center to provide guidance on emergency management training and execution.

ASSESSMENT AND CONCLUSION

As with any program, the need to develop comprehensive assessment tools to determine the effectiveness of the program is important to its overall success. The CAT conducts after action reviews after real-world and training exercises and maintains a record of the reviews within the ECATS. To prevent the reviews from turning into "blame" or "finger-pointing" sessions, the format of the review is not rigid or formalized and allows team members to speak openly about things that need improvement or refinement. An idea not yet put in place within the framework of the incident preparedness plan and the Crisis Action Team is working with outside agencies to provide assessment and evaluation of training exercises.

Never a perfect world, the university's respected reputation for its comprehensive approach to emergency management is constantly challenged by the fact *if something can go wrong, it most likely will*. Because of our uncertain world, the university will continue to scrutinize and improve its policies, procedures, and systems associated with emergency management always realizing that the most important asset is trained, knowledgeable leaders.

REFERENCES

FEMA. (2008). National response framework. Washington, DC: U.S. Department of Homeland Security. Retrieved from http://www.fema.gov/nr

Mississippi State University Policies, Presidential Matters. (2009). *Emergency Operations Policy 01.04.*

U.S. Department of Homeland Security. (2011). *National incident management system: Training program.*

INDEX

Printed in the United States
by Baker & Taylor Publisher Services